OPTIONS
AND
PERSPECTIVES

OPTIONS AND PERSPECTIVES

A Sourcebook of Innovative
Foreign Language Programs in Action, K-12

F. WILLIAM D. LOVE   **LUCILLE J. HONIG**
Project Director, Co-Author   *Project Assistant, Co-Author*
THE AMERICAN COUNCIL ON THE TEACHING
OF FOREIGN LANGUAGES

BELA H. BANATHY   **SHARON ENTWISTLE**
Principal Investigator   *Project Coordinator*
FAR WEST LABORATORY FOR EDUCATIONAL
RESEARCH AND DEVELOPMENT

Published by
THE MODERN LANGUAGE ASSOCIATION OF AMERICA

New York · 1973

The research reported herein was performed pursuant to a contract with the Office of Education, U.S. Department of Health, Education, and Welfare. Contractors undertaking such projects under Government sponsorship are encouraged to express freely their professional judgment in the conduct of the project. Points of view or opinions stated do not, therefore, necessarily represent official Office of Education position or policy.

The American Council on the Teaching of Foreign Languages, as a nonprofit individual membership organization, promotes the study of foreign languages and provides services to those concerned with foreign language education.

The Far West Laboratory for Educational Research and Development is a nonprofit public organization supported in part by funds from the United States Office of Education and the National Institute of Education, Department of Health, Education, and Welfare.

Library of Congress Catalog Card No. 73-78994
ISBN 0-87352-070-x

The Modern Language Association of America
62 Fifth Avenue
New York, New York 10011

Designed by The Etheredges

ACKNOWLEDGMENTS

The authors wish to thank Julia Petrov, Chief of the Research Section of the Division of Foreign Studies of the Institute of International Studies at the U.S. Office of Education, for her role in developing the survey. We would also like to thank Maria Swanson for her work as a consultant, the members of the committee that reviewed sample program descriptions prior to publication, *all* the program directors who responded to the survey questionnaire, and—for both their good ideas and programs and their extensive cooperation—the directors of the programs chosen for description in this book. Finally, we would especially like to thank C. Edward Scebold, Executive Secretary of the American Council on the Teaching of Foreign Languages, for providing valuable practical assistance and moral support.

FWDL
LJH

CONTENTS

CONTENTS – ix

x – CONTENTS

INTRODUCTION

Communication among people involved in the various facets of foreign language education received much attention during the late fifties and early sixties, and numerous projects were launched by various agencies with U.S. Office of Education and foundation support to aid in disseminating information on instructional materials and programs. In those years, the major concern was the development of materials and support of the newly evolving audio-lingual approach. In recent years, however, there has been a shift away from a single approach to language learning at the same time that learning styles have become a primary concern. We have begun to take into account and make adjustments for student differences in interest, ability, and motivation. As a result, experiments in foreign language instruction—many validated by follow-up studies and research-based evaluation—have opened up new possibilities. Exciting new programs have evolved from these experimental programs and from other projects devoted to expanding the horizons which have restricted foreign language study to primarily linguistic objectives. Furthermore, individual schools and districts are taking the initiative more and more in devising original programs for their students. All of these recent developments indicate that a comprehensive look at the nature of the programs that have come into being is long overdue. The purpose of this report is to take such a look.

Foreign Language Annals (the journal of the American Council on the Teaching of Foreign Languages), *The ACTFL Review of Foreign Language Education,* the *Modern Language Journal,* and other publications have periodically provided information on innovative programs and projects. This report incorporates and extends the efforts of those publications and summarizes further developments. It presents information on current innovative foreign language projects and programs for grades K-12. *Its intent is only to provide information and not to mandate, or even necessarily promote, change.*

The report is the result of a project supported by the Research Section of the Division of Foreign Studies, Institute of International Studies, of the U.S. Office of Education. The project was a joint venture of the Far West Laboratory for Educational Research and Development and the American Council on the Teaching of Foreign Languages.

Since 1968, the Far West Laboratory for Educational Research and Development has been engaged in preparing "information products" in a variety of curriculum areas and has produced both multi-media and print-only reviews and reports. Many of the techniques and procedures worked out by the Laboratory in its previous projects have been used in developing this report. As an offshoot of previous efforts, cooperative ventures of the Laboratory and other agencies have also been undertaken. Given its professional leadership position in foreign language education and its relationship to the ERIC Clearinghouse on Languages and Linguistics (MLA/ERIC), the American Council on the Teaching of Foreign Languages was the obvious choice as a partner in conducting a survey of innovative foreign language programs. The project was initiated in March 1972 and was completed in April 1973.

The project entailed the collecting, selecting, organizing, analyzing, and reporting of information on innovative foreign language programs and projects in grades K-12. In our survey, we looked only for foreign language programs (not bilingual) and only at programs in which the primary emphasis was on teaching foreign *language*. Furthermore, we looked only for "innovative" programs, rather than for "successful" programs per se and tried to include only those "innovative" programs which we saw also as "successful." Keeping these distinctions is important. For example, during the course of the project several people have asked when we were going to come out with the descriptions of the 50 "best" foreign language programs in the country. Obviously, this report does not respond to that question, even though programs reported here may be among the best. Nor can we say that every innovative program in the country was identified: in many cases, the survey questionnaires were not returned; some programs could not be located, and others undoubtedly never came to our attention.

Collection of Information. To identify prospective programs for the survey, a number of routes were followed: announcements in state and regional foreign language journals and newsletters; announcements in national publications; form letters to state foreign language supervisors and some district coordinators; personal letters to a large number of people in the profession; an ERIC search; a search of the professional literature over the past five years; attendance at meetings and workshops; word-of-mouth; and personal knowledge of the project staff. As a result of these initial contacts, over 250 programs were identified and were sent questionnaires. Approximately 150 questionnaires were completed and returned to the survey staff.

Selection of Programs. A maximum of approximately 50 programs was established as the number which would represent a good cross-section and which could be dealt with in a conveniently-sized book. The following guidelines were formed as the broad framework for selecting programs to be described: (1) The program is on-going, (2) it is "innovative," (3) it is consistent with its stated goals (implying that it has definite goals and objectives), (4) program outcomes give evidence that it works, and (5) the program is articulated vertically (applicable to programs whose sequence is longer than one year).

The term "innovative" is not easy to define. For several years we have been witnessing a move away from traditional textbook-based and teacher-centered instruction toward programs with a variety of orientation. Our survey uncovered a range of innovations on the following dimensions: (1) patterns of organization, (2) means of instruction, (3) locales of study, (4) subject matter, (5) motivational incentives, (6) special target groups, and (7) instructional resources.

Organization, Analysis, and Reporting. After the information was collected, it was organized and analyzed, and then came the task of reporting. Some programs required extensive coverage; less complex programs were reported in shorter formats. Long reports were generally organized into sections on such topics as: (1) an overview of the program, (2) program development and present status, (3) target audience, (4) program goals and/or goals for students, (5) student grouping and scheduling arrangements, (6) methodology and representative content, (7) credit and articulation, (8) materials and facilities, (9) roles of teachers and other personnel, (10) training requirements, (11) role of community, (12) program evaluation, (13) funding and costs, (14) adaptability of concept to other places, (15) available descriptions, and (16) contact person. Short reports consist of a narrative description of the program and one paragraph on any of the section titles cited above, as appropriate. However, every report lists a contact person. Midway through the project we tested the approach and the content of sample program descriptions to be included in the book. A group of foreign language teachers, coordinators, and professors of foreign language education were given a set of preliminary draft reports and an overview of the goals of the project and were asked if the project and reports were on the right track. In addition to making many valuable suggestions for revision and improvement, the reviewers reported that the book should be useful and of interest to the profession.

The Utility of the Report. The report should have utility for the foreign language profession in general. For individual teachers, schools, and/or school districts the report may be: (1) a source of enough detailed information about specific programs to permit administrators and teachers to decide if there are ideas which are adaptable to their own situations and which they would like to pursue, (2) a stimulus to administrators and teachers for organizing programs of their own design, (3) a source of examples that demonstrate the feasibility of changing foreign language programs, (4) a source of new ideas for using and adapting commercial materials and/or creating one's own materials.

In teacher training the report can be used (1) as a springboard for methodology courses, (2) as a way of making trainees aware of the diversity of approaches to foreign language education, (3) as a case-study approach to curriculum and how some schools solved some of their problems, (4) as a way of giving trainees new ideas in organization and approaches to foreign language instruction, and in helping them to become responsive to school and student needs, and (5) as a source of case descriptions for practice in evaluating program format and research results.

In a general way, the report serves by (1) improving the "image" of foreign language instruction among administrators, parents, and college students, (2) informing colleges and districts of possibilities for preservice and inservice teacher-training programs, (3) providing background information for people involved in foreign language consultant work, and (4) providing a base for individuals to compare what they are doing with what others are doing.

Some words of caution and suggestions are in order for those who wish to consider adapting or adopting programs reported here. Some of the programs have been developed to solve problems; others have been developed through fortuitous circumstances, an outburst of energy, or simply a desire to do something different. While some programs have been created to solve given problems, they may in turn have created other problems, or might create similar problems in a different setting (the problem of replacing "lockstep frustration" with boredom and indirection in students' individualized work, for instance) unless possible negative effects are anticipated and dealt with. Where we were given information on specific problems or fortuitous circumstances, we provided it in the program reports.

It may not be desirable or even feasible to adopt programs in toto. In most cases, adjustments will have to be made in fitting programs into new environments. Most of the programs reported here can be transferred across languages, and some might be transferred across grade levels. In some cases, especially those involving methodology, it would be advantageous to do background reading and even to visit the programs. Finally, innovative programs as a rule need a good deal of administrative support in their early stages.

In closing, we wish to invite the reader to share findings, comments, or observations with us. Even though the project is completed with the publication of the report, we hope to have the opportunity to make available similar reports in the future. Your contribution will facilitate our work. Please send your comments to either of the two addresses given below.

BELA H. BANATHY
Far West Laboratory for Educational Research and Development

C. EDWARD SCEBOLD
American Council on the Teaching of Foreign Languages

Executive Secretary
The American Council on the Teaching of Foreign Languages
62 Fifth Avenue
New York, New York 10011

Information Products
Information Utilization Division
Far West Laboratory for Educational Research and Development
1855 Folsom Street
San Francisco, California 94103

SECTION I

AFRICAN STUDIES IN FRENCH FOR THE ELEMENTARY GRADES

ABSTRACT

African Studies in French is the second phase of a "twinned class-room" approach that integrates into FLES instruction a prolonged exchange of slides, tapes, realia, and letters between American children and their peers in a French-speaking country. The program's first phase was begun in 1966 in the hope that personal contact and identification with children of a different culture would motivate FLES students to continue French for five or six years. A second-grade class in Cincinnati was twinned with a class in France and had monthly exchanges with classes in different regions of France over a three-year period, devoting one-half of French instruction time to the exchange activities and the other half to formal language study. The fourth year, French was combined with social studies and the class began to exchange messages with French-speaking students in a completely contrasting culture, that of Upper Volta, in Africa. The American program director went to Upper Volta and for two years presented the monthly American messages to the selected classes there, helped them prepare messages to send to the class in Cincinnati, and did field work. The materials from Africa were studied in the American students' social studies classes as well as in French. A series of tests and attitude inventories indicated that the exchange activities were instrumental in the low attrition rate of 2% over the five-year period. At the end of the sixth grade the students requested more French classes, and, despite the termination of the project grant, lessons were provided for another two years. The materials collected by the researcher in Africa have been assembled into cultural units available to teachers of French, Black Studies, and anthropology.

PROGRAM DEVELOPMENT

PHASE I The project began in 1966 with a grant from the U.S. Office of Education to try "an approach to foreign language study based not only on the nature of language and how it is learned but also on the nature of the child and why he wants to learn."[1] Two French instructors from the College of Mount St. Joseph served as program director and teachers for students in two elementary schools in the Cincinnati area. An experimental class (E) of 42 boys and girls who were beginning French in grade 2 was twinned for three years (1966–69) with a class of boys and a class of girls in France who knew no English. Each year the classes in France were located in different regions of the country. Slides and tapes in French were prepared under the supervision of the classroom teachers abroad and the French instructors in Cincinnati, and class exchanges were made about once a month. Individual pupils also exchanged photos, drawings, postcards, and small gifts on their own initiative. The control group (C), 42 students matched with the E group on the bases of age, sex, I.Q., and language aptitude, began the study of French in grade 2 under the same teacher. The same materials and techniques were used in both groups, but the Cs did not enter into an exchange. For them, the materials from France bore no personal associations and were like commercially-produced materials.

At the end of the three years a battery of inventories and tests was administered. Ninety-eight percent of the E group, as compared to 85% of the C group, indicated that they still liked French and wanted to continue studying it. On language achievement tests the Es performed slightly better than the Cs in listening comprehension, reading, and writing, and did significantly better in speaking and overall achievement. An inventory of preferences of materials used in class indicated that the slides and tapes ranked highest with 78% of the E group as compared to 61% of the Cs. It was decided to withhold judgment on the effects of the twinning approach until it had been tested for two more years.

PHASE II During the first phase, language learning had been the final goal and cultural interest a means of achieving it. But in the fourth year the program staff decided to try making language a real means to cross-cultural understanding, so that the children would identify not just "with peers in a similar culture, but with peers in a contrasting one." Upper Volta was the country selected, and the town of Ouahigouya, the capital of the ancient Mossi kingdom, was chosen as the center of operation. Upper Volta's economy is 95% agrarian, chiefdoms thrive within a republican form of government, only 10% of all children attend school, medical facilities are often nonexistent, Islam and Animism are the major religions, the climate is hot year-round . . . in short, it is a country that contrasts in almost every way with the world known to children in Cincinnati.

The program director took a two-year leave of absence to serve as researcher and facilitator in Upper Volta. On her way to Africa, she spent several weeks in Paris, where she interviewed people who had worked and lived in Upper Volta and got initial clearance for the project from the country's ambassador to France. Once in Upper Volta, she did field work in cultural anthropology, arranged to have two classes in Ouahigouya participate in the exchange, assembled the messages prepared with these children, and presented the American messages to them.

Both groups in Cincinnati had French instruction daily for

30 minutes. The first slide unit from Upper Volta was a tour of the capital, "guided" by the students, that showed "modern public buildings of Western design and other signs of civilization as American children knew it, to ease them into a culture almost every aspect of which is in unsettling contrast with their own." Other units dealt with the school and the children themselves, and, over the two-year period, the American children saw slides of all the different classes and castes of the Mossi civilization in action, "from the Emperor of Yatenga to the chiefs of the village of Nyinga; from the peasant planting his millet and weaving bands of cotton cloth, to the blacksmith making an iron daba or bronze figurines; from the medicine man of Zogore to the dancers of Goni." A case of Mossi realia and artifacts—native clothes, tools, weapons, household utensils, musical instruments, carved wood masks—was also sent for student examination. The social studies teachers sat in on the presentations in French class and later presented the slides again with more in-depth discussion in English.

The E group sent its own messages to Upper Volta: tapes prepared in French by the students and teacher accompanied slides taken by the teacher, some pictures from the children's family collections, and products of occasional group picture-taking expeditions. The first unit prepared in Cincinnati focused on the class in school and showed details of clothing, hairstyles, and classroom furnishings, all of great fascination to the children in Africa. Subsequent units dealt with such topics as the city and its skyscrapers, suburban homes and shopping centers, a visit to a farm, the preparation of a meal, a birthday party, and snow. One African unit described a student's accident and broken leg, set by a native bone-setter; the American children responded with pictures of three of their own classmates who at that time were wearing plaster casts. Gifts like costume jewelry, T-shirts, and miniature car model kits were also sent from Cincinnati, as well as drawings of each student's home and personal photos.

Again, in Phase II, the C group viewed the materials sent from Africa in both French and social studies classes, but did not prepare its own messages. However, an accidental "spill" of information by an E student to a cousin in the C group tipped off the latter group about the personal exchanges. They protested strongly that they were being discriminated against and made the atmosphere so tense that in September 1970 it was decided to make them an E-2 group and to include them in the exchange dialogues. The experimental design was necessarily altered to include new control factors. Results of the tests and inventories administered at the end of the two-year African phase indicated that the exchange, while contributing insignificantly to the rate of language learning, did motivate and sustain student interest in language over the desired length of time.

PRESENT STATUS

The project grant was terminated after the second year of the African phase, but all participants asked to continue with French instruction in grade 7. Since there was no special class time allotted to French and the original groups had been dispersed among several different seventh-grade classes, the program director and her associate each taught one group daily for half an hour before the school day began. Attrition naturally increased when students had to get up half an hour earlier and find their own way to school. French instruction was limited to the use of the original text, since lack of funds prevented the purchase of new books or a continuation of the African exchange; in fact, in Upper Volta, even the price of postage would have been an impossible luxury without the assistance of the American director and the project grant. As it was, the two instructors taught their seventh-grade classes with no pay for themselves. The following year the director left the area for an extended stay in Africa, and the remaining instructor planned to discontinue classes. But the students insisted. He capitulated, taught each class twice a week, again before the school day began, and asked parents to contribute one dollar for each student for each week of instruction as his salary. In their seventh year of French, 34 students from the original two groups were taking French in spite of the awkward scheduling and added expense.

STUDENT GROUPING AND
SCHEDULING ARRANGEMENTS

The E and C students were kept in separate and self-contained groupings throughout the five years of the project. One reason the approach was not tried again in a second-grade class was the school administrators' unwillingness to maintain such rigid class groupings over a five-year period. Another problem has been time; originally it was hoped that class sessions could be 40 minutes long, but to make even 30 minutes available for French instruction, either the lunch period had to be shortened or the school day lengthened.

METHODOLOGY

The French instructor previewed the slides, tapes, and researcher's notes before presenting the African units. Each unit was introduced in English and then the slides were shown without the recorded dialogue. The French tapescript was first given to students on mimeographed sheets and used as a reading lesson. Then it was played on the tape recorder as an exercise in listening comprehension. Finally the slides were shown again with the correlated tape. Most units were too long for one class period and were divided into segments. Sometimes the students had a show-and-tell session in which they replaced the voices of the African children with their own comments. In social studies the slides were used without the tapes; the social studies teacher used the notes the researcher provided with each set of slides to expand the cultural content of each unit.

MATERIALS

Thirty units (tapes and 500 slides) were sent from Ouahigouya to Cincinnati during the two-year period; 24 units were sent from Cincinnati. Some of the units were in the form of the narration of an event; others were descriptive or expository. Most of the African tapes were recorded in simple French by the children and were accompanied by the researcher's explanatory notes in English, intended mostly for the social studies teachers. Some units dealing with problems in African education were prepared expressly for teachers. The researcher photographed and documented much more material than could be edited and used during the two-year period. On her return, she classified 650 additional slides and worked them into 11 supplementary units.

ROLE OF ADMINISTRATORS

(1) The project director, who also served as an instructor, acted as liaison with the U.S. Office of Education, with administrators and teachers in the cooperating schools, and with the parents of participants. While she was on leave in Africa, her associate assumed these responsibilities in addition to teaching both groups of students. (2) The Ministry of Education in Upper Volta gave final approval for the researcher-facilitator's work, and the Inspector of Elementary Education for Ouahigouya assigned a group of 40 boys and 40 girls in classes corresponding to the fifth and sixth grades to participate under the direction of the researcher-facilitator.

ROLE OF PARENTS

Evening meetings were held about once a month for the parents of the participating American students to acquaint them with the project materials and activities. Parents also participated in an evaluative survey regarding their children's attitudes toward the project.

ROLE OF SPECIAL CONSULTANTS

In constructing the experimental design and evaluative procedures, consultants were employed in language pedagogy, language sequence, Mossi culture, anthropology, testing, sociopsychology, and African studies.

PROGRAM EVALUATION

Numerous tests and inventories were administered at the end of the African phase (May 1971) to both experimental groups, parents of the participants, and the participating students in Africa, as well as to new control groups that had not been involved in the cultural study at all. Only a small portion of the results can be presented here; complete results and test descriptions may be found in the *Technical Report* (see Available Descriptions).

Students completed inventories on their attitude toward African studies and French instruction, as well as a free-response evaluation of both. The results of the last indicated that the two E groups were pleased with both French instruction and African studies; their answers corroborated the findings on the first attitude inventory, which indicated a positive response to, and reasonable understanding of, African life and African people. In response to the question "Do you like French?" only 2% of all the Es said they did not, as compared to 20% in a control group (C) that had had French for an equal number of years without the formal study of a contrasting culture. Fifty-four percent of the Es said they liked French very much, as compared to 22% of the Cs. In response to the question "Do you often tell your parents about what you are learning in French class?" 84% of the Es and 42% of the Cs responded "very often" or "sometimes," while none of the Es and 36% of the Cs said "never." Seventy-six percent of the Es said they sometimes spoke French outside the classroom, as compared to 35% of the Cs.

Student achievement was evaluated by the Common Concepts Foreign Language Test. Since only about one-half of the class time for the Es was spent on formal language instruction, the students were compared with a norm group of junior high school students who had completed two semesters of French. The following figures represent the results.

E-1   Mean standard score 47   Percentile 38
E-2   Mean standard score 49   Percentile 46

Although the twinning factor apparently did not have a significant effect on the rate of language learning, it does seem to have been a "contributing factor to the extraordinary degree of perseverance of the students." The director notes that "it is probably safe to say that in no other FLES program have 98% of the beginning students ever opted to continue through five consecutive years of instruction." From the result of all test evidence she concluded that "twinning is appreciated by American children not only when the partners live in 'advanced' cultures similar to their own, but also when they live in a so-called 'primitive' culture of the Third World."

In an inventory of students' attitudes as seen by their parents, conducted in May 1971, 96% of the E-1 parents said their children showed equal (55%) or greater (41%) interest in studying French as compared to the preceding year. One-hundred percent of the E-2 parents said their children were at least as interested in French as they had been the year before, with 65% saying their children displayed even greater interest. Ninety-seven percent of E-1 parents and 100% of E-2 parents said their children seemed to be eager or willing to continue with French the following year. Parents also completed an evaluation form of the program. In response to "What, in your opinion, are the strongest points of the French-African classes?" all but two parents cited the cultural aspects. In response to "Whát was the weakest point in the program?" all parents answered that there was not enough time allotted to the class sessions. In response to a question asking for suggestions for improving the program, most parents left the space blank, while those who did write suggestions wanted to increase the project's scope: for example, exchanging even more slides, letters, and gifts, and involving black people in the local community. In annual surveys of attitudes toward the project, both the students in the E-2 group (originally the first control group) and their parents showed a steady rise in enthusiasm from the time the group entered into the actual exchange activities until the project's termination.

FUNDING AND COSTS

All project costs were funded by a grant from the U.S. Office of Education. For the African phase (1969-1972, including time for preparing the final report), total funding amounted to about $100,000. A breakdown of expenditures is:

Supplies and materials	$ 3,118
Travel (*for researcher and consultants*)	3,172
Salaries (*director, associate director, two local school coordinators, consultants; plus benefits*)	88,223
Communications and services	690
Statistician	480
Testing	400
Film processing and duplicating	600
Equipment (*tape recorders, cameras, slide projectors, screens for use in U.S. and Africa; car for researcher's transportation in Africa*)	2,627

ADAPTABILITY OF CONCEPT TO OTHER PLACES

Obviously a twinning program as elaborate as the one described could not be conducted without extensive funding. However, twinning that involves a European country, for example, could be conducted with minimum expense once teachers and schools willing to participate have been found. Ministries of education, local governments, and regional educational offices in the foreign country, as well as agencies involved in cultural or educational exchange programs, could be used for finding cooperating schools abroad. At least one modified twinned approach in the secondary grades has been arranged through an American teacher's personal contacts in France. And without the expense of a researcher in a foreign country, transportation, elaborate testing, extensive reporting or material development, even the cost of a program involving a Third World country would be greatly reduced if a cooperating teacher in the foreign country were found and the foreign language teacher in America were able to develop the program with existing personnel. The program director notes that "care should be taken that the selection and presentation of the audio-visual elements in each country be made under the guidance of someone who understands and is sympathetic with the culture of both countries. Otherwise misunderstandings, alienation, and hard feelings may arise. . . . In Third World countries the cultural adviser might well be a successful Peace Corpsman or a native who has studied or worked in the U.S. and has returned to his country with good feelings toward both his native culture and that of his erstwhile hosts." The director also recommends that: (1) the cultural locale be varied from time to time; (2) the twinning procedure be carried beyond the elementary grades; (3) in cases where the partners abroad are studying English, the American students record their messages in English; (4) materials be made available to students for use after class and to all social studies teachers. She notes that the success of the exchange materials in class depends to a large degree on the teachers who use them, who "must not only be sensitive to the needs and reactions of American students, but also to the values of the foreign culture. A sense of timing is also very important, knowing when and how long to use certain visuals and tapes. However, the children themselves did not agree on how much time should be spent on any of the cultural or linguistic aspects of the program." Finally, she notes that the 30-minute time slots allowed for French were inadequate and that it took two years, instead of the one year anticipated, to complete the basic text.

AVAILABLE DESCRIPTIONS

(1) Sister Ruth Adelaide Jonas, "The Twinned Classroom Approach to FLES," *Modern Language Journal*, 53 (1969), 342–46. (2) A collection of over 1200 original color slides, arranged in sets according to cultural themes, and correlated tapes recorded by African children in French and by the researcher in both French and English are available for short-term use or for duplication from: African Project, Modern Language Department, Mount St. Joseph College, Mount St. Joseph, Ohio 45051. There is a minimal fee for borrowing slides and tapes to cover loss, deterioration, handling, and postage. The fees vary according to the number of slides involved and are indicated in the Index, a

three-page list of the slides and tapes available free of charge from the above address. (3) A report, "African Studies in French for the Elementary Grades: Phase II of a Twinned Classroom Approach to the Teaching of French in the Elementary Grades," prepared for the Office of Education by Sister Ruth Adelaide Jonas, is available *only* from ERIC: Volume I, a Technical Report (90 pages) (ERIC ED 006 993), and Volume II, Dialogues and Essays (263 pages) (ERIC ED 006 994). (4) Also available from ERIC are the final report of the first (French) phase of the project (ERIC ED 041 528) and a transcript of the dialogues from the first phase (ERIC ED 041 529), both written by Sister Ruth Adelaide Jonas.

PROJECT INITIATOR

Sister Ruth Adelaide Jonas, S.C., College of Mount St. Joseph-on-the-Ohio.

CONTACT PERSON

Stanley G. Thom, Chairman, Department of Foreign Languages, College of Mount St. Joseph-on-the-Ohio, Mount St. Joseph, Ohio 45051 (513) 244-4200

NOTE

[1] All quotations are from Sister Ruth Adelaide Jonas, "African Studies in French for the Elementary Grades: Phase II of a Twinned Classroom Approach to the Teaching of French in the Elementary Grades," I: Technical Report (Mount St. Joseph, Ohio, 1972).

BUTLER
AREA
LANGUAGE
SATURATION
PROGRAM

ABSTRACT

Many elementary school students may study the concept of equal sets, perform a dissection of an animal's eye, or enact the adventures of Jacques Cartier in the Canadian wilderness, but sixth-grade students at the Emily Brittain School in Butler, Pennsylvania have had the opportunity to do all these things—and more —in French. A Language Saturation Program for "academically talented" students uses French as the language of instruction in a different subject area of the regular sixth-grade curriculum each marking period. Each year for the last six years, 25 sixth-graders have studied math, social studies, science, health, language arts, and the fine arts in French. Using texts from France and Canada, teacher translations of English texts, instructional films "dubbed" in French, and a variety of visual aids, the program aims at developing the language skills students have acquired during three years

15

in the regular FLES sequence by putting the skills to use 40 minutes a day in a challenging and practical way.

BUTLER AREA FLES FRENCH PROGRAM

The Language Saturation Program is only one school's "enrichment" supplement to the Butler Area FLES French Program. This district-wide FLES sequence, in its entirety, involves eight teachers and over 3500 students in 17 elementary schools, including some students in learning disability and special education classes and one fifth- and one sixth-grade class of academically talented students. All FLES students receive 15 minutes of instruction daily from grade 3 through grade 6. (Until this year, the two classes of academically talented students had 40 minutes of French each day.) Lessons are conducted with audiolingual dialogues and drills, and an enthusiastic and lively teacher approach is combined with frequent changes of techniques and visual aids—songs, flashcards, films, puppets, and playlets—to develop conversational skills and sustain student interest in foreign language. At the end of the sixth grade, 80 percent of all Butler FLES students do, in fact, choose to continue the study of French in junior high school.

Language skills in the FLES sequence progress from the mastery of basic phonology and simple pattern structures in the third grade to comprehension of long narrations, spontaneous response, and pre-reading exercises in the sixth. At all levels the emphasis is on speaking the language, in areas of interest particular to each age level, using idiomatic expressions and natural conversation patterns comparable to those used by students of the same age in France. And, in addition to introducing one or two new speech patterns, each lesson deals in some concrete way with an aspect of French culture. In the third grade, for example, students don the hats, capes, and sticks of the French policeman's uniform as part of a dialogue exchange, while in the sixth grade each student creates his own three-dimensional miniature French village, complete with street signs and labeled stores. All teaching in the program is in French, and comprehension is developed through pictures, gestures, or any other clues that help avoid direct translation into English.

Each participating Butler school has, to some extent, supplemented this basic FLES program: the Christmas and spring holiday programs of most schools are either all or partly in French; many sixth-grade classes go to the Buhl Planetarium in Pittsburgh to see the sky show in French and to participate in the program of French skits that follows. Some schools have had French food "tasting parties," and in several schools students make puppets, adapt dialogues for shows, and have French puppet contests. But the Emily Brittain School, with "enriched" classes involved in a more intensive study of the language in the fifth and sixth grades, seems to have come up with the most innovative variation on the FLES theme.

DEVELOPMENT AND PRESENT STATUS OF THE LANGUAGE SATURATION PROGRAM

Seeing that the "enriched" class was bored with the regular French lessons, and that their 40-minute sessions could lend themselves to more varied work than the usual 15-minute sessions, the school principal, classroom teacher, and French teacher planned a saturation program that would use French as the language of instruction in several sixth-grade curriculum areas. The French teacher would present these areas during the 40 minutes allotted to French classes. Rather than teach all subjects in French at the same time, it was decided that a different subject would be conducted in French each six-week marking period in order to avoid discouraging students whose difficulty with one particular subject might be complicated by the use of a foreign language over a longer period of time. The French teacher worked closely with the classroom teacher to assure that all subjects chosen for the program would be standard areas of the district's regular sixth-grade curriculum. The only variations were that French was spoken in the classroom, French and Canadian texts were used in conjunction with French translations of English texts, and the language arts and "cultural" periods focused on topics pertaining to France.

The Saturation Program operated successfully for six years but was discontinued after the 1971–72 school year because of budgetary problems that caused the cancellation of the 40-minute enrichment sessions at the Brittain school. Fifteen-minute sessions were considered insufficient for the Saturation Program, and the regular FLES sixth-grade program was resumed in its place. However, some interdisciplinary aspects of the Saturation Program have been incorporated into the FLES sequence throughout the Butler area. For example, in the third grade the French unit on numbers and mathematical statements has been extended to include a review in French of the math concepts learned in English. In the sixth grade, visits to the French sky show at the planetarium are preceded by units focusing on science vocabulary and appropriate sentence patterns in French, as well as the preparation of skits. The district-wide sixth-grade FLES curriculum also includes a unit on the province of Quebec, and the French teachers approach this unit with a view toward reinforcing and supplementing the social studies units on the same subject.

Although the Saturation Program itself has been suspended, plans are being made to introduce a similar program at the secondary level and at the sixth-grade level in September 1973. The description which follows refers to the Saturation Program as it was conducted for six years.

TARGET AUDIENCE

"Academically talented" students in grade 6, selected through I.Q. tests, achievement tests, reading levels, and teacher recommendation, who have completed three years of FLES language study.

MAJOR GOALS FOR STUDENTS

(1) To develop proficiency in the aural-oral skills of French by using the language in a variety of subject areas; (2) to develop some proficiency in reading and writing skills in French; (3) to

learn the content of the various subject areas as well in French as in English; (4) to develop a favorable attitude toward foreign language learning; (5) to develop an understanding and appreciation of cultural differences.

STUDENT GROUPING AND
SCHEDULING ARRANGEMENTS

The 25 students in the "enriched" class meet together for language saturation courses for 40 minutes a day, five days a week, during the time allotted for "enrichment" French. The school year is divided into six six-week marking periods; mathematics, language arts, "culture," and social studies are taught in the foreign language for one six-week period each, and science and health are taught jointly for two six-week marking periods.

REPRESENTATIVE CONTENT

(1) Modern math is taught for the first six weeks, since students already have a sound background in French numbers and little reading is required. Math units in English are translated by the teacher into French, and, with daily demonstrations involving the overhead projector, students develop an understanding of such concepts as billions, sets, Roman numerals, and approximations. A few minutes are devoted each day to mental arithmetic and brain-teasers. (2) The next six-week period is devoted to the study of the history, geography, and culture of Quebec, using French-Canadian geography texts, frequent films dubbed in French, and student-prepared skits. (3) The next twelve weeks entail a correlation of the science and health areas in a study of the parts of the body and their functions. Students use dittoed sheets prepared in French by the teacher to accompany text units, and perform and observe experiments involving real animal organs. For each of the five health-science units presented in French, a related film is shown. (4) The following six weeks are used to

study fables, legends, and fairy tales of France and French-speaking countries. For example, students read selections from the fables of La Fontaine, a story from *Première Étape* (D.C. Heath), and "P'tit Jean s'en va au chantier." (5) During the final six weeks, called the "cultural period," students spend one day a week on French sports; another day on art appreciation, in which they see slides and copies of works of such French artists as Monet and Renoir and learn about the artists' lives; another day devoted to French music and the composers' lives; and one day viewing slides of France.

A typical example of a unit taught in French is the science and health unit on vision. A diagram of the eye is given to each student, and, using a wall chart, the teacher explains the physical structure of the eye. After three or four sentences of explanation, she asks several questions to see if students have understood. Each day the teacher does several "exercices d'observation"— short experiments, similar to those in the students' English science books, which the teacher has prepared in French. At the end of the unit students also prepare an experiment or a report on vision; one student, for example, explained the Braille system in French. Classroom activities also include the examination of a model eye, the dissection of a pig's eye, and the viewing of the film, "The Eyes and Their Care" (Encyclopædia Britannica), "dubbed" in French by the teacher.

METHODOLOGY

Comprehension of concepts in the subject area is achieved through the use of explanations in French based on previously learned vocabulary and structural patterns, frequent questioning, and visual aids such as charts, maps, filmstrips, slides, films, and pictures. New speech patterns and vocabulary are introduced gradually, in context, and are reinforced with brief oral drills and repeated use in context. Basic reading skills are developed through the use of labeled charts and maps, quizzes involving the matching of words with diagrams, pictures, and numbers, short stories adapted and mimeographed by the teacher, and simple texts in

French. Students frequently put on skits related to the history of the French explorers in Quebec or depicting stories they read. Excerpts from stories are regularly read aloud by students and recorded on tape for reading and pronunciation practice. Students also present frequent short oral reports, simple scientific demonstrations, or brief explanations of maps, pictures, and objects. Two minutes at the end of each class session are reserved for student questions in English.

MATERIALS

For science and health, units from the English texts are translated and correlated with dittoed sheets adapted from *Manuel de Zoologie* (Quebec: Editions Pédagogie Inc.). Desk charts for the study of anatomy are obtained for each student from La Librairie Canadienne in Montreal. For math, the teacher translated the standard English math text, using a text from France as a reference. For the social studies unit on Quebec, each student has a copy of *Géographie, Cours Elémentaire*, Volume I (Montreal: Centre de Psychologie et de Pédagogie). In addition, a variety of films are shown, with the English narration muted and a French translation recorded on tape by the teacher played instead. Other materials used are film, slide, and overhead projectors; slides of Quebec and France; and records of French music.

GRADING

Students are evaluated by the French teacher both in French language and in the subject areas. Grades of A, B, C, etc. for French are determined by the evaluation of students' language proficiency in class participation, tape tests, and oral tests administered by the teacher. Grades in the subject area are determined in the traditional manner, based on performance (in French) on picture and number quizzes, oral quizzes, oral reports, and experiments.

ROLE OF STUDENTS

Students speak only in French in each of the subjects taught in that language. Student responsibility for completing experiments, reports, and other classroom activities is the same as in the regular sixth-grade classes in English. Students are encouraged to ask the French teacher for a conference when learning problems related to language difficulties occur.

ROLE OF TEACHERS

The French teacher, who is also the department chairman for foreign languages, translates units from math and science texts, prepares worksheets, charts, and French narrations for English films, and selects appropriate readings, slides, and films. She is familiar with all areas of the sixth-grade curriculum that she teaches in French, and conducts all testing and evaluation of language proficiency as well as progress in the subject areas while they are part of the Saturation Program. She works daily with the classroom teacher, who helps select topics to be taught, approaches, and areas for testing, sits in on classes in French, and shares the responsibility for preparing some materials.

ROLE OF ADMINISTRATORS

The school administrators are responsible for determining the enrollment in the enrichment classes and for scheduling 40 minutes daily for their language instruction, as opposed to the usual 15-minute FLES period. The principal originally proposed the idea of a saturation program and met with the French teacher and the classroom teacher to select the areas to be taught in French; she observes the classes regularly.

ROLE OF PARENTS AND COMMUNITY

Parents are invited to observe the saturation class. Both local newspapers, the Butler *Eagle* and the Pittsburgh *Press*, sent reporters to observe the program and published articles describing it. The local radio station invited the French teacher to explain the program on the air.

PROGRAM EVALUATION

Saturation students generally did as well in each subject area as they had previously done in the same areas in English, and there was no problem of "catching up" when they returned to instruction in English. In the first "trial" marking period of mathematics, two students received Cs while the rest received As or Bs; the two C students, it was discovered, had been consistently weak in math. Student participants were asked in individual conferences with the French teacher whether they preferred the "saturation" approach or the standard audiolingual approach that had been used in grades 3–5. Students preferred the new approach, and teacher appraisal of student attitudes confirms that their reaction was more enthusiastic than it had been in the regular FLES classes.

Although no formal outside evaluation has been conducted, representatives of the Pennsylvania Department of Public Instruction visited the program in 1968 and were so favorably impressed that they initiated an amendment to the state's education laws that gives legal status to the teaching of non-language courses in a language other than English.

FUNDING AND COSTS

The program has been funded through the regular school budget. Costs particular to the Saturation Program include the initial cost of geography books for each of 25 students, reference books in French for teacher use, foreign language charts and maps, slides and pictures, and the French teacher's salary. Audio-visual equipment, films, and English language texts are part of the regular school materials and incur no additional expense for the Saturation Program. Specific costs for books, charts, pictures, and maps were not available.

ADAPTABILITY OF CONCEPT TO OTHER PLACES

The foremost consideration for adapting a sixth-grade saturation program would be the students' previous foreign language education and proficiency. A strong FLES sequence, begun several years earlier, would be necessary for the comprehension of and participation in discussions in French in a variety of subjects. Other considerations would be: (1) state laws permitting the instruction of non-language subjects in a foreign language; (2) administrative approval for the program, as well as the support and cooperation of the classroom teacher; (3) a French teacher capable of adapting English materials to the target language, of presenting a variety of subject areas in the curriculum, and of using audio-visual aids effectively; (4) a high level of student interest and ability to use the foreign language; (5) a sixth-grade curriculum with areas that can feasibly be approached in a foreign language (for example, the study of Quebec in social studies), or administrative and parental approval for minor changes in the curriculum for limited periods of time; (6) available print and visual materials in the target language, or the possibility of developing them in several subjects.

A similar program, or a modified version of it, could also be conducted at the secondary level, with the language teacher assuming responsibility for teaching other subject areas in the target language for short periods of time. A French teacher could, for example, arrange with a social studies teacher to conduct in French a regular social studies unit on European history, or take over the regular art teacher's presentation of a unit on impressionism for French classes.

AVAILABLE DESCRIPTIONS

A description of the Saturation Program appears in the 1969 *Journal* of the Pennsylvania State Modern Language Association.

CONTACT PERSON

Stella Emrick, Chairman of Foreign Languages, Emily Brittain School, Butler, Pennsylvania 16001 (412) 287-8721

CHINESE-RUSSIAN STUDY CENTER

ABSTRACT

Four classrooms and a library-resource center in one high school and a teaching staff of six have given students from almost 40 schools in the Toledo, Ohio area the chance to study Chinese and Russian language and culture. Each year more than 300 students enroll in courses offered by the Chinese-Russian Study Center in four levels of Mandarin Chinese and Russian language and literature, the history of Russia and China, and Asian studies. Students who do not come directly to the Center can still benefit from its resources through a service that sends staff members to teach at area schools and speak to any interested school or community group. An interdisciplinary approach to language study, an extensive library, teacher-developed syllabi in all 13 courses offered, and close cooperation with community organizations enable the Center to provide instruction in the languages and cultures of

26

two areas that are increasingly important in contemporary world affairs.

PROGRAM DEVELOPMENT AND PRESENT STATUS

Until six years ago no secondary student in the metropolitan Toledo area could study Chinese and Russian language and culture—simply because they were not offered at the secondary level. In 1966 the Toledo schools received an ESEA Title III grant to establish a Chinese-Russian Study Center. The grant was renewed each of the next three years. With these funds, an area of one school was remodeled for the Center, a six-member staff was hired, consultants were employed to help develop the curriculum and choose materials, and a recruitment and publicity campaign was launched. "One of the first problems encountered and to be dealt with was the mistaken conception that the courses offered by the center would not attract a significant number of interested students."[1] It was assumed that these subjects were too difficult to be taught successfully to high school students and that they would be best introduced at the university level. But over the six years the Center has operated, enrollment has increased at an unexpectedly rapid pace. To publicize the Center and gain enrollment, a brochure is sent to all area schools, articles are published in local newspapers, and the staff speaks to community groups, teachers' conferences, and students at all Toledo schools. A catalogue of Center resources is distributed and the program is explained at Open House for parents and prospective students. In 1969 the local educational television station presented a program on the Center in prime time, just before the President's State of the Union Address.

A major problem encountered in the first two years was the trouble students had in finding time for classes at the Center. Courses were offered until 4:30 p.m., and students were beleaguered by conflicts between Center classes and extracurricular activities at their "home" schools. The Center staff wanted their program to be regarded as an integral part of the academic program of the participating schools, not as "extra" work. By the third year the participating schools agreed to give their students time to study at the Center during the school day. But transportation to the Center was a problem that could not be solved, and during the past three years classes have been offered in five area high schools in addition to the Center itself. Each member of the staff, therefore, teaches Center courses part-time in another school. Another problem was the difficulty in finding an "exceptionally qualified" teacher of Chinese with experience in secondary teaching, but finally a native of Taiwan meeting these requirements was hired. Finding materials suitable for use at the secondary level was a continuing problem; those available were geared mostly toward college, requiring adaptations and teacher-created supplements. Throughout the first four years of the program, the staff members wrote—and tested in their classrooms—syllabi for each of the courses and assembled them into booklets with performance objectives for students, course overviews, materials, and specific topics and activities.

During the program's first year the "speaker service" reached 5000 students in over 25 high schools. And, although it was originally intended only for schools, the service was expanded, at community request, to include public groups as well. In 1968-69 an unexpected increase in enrollment necessitated a full teaching load for each staff member, but the full speaker service was still offered. Requests for information about the program have been received regularly from all areas of the U.S. as well as from Germany and Australia. The director notes that the lack of criticism from the Toledo community toward a program that deals with sensitive political topics and countries that are considered hostile to the United States "indicates a sophistication in education for which the project would like to claim some credit." At present there are six staff members at the Center, including the program director, who also teaches Asian Studies, and a librarian.

TARGET AUDIENCE

Students of all abilities, grades 9-12. Participation is voluntary. In 1972–73, there are 160 students enrolled in four levels of

Chinese or Russian language and literature and more than 150 in social studies courses. These students come from seven schools; a total of 17 schools have sent students to the Center in the past.

PROGRAM GOALS

(1) To provide an opportunity for students in the Toledo area to take courses in the history, culture, and language of China or Russia; (2) to create a library of resource materials specializing in China and Russia that will be open to the entire educational community; (3) to make available to the schools speakers from the Center staff.

STUDENT GROUPING AND
SCHEDULING ARRANGEMENTS

Students meet for 55 minutes a day, five days a week, in language classes grouped according to level. Students may take language or history only, or both combined. Half of the Center's students come from schools which agree to let them finish the school day at the Center or give them travel time to attend the Center and return. The other half of the students attend classes scheduled at their "home" schools taught by "visiting" members of the Center staff.

METHODOLOGY AND REPRESENTATIVE CONTENT

Students are urged to take four years of language and at least one year of related social studies courses. At the first level of language, the approach is audiolingual, with about three-quarters of instruction time devoted to listening and speaking. In the course syllabi, there are stated objectives for students for each level. For example, in Mandarin Chinese I students are expected:

1. To be able to pronounce all the sounds of Mandarin Chinese.
2. To develop the ability to speak and understand short and simple Chinese.

3. To be able to read and write correctly about 200 Chinese characters.
4. To be able to write simple sentences based on sentence patterns.
5. To understand some aspects of the life and customs of Chinese people.

Students work with pattern drills, folk songs, pronunciation drills, and basic dialogues. The dialogues are memorized, reinforced with tapes recorded by native speakers, and adapted in role-playing situations. Chinese characters are introduced only after the students have command of basic sound patterns and some dialogues, and students read only what has been previously learned orally. Each character is practiced in writing about 20 times; then students are asked to copy sentences and finally whole dialogues. This is followed by dictation, translating sentences into English, and writing short compositions or letters. The first-level Chinese course also devotes some time to values, attitudes, ethics, and other aspects of daily life in China; films and filmstrips are shown, and there are occasional outside readings in English. At the second level of Mandarin Chinese, students learn 250 more characters, and there is more emphasis on reading and writing. At level III, students are expected to understand rapid standard speech, speak with intonation and pronunciation "approximating native speech" in a variety of contexts, read magazines and newspapers with reasonable ease, do more translating, and gain a broader understanding of Chinese history. By the end of level IV, students have learned over 1200 characters, have more practice in translating from Chinese to English and English to Chinese, carry out lengthy discussions in Chinese on contemporary China and world affairs, and write compositions and summaries of discussions.

In Russian I, listening and speaking skills are developed through dialogue and vocabulary work. Students learn 800–1000 words and about 70 idioms, "basic declensions, the function of the perfective aspect, declension of personal pronouns, and ordinal and cardinal numbers." They are expected to understand simple spoken sentences and paragraphs in Russian and eventually to write them. The Russian alphabet is analyzed, the language is compared to other Slavic languages, and the relationship between Russian history and the development of the language is discussed.

Students read only material that has been learned orally. Writing exercises begin with letters and letter elements, then progress from straight copying, dictation, and guided composition to free composition in level III. By the end of level III, students are expected to read and report on short stories from Russian history and literature and understand fluent spoken Russian. The fourth level is a literature course with readings, class discussions, written and oral reports, and "trials" where literary characters are accused and defended by students. They read excerpts and entire works dating from the time of the introduction of Christianity to Russia through Pasternak, and often comparisons are made with literature of other countries. For example, Chekhov's *Cherry Orchard* is compared with Mitchell's *Gone with the Wind*.

In social studies, courses are conducted in English and are based on readings and discussion. Each course is one semester long. Asian Studies attempts to "illustrate the cultural diversity of the Asian world," covering the history, religions, and cultural achievements of India, China, and Japan. Imperial Chinese History focuses on the development of China until 1644 (the year of the Manchu conquest), as well as traditions, legends, religion, philosophy, literature, and art. Modern Chinese History includes such topics as the geographical and cultural conditions that tended to isolate China from other countries, the influence of geography on China's way of life, the Nationalist-Communist split, the impact of China's cultural heritage on its present, and the relationship between China and its Asian neighbors. Imperial Russian History emphasizes the relationship between Russia's past and present, and parallels the evolution of Russian society with that of the U.S., beginning with the founding of the first Russian state and ending with the fall of the Romanovs in 1917. Soviet Russian History covers the revolutionary movement, life and politics in contemporary Russia, and the relationship between Russia and other countries.

There are also special activities related to the language and history courses: culture days, field trips to such places as the Toledo Art Museum, the celebration of Chinese New Year, and visits from members of the Toledo Ballet Company who discuss the Russian ballet and give performances. The Russian teacher has even taken some students to Russia.

MATERIALS AND FACILITIES

In addition to the teacher-prepared syllabi, the Center has assembled a large collection of books, periodicals, newspapers, films, filmstrips, slides, transparencies, and records. A catalogue and supplement on audio-visual aids is available for use in the participating schools and the Center classes. The library-resource center contains movie and filmstrip projectors, tape recorders, and record players and is furnished with tables, bookcases, and comfortable armchairs.

CREDIT AND GRADING

Students are graded A through F by "subjective teacher analysis." They receive one full credit for each year of work, a system approved by the North Central Association and accepted by the "home" schools.

ROLE OF TEACHERS

Teachers work closely with one another to integrate the study of language with that of history. At times the language teachers give lectures to the social studies classes in English. Teachers also talk to classes and community groups throughout the city as part of the speaker service.

ROLES OF PROGRAM DIRECTOR AND CONSULTANTS

The director of the Chinese-Russian Study Center teaches the course in Asian Studies and is responsible for hiring and supervising staff members, arranging class schedules, and managing the budget. He takes part in the speaker service and arranges for special activities and guest speakers. He visits administrators and counselors in the participating schools to discuss any problems in scheduling and the means of promoting enrollment. Consultants in social studies, Russian history and language, and Chinese history and language assisted in curriculum development, selection of textbooks and resource materials, selecting personnel, and publicity.

ROLE OF COMMUNITY

The Chinese-Russian Study Center has been involved extensively with the community through its speaker service and publicity campaigns. A Citizens' Advisory Committee advises the Center on promotional activities and program improvements. Finally, there is continuous interaction between the Center and educational and cultural organizations. For example, the Center helped organize a Symposium on Asia and Africa for social studies teachers with the Toledo Council of World Affairs, conducted a China Night with the International Institute, and, in cooperation with the U.S. Information Agency, prepared an exhibit of photographs for a cultural exchange exhibit on American education that toured the U.S.S.R. A Chinese instructor from the Center prepared a show for a local television station on how to teach children the use of the abacus. The League of Women Voters used staff members as resource people while doing a study of China and sent copies of the results of the study for use at the Center. The University of Toledo often sends students to observe classes at the Center as part of their teacher-training program and sends intern teachers to work in the library-resource center.

PROGRAM EVALUATION

Studies of the program that were available were done at the end of the program's second year. An enrollment of 424 students in 1968–69 represented an increase of 59.6% over the previous year. In informal opinion surveys, the students said that they did not find the study of the languages especially difficult. "The grades earned . . . indicate that the performance of the students [was] above average. More than half of the students earned either an A or a B in Center subjects. Most of the first-year language students indicate they will continue the study of the language in the next school year." A questionnaire was sent to all students who had completed courses at the Center and graduated from high school. Two hundred were sent and 72 were returned. The students rated the content of Center classes as follows: outstanding—61%; good —36%; and fair—-3%. None rated it poor. Instruction was evaluated as outstanding by 75%, good by 22%, fair by none, and poor by 3%. Asked to what degree their attitude toward China or Russia was influenced by their work at the Center, all students indicated that they were influenced, 71% greatly, 29% somewhat. Forty-seven percent said their work at the Center influenced their choice of university courses, and 85% of those who went to college said the Center courses were "very helpful" in their college work.

Many consultants have visited the program and commented favorably. Jean Tilford, Supervisor of Social Studies in the Cincinnati Public Schools, noted, "The establishment of the Center, physically, within an existing high school appears to have been accomplished with a maximum return on investment and planning. It is recognized as a most innovative educational experiment by persons who work in the area of social studies throughout the nation." David Tavel of the University of Toledo stated, "There are features of uniqueness in the Center, such as the appeal to all pupils rather than just the academic elite, which render the program all the more notable." Many consultants mention the fine library holdings, commend the physical arrangements in the classrooms and resource center, and note that the program appears appealing to students. Finally, members of the Center staff have been invited to explain the work of the Center at the National Council for the Social Studies, the Modern Language Association, the American Association of Asian Studies, the American Association for the Advancement of Slavic Studies, and the Ohio Council for the Social Studies.

FUNDING AND COSTS

Title III grants amounting to more than $380,000 from June 1966 to June 1970 plus some local funding financed all developmental aspects of the program: establishment of the physical facilities, consultant fees, curriculum development, hardware, instructional materials, an extensive library collection, publicity, the speaker service, publication of syllabi, and staff salaries for the first four years. Since then, funding has been assumed by the Toledo Public Schools; besides salaries, additional costs have been $2000 for "software" materials, $200 for equipment, and $1000 for the maintenance of the Center's office, located with the classrooms and library.

ADAPTABILITY OF CONCEPT TO OTHER PLACES

The director notes that it would be difficult for a single school to establish such a program because of limited student demand; the "rationale for the project was predicated upon the idea of creating one central place to which students from almost 40 secondary schools" could come. A "magnet" center for the study of less commonly taught languages and related subjects in the social sciences could be established, like the Chinese-Russian Study Center, within an existing school facility by a group of schools or a school district. Cooperation among participating schools and the center is needed for scheduling, release of students, and credit. Funds for a resource center and library, publicity, curriculum development, and staff salaries, as well as the availability of qualified teachers in "critical" languages, are also major considerations.

AVAILABLE DESCRIPTIONS

The Center has been the subject of articles in the January 10, 1972 issue of *Scholastic Teacher* and the January 21, 1972 issue of *Ohio Schools*.

CONTACT PERSON

Norman Klee, Director, Chinese-Russian Study Center, Toledo Public Schools, 3301 Upton Avenue, Toledo, Ohio 43613 (419) 475-5092

NOTE

[1] All quotations are from "Application for Federal Continuation Grant Under P.L. 89–10, Title III ESEA: Project Title Chinese-Russian Study Center, Project Number 67-3357" (Toledo: Toledo, Ohio City School District, 1968–69, 1969–70).

CONTACT
STUDY
OF
MEXICO

ABSTRACT

Students at Woodrow Wilson High School in Tacoma, Washington can learn Spanish both in the streets of Mexico City and the classrooms of Tacoma through an exciting program that brings foreign study into the school's regular curriculum. The Contact Study of Mexico gives students the opportunity to spend seven weeks in Mexico, where, during the final 12-week quarter of the school year, they live in private homes, attend local schools, do independent research, and travel within the country.

PROGRAM DEVELOPMENT AND PRESENT STATUS

The program was developed by the Spanish faculty at Woodrow Wilson High School in cooperation with the Coordinator of

Foreign Languages for the Tacoma Public Schools and the Ibero-american Cultural Exchange Program (ICEP), a private nonprofit organization. The Office of the State Superintendent of Public Instruction approved the program in October 1971, and it was put into operation the following spring. The program is open to students in the school who have completed two years of high school Spanish, have been recommended by a teacher in the Spanish department, and agree to the standards of conduct established by the high school and the ICEP. Twenty-six students in grades 11 and 12 participated in 1972; an equal number is expected in the spring of 1973.

MAJOR GOALS FOR STUDENTS

(1) To gain an understanding of a foreign culture through real immersion and involvement in it; (2) to develop proficiency in the Spanish language through intensive contact with native Spanish speakers; (3) to appreciate their own country, its values, culture, and political system; (4) to be involved in "activities relevant to solutions of problems of intercultural misunderstanding";[1] (5) to learn first-hand the geography of a neighboring country; and (6) to gain in-depth knowledge of an aspect of Mexican life through independent research.

PROGRAM GOALS

(1) To develop a mutual feeling of international friendship; (2) to help Mexicans understand Americans and their culture by giving them close contact with young Americans; and (3) to serve the nation's needs by increasing interest in international understanding, diplomacy, and competence in foreign languages.

ORGANIZATIONAL ARRANGEMENTS

The school year in Tacoma is divided into three 12-week quarters; Contact Study of Mexico takes a full quarter. The program consists of five stages; (1) three weeks of full-day orientation in Woodrow Wilson High School; (2) one week of orientation in Mexico City; (3) homestay with Mexican families and attendance at local preparatory schools for five weeks; (4) one week of field trips in Mexico; and (5) two and a half weeks of "culminating activities" in Tacoma.

REPRESENTATIVE CONTENT

During orientation in Tacoma, students work with (1) the four language skills, Mexican slang, and vocabulary for specific situations they are likely to encounter; (2) Mexican history and geography, especially of those areas they will visit (altar pyramids of the Aztecs, tropical agricultural areas), and the system of land reform; (3) contemporary events in Mexico (the political system, the riots at the 1968 Olympics, attitudes toward the U.S. and Cuba); (4) Hispanic values and customs (handshaking, vocal intonations, traditional family relationships); (5) shopping practices (street vendors, haggling over prices); (6) the fine arts and handicrafts; and (7) readings and recordings by W. Clement Stone, Dale Carnegie, and Norman Vincent Peale to provide motivation and self-confidence. In the orientation period in Mexico City, students are given more detailed and specific cultural information (family relationships, operation of schools, exchange and handling of money, health measures), as well as historical information about the monuments, churches, universities, theaters, museums, pyramids, and other places visited in Mexico City. Relevant and necessary vocabulary and expressions are explained.

During the homestay students develop their listening and comprehension skills by living with Mexican families and attending local schools. The students choose their projects for independent research from among topics suggested by the program staff. In the past, these suggestions have included the roles in Mexico of the military, the church, students in politics, the Ejido system of land reform, the one-party system, the middle class, foreign capital, technology, modern education, races and racism, arts, religion, significant people in Mexican history, or significant historical periods. The final form of each student's project is a report, written in Spanish, combining research findings and on-site observations with related pictures taken in Mexico.

Following the homestay, the group unites for a week of field trips, during which they visit such places as the ceramic and tile pottery manufacturing shops of Puebla, the forts of Loreto and Guadalupe, the tropical coast, several Indian villages, and Chulula, former center of the Toltec empire. They then return to Tacoma, where the remaining two and a half weeks of the quarter are spent coordinating pictures and information gathered in work on individual projects for a group presentation to other classes in the school, assemblies, and to elementary and high schools in the area. Last year over 100 presentations were given. Discussions are held to formulate ideas for future groups conducting similar programs.

METHODOLOGY

In pre-departure orientation, language study is approached through audiolingual drills in vocabulary and grammar, small-group conversation sessions conducted by advanced students, written drills and reading exercises, songs and games, dramatized dialogues, correspondence with host homes and schools in Mexico, and oral reports. History, geography, and culture are presented through individualized readings, talks by native Mexicans, lectures, films, maps, slides, recordings, and individual and group study of Mexican newspapers. Students take extensive notes. All activities are conducted in Spanish.

The orientation in Mexico consists of lectures and group discussions given by the ICEP director and representatives with the assistance of Mexican teachers and high school and university students. Daily study tours in the city provide direct contact with local history and culture.

Students work independently on research projects during the orientation and homestay periods. The supervisor-counselor visits each student periodically to give guidance.

MATERIALS

The basic texts used in orientation are *Spanish for Communication* (Boston: Houghton Mifflin Co.) and *Muchas Facetas de México* (Skokie, Illinois: National Textbook Co.). A wide variety of supplementary texts and reference books in Spanish and English, workbooks, Spanish magazines and newspapers, readers, films, filmstrips, and slides are used in orientation, as well as tapes, tape recording booths, film and slide projectors, maps of Spanish-speaking countries, and posters.

CREDIT AND ARTICULATION

Students at Woodrow Wilson High School receive four credits in each of the three quarters of the school year. In the quarter devoted to the Contact Study of Mexico, participants earn full credit: two credits in foreign language, one in social studies, and one in the project area. Students are evaluated during orientation on the basis of performance on oral and written tests, oral class presentations, written assignments, and notes; individual projects are evaluated by the teacher on the basis of preparation, content, and presentation. Letter grades (A, B, etc.) are given, as in all other courses in the school.

A course in Latin American Civilization and Culture is now given in the winter preceding the Mexican trip, and participants are encouraged to take this course for advance preparation. When they return from Mexico, students may continue in advanced courses in the regular Spanish sequence, or they may act as teaching assistants in Spanish classes in the school and as cross-age tutors in the district's elementary and junior high schools. One student helps out in a local Mexican restaurant and her time there counts as class time.

ROLE OF STUDENTS

In Mexican schools students may attend classes as visitors or participate actively as tutors or teaching aides in English classes.

Students are considered members of their host families, assume their share of household duties, and adhere to family rules. Students obey standards of conduct established by the program directors and respect and adjust to local modes of behavior, customs, and values. They use Spanish as much as possible during the orientation weeks and speak in Spanish in their Mexican homes and schools. Students tutor members of their family interested in learning English.

ROLE OF SUPERVISOR-COUNSELOR

The supervisor-counselor conducts the major part of the orientation session and administers proficiency tests before and after the trip. During the week of travel and the orientation session in Mexico, this teacher acts as general supervisor, counselor, chaperone, and resource person, and is available 24 hours a day. During the homestay period he visits five or six students daily to help with projects and personal problems and makes himself available to any student who needs him by posting his itinerary at all times at his hotel. Although no special training is necessary for this position, it is evident that the supervisor-counselor must be well versed in Mexican culture, geography, and language, and able to counsel students on a wide range of academic and personal problems. Following the Mexican trip, the supervisor-counselor helps arrange visits and presentations in other schools.

ROLES OF TEACHERS AND TEACHER AIDES

The four Spanish teachers in the school recommend students for participation in the program, assist in orientation, and give guidance in selecting topics for independent study. Teachers from other departments supply references and information in history, geography, art, and music. Two or three Mexican students attending Woodrow Wilson High School through the ICEP assist during orientation in teaching Mexican history and tutoring language.

ROLE OF SPECIAL STAFF

The Iberoamerican Cultural Exchange Program determines standards of conduct and health, arranges the transportation to Mexico and travel in the country, and arranges hotel accommodations, homestays with families, attendance in Mexican schools, and accident and health insurance. The ICEP director and representatives conduct lectures and discussions with students during orientation week in Mexico City and accompany them on tours of the city during orientation week and on the field trips. Mexican teachers and high school and university students, working voluntarily in cooperation with the ICEP, also take part in discussions and field trips, providing information, supervision, and practical assistance.

ROLE OF ADMINISTRATORS

The Office of the Superintendent of Public Instruction of the state of Washington gave final approval of the Contact Study of Mexico through the coordinating efforts of the Administrator for Secondary Education of the Tacoma Public Schools. The district's Coordinator of Foreign Languages cooperated in developing and promoting the program. An assistant, the Area Chairman in Foreign Languages, assists in teaching during the orientation session in Tacoma and arranges for student presentations in schools after the group returns from Mexico.

ROLE OF PARENTS AND COMMUNITY

Parents of participants give written permission for the students to travel and study abroad and agree to the terms of conduct and organization as determined by the school and the ICEP. Parents and members of the community contribute to the money-raising projects organized for the program. Each elementary and junior high school in the area, each high school teacher, and many community organizations are contacted for student visits and presentations.

PROGRAM EVALUATION

After the 1972 trip, participants filled out a questionnaire, intended to evaluate the program organization and the students' experiences in Mexico as well as survey their attitudes toward the foreign country and people. All students were highly positive toward Mexico and Mexican people and said living with the families had helped them feel truly involved in Mexican life. They noted a wide range of valuable experiences—making friends and sharing in family life, tutoring English, and feelings of satisfaction at their increased fluency in Spanish. "Before I went I thought of Mexicans just as people of a foreign country. Now I think of them as my friends," wrote one girl. Another student noted that "through the family I made friends and gained an understanding and appreciation of Mexico that I could have received by no other means." All students felt more open-minded and patient as a result of the trip. They had grown to appreciate the high standard of living, sanitation conditions, educational system, and freer family relationships in the U.S., but, at the same time, found the easygoing attitudes of Mexicans, their open friendliness and warmth, and the slower pace of Mexican life very attractive. Students suggested that a more careful screening of host families could be done, that orientation in Tacoma be shortened or made less intensive and carried out over a quarter, and that the orientation period in Mexico City be lengthened.

Before and after the trip, students were given the Pimsleur Listening Comprehension Test, Form C, and the MLA Listening and Reading Comprehension Tests, Form MA. As a group the students performed slightly better on the post-tests than the pre-tests, indicating some improvement in the "passive" skills of listening and reading during the seven-week stay in Mexico. The improvement, however, was not statistically significant. Speaking and writing skills were not tested. The most important effect of Contact Study of Mexico seems to have been in the participants' attitudes toward the Spanish language and the Mexican people and culture.

FUNDING

Those parts of the program conducted at Woodrow Wilson High School, as well as reference books, texts, and audio-visual materials, are financed through the regular school budget. The average annual expenditure per pupil for the district is $1130. Transportation, ICEP services, and homestays are financed entirely by the students, with the help of parents, part-time jobs, and money-raising projects arranged through the Spanish department: car washes, rummage and decal sales, dinners for the community, and painting projects. The supervisor-counselor's travel and hotel expenses of approximately $500 are met through student fees, and his regular salary is provided by the school district.

COST

The total cost for each participant is estimated at $643.

$150	ICEP fees for services provided by ICEP, including 5-week homestay Host families provide room and board
39	Thirteen nights in hotels
12	Health and accident insurance premium
16	Bus fare for field trip
20	Estimated portion of accompanying teacher's expenses
10	Reserve fund to meet unforeseen expenses; refundable if unused
280	Round-trip air fare
39	Estimated cost of meals, exclusive of homestay
7	Estimated cost of local transportation
10	Admission fees to museums, movies, etc.
60	Estimate of additional personal spending money needed

The special texts used for orientation, *Spanish for Communication* and *Muchas Facetas de México*, are purchased through the school budget, an initial cost of $246 for 26 pupils. All other texts, reference books, and audio-visual materials are used in the regular Spanish sequence and incur no additional expense to the school or to individual students for the contact program. The school provided cameras and film supplies for the production of the group's film, and editing was done by the supervisor-counselor during the summer at his own expense.

ADAPTABILITY OF CONCEPT TO OTHER PLACES

Considerations in adapting the concept of a contact program would be: (1) local and/or state administrative approval of prolonged student and teacher absence during the school year (in Tacoma, the program is given the status of an extended field trip); (2) arrangements for transportation, hotel accommodations, travel, health, and accident insurance, homestays, and attendance in schools in the foreign country; (3) the availability of qualified supervisor-counselors; (4) assurance and evidence for parents that students will be suitably supervised and housed and that adequate medical attention and counseling will be available; (5) establishment of standards of health and conduct acceptable to American parents and host families in the foreign country; (6) parental approval; (7) ability to finance the trip through special projects and student, parent, community, or school resources; (8) scheduling allowances and approval from other departments for release of students from other courses for orientation as well as foreign residence. Orientation could be offered as a full semester or quarter course one period a day to minimize student absence from other subjects.

The 30 secondary schools of Jefferson County, Colorado have worked with foreign ministries of education, departments of tourism, and other government agencies in setting up a somewhat similar study-abroad program, called Third Quarter Abroad (QA3). The program takes place during the entire third quarter of the school year, which is four quarters long. Participants are required to be able to function in the language and have both the recommendations of their counselors and the permission of their teachers for the third and fourth quarters. Following a week of orientation and travel, they spend almost seven weeks living with host families in Clermont-Ferrand, France; Tehuacan, Mexico; or Alejuela and San Jose, Costa Rica. Special QA3 language and culture courses, taught by native teachers, are given in the mornings, while lectures, field trips, and theater-going fill the afternoons. Occasionally students visit regular classes in local schools. After the homestay period, the students tour the countries for nine or ten days, visiting the capital cities and seeing some of the sights in the countryside. Another component of the QA3 program is Classical Studies, for which there is no language requirement. Groups of students accompanied by Jefferson County teachers travel through Italy, Greece, and the Aegean Islands; they explore the remains of Classical and Renaissance cultures and go to museums, monuments, and plays. The costs of the programs are $910 for France, $550 for Mexico, $735 for Costa Rica, and $1150 for Classical Studies. These costs do not include personal spending money. Participants earn one and a quarter Carnegie units of credit in languages and humanities.

AVAILABLE DESCRIPTIONS

"A Contact Study of Mexico," a film and tape recording produced by the participants of the 1972 program, edited by Ralph Emerson, is available from the contact person for a $15 rental fee.

SENIOR PROJECT STAFF

Carl Dellaccio, Coordinator of Foreign Languages, Tacoma Public Schools; Cenobio Macias, Area Chairman in Foreign Languages; Ralph Emerson, Spanish teacher; James O'Neill, Spanish teacher; Gerald Aurand, Director, Iberoamerican Cultural Exchange Program.

CONTACT PERSON

Carl Dellaccio, Coordinator of Foreign Languages, Tacoma Public Schools, P.O. Box 1357, Tacoma, Washington 98402 (206) FU3-1881 Ext. 470

Larry McWilliams, Coordinator of Foreign Languages, Jefferson County Public Schools, 809 Quail Street, Lakewood, Colorado 80215 (303) 237-6971

NOTE

[1] All quotations are from Ralph Emerson et al., "A Contact Study of Mexico: Using the Spanish Language" (Tacoma: Woodrow Wilson High School, 1972).

FOREIGN LANGUAGE EXPLORATION PROGRAM (FLEX)

ABSTRACT

When a ninth-grade student is faced with a choice among five foreign languages he may study for several years, how does he decide which one to take? Does he take the one they say is easy, the one his mother and father took (or wished they had taken instead of the one they did), the one his best friend takes, the one with the friendliest teacher? Or does he take the one he really likes? In a Foreign Language Exploration Program in the junior high schools of Topeka, Kansas, students have a chance to discover their own preference in foreign languages by getting a "taste" of German, Russian, French, Latin, and Spanish for six weeks each. After learning some basic vocabulary, sentence structures, cultural associations, and linguistic idiosyncrasies of each language, the students are ready at the end of the year to make a reasonable choice of a language (if any) to study in high school

on the basis of real experience, real success or failure, real likes
and dislikes, and real knowledge.

PROGRAM DEVELOPMENT AND PRESENT STATUS

In order to shift the decisive factors in student choice of
foreign language away from prejudice, hearsay, parental or peer
pressure, whimsy, or indifference, FLEX was begun as a pilot
program in the fall of 1970. Sixty students in two seventh-grade
classes in two schools volunteered for FLEX classes, and by the
end of the year all six staff members agreed the program had been
a success. The following year over 250 students in nine classes in
seven of the district's 12 junior high schools were involved, and
the staff was expanded to ten—an average of two teachers in each
language. By 1972–73, ten FLEX teachers were giving language
instruction to a total of 461 students in 17 classes in 11 Topeka
junior highs, and, under a system of rotating teachers, almost
every class is exposed to five different teachers as well as five
different languages.

STUDENT GROUPING
AND SCHEDULING ARRANGEMENTS

All FLEX classes in the 11 schools are scheduled at the
same block of time during the day in order to allow for the rotation of teachers every six weeks; the only exception is where one
teacher teaches all five languages to two classes for the entire year.
The first three weeks of the year are used for a general introduction to language, then six weeks are devoted to each of five languages and the last three weeks of the year to summary and
comparison. Class meetings are held for one hour each day.

REPRESENTATIVE CONTENT

For the first three-week phase on the philosophy of foreign
language study, students discuss such concepts as "written" vs.
"verbal" language, speech, and language without sound. They see

a filmstrip "Impact of Communication" and listen to the tape "A Word in Your Ear." They may play charades, begin pronunciation of words in various languages, discuss the importance of studying foreign languages, and see the filmstrip "Why Study Foreign Languages." Students then begin the first language; there is no set order to the sequence of languages. Basically the same vocabulary is learned in each one to allow students to make a comparative analysis of all languages studied. In all five, students learn to count to 31, tell time, name classroom objects, respond to basic commands, and recognize the language orally and visually. They become acquainted with certain grammatical idiosyncrasies of the languages and learn to carry on two very basic conversations in each. For example, each teacher is asked to include somewhere in the six-week unit the following dialogue:

A. Good morning.
B. Hi, how are you?
A. Fine thanks, and you?
B. Not so well; I have a cold.
A. Gee, that's too bad. I hope you feel better soon.
B. Well, I have to go now. I'll see you later.

Students are also introduced to cultural aspects of the peoples and countries represented by each target language; the focus of the cultural unit is left to the individual teachers. Some may concentrate on music and art, while others, such as a teacher whose class met in the home economics room, might have their students do some "native" cooking, but certain basic customs are explained to each class and songs are sung in each language. The final three weeks are devoted to a comparative analysis among all five languages and English. Students fill out a questionnaire telling which languages they liked most and least, how difficult they thought each language was, and which language they would like to continue.

METHODOLOGY

The approach is mainly aural-oral, with very little emphasis on reading and writing. The teacher introduces an oral structure through a pattern drill accompanied by a visual aid. The students learn the pattern, and visual substitutions are made; each time a visual substitution is made, the previous aids are reviewed. A second review may be made through a question-answer period, with the teacher first asking students questions. Then students can "play teacher" and ask each other the same questions, while the teacher walks around the room listening to individual answers. Many "lingua" games and audio-visual aids are used; each teacher has a tape recorder, overhead projector, and record player, and uses them as he sees fit.

MATERIALS

FLEX teachers have at their disposal hundreds of records, filmstrips, tapes, and overhead transparencies from the district's audio-visual center. Teachers vary the materials from six-week period to six-week period and from year to year. Texts are used only for the introductory phase; for each language teacher-prepared worksheets and diagrams supplement the oral and visual presentations.

CREDIT AND ARTICULATION

A special FLEX report card lets parents know at the end of each language phase if the student is doing well, doing satisfactory work with certain reservations, or doing unsatisfactory work. No letter or number grades are used. Evaluation is based on daily work, conversations, and cultural projects, and students are reminded that it is natural to do better in some languages than in others. One unit of credit (two semesters of attendance) is awarded upon completion of the course, provided the student satisfactorily completes at least four of the six phases.

The FLEX program is the first foreign language offering in the district. In most schools, no individual language is offered until the ninth grade; at this time, a student may select the language he found he liked best in FLEX.

ROLE OF STUDENTS

Students enroll in the FLEX program voluntarily and by the end of the program are expected to be able to make a reasonably intelligent comparison of the languages and decide on their personal preferences.

ROLE OF TEACHERS

Each FLEX teacher but one is responsible for only one language, and there are two teachers in each language. All ten are teachers in the district's secondary schools and have one or two FLEX classes in a different junior high school each six-week period. One teacher additionally teaches all five languages to two different classes in two schools, and remains with these classes all year. The teacher who teaches a class's first language also conducts the introductory phase for that class. The last language teacher of a class gives the three-week final session.

ROLES OF DEPARTMENT SUPERVISOR
AND SCHOOL PRINCIPALS

The department supervisor also teaches Russian in the FLEX program. He establishes the rotating teacher schedules, the basic curriculum outline, and course goals, conducts training sessions for teachers, and makes periodic classroom visitations. Junior high principals are responsible for enrolling their classes in the FLEX program. They talk to sixth-grade classes to describe each elective seventh-grade course, such as FLEX, and sometimes the department supervisor goes with the principal to answer specific questions.

ROLE OF PARENTS AND COMMUNITY

The department supervisor is on call for parent meetings when FLEX is on the agenda. Parents receive special report cards for their students' progress in FLEX. At least one feature article in the leading local newspaper focuses on the program each year, and at least one article in each issue of the city foreign language newsletter concerns FLEX.

TEACHER TRAINING

FLEX teachers meet with the department supervisor three or four times before the school year for an orientation workshop, and meet with him within three days after each phase of the program begins to discuss curricula, approaches, and problems.

PROGRAM EVALUATION

An in-depth study to evaluate the total FLEX program will begin in 1973–74. By that time, those students in the pilot program and the first year of extended enrollment will be far enough along in school to determine the effectiveness of FLEX in terms of student interest, perseverance, and proficiency in foreign languages. Meanwhile, the growth of the program from 60 students in two schools to 461 in 11 within three years is an indication that students and administrators, who all participate on a voluntary basis, find the program valuable. Only one Topeka junior high does not participate in the program. In an item entitled "Believe It or Not" in the December 1972 Topeka foreign language newsletter, it was noted that overall foreign language enrollment in the city rose between 1971–72 and 1972–73 and that the largest enrollment increase between the two years was in the FLEX program, which grew from 251 students to 461.

FUNDING AND COSTS

The average annual expenditure per pupil specifically for the FLEX program is $73. This district funding covers all costs of salaries of FLEX teachers, materials, and curriculum development.

ADAPTABILITY OF CONCEPT TO OTHER PLACES

A program similar to FLEX could be initiated in any school district (or even in one junior high school cooperating with the language department of the high school into which it feeds), depending on available time, money, and personnel. Scheduling in the junior highs should permit one period each day for each class in the program, and language teachers from the high school(s) should be free to teach at the junior high(s) for one or two periods daily, unless additional staff is hired expressly for the program. If several junior high schools are involved, it is best to schedule these classes during the same block of time, to facilitate teacher rotation. Personnel and released time should be available for curriculum development. Teachers should not only be qualified in their respective language or languages, but trained in the methods and curriculum chosen for the program so that presentations in each language, though varied in certain materials and activities, will be consistent enough in approach and content to allow students to make a fair comparative analysis. It has been found in Topeka that rotating teachers helps students to avoid choosing a language on the basis of teacher personality. If a high school offers only two or three languages, a half-year junior high exploration program could be given.

CONTACT PERSON

George M. Rundell, Supervisor of Foreign Languages, The Topeka Public Schools, Instructional Resource Center, 1601 Van Buren, Topeka, Kansas 66612 (913) 357-0351 Ext. 46

FOREIGN LANGUAGE INCENTIVE PROGRAM (FLIP)

ABSTRACT

The Foreign Language Incentive Program is a three-day summer institute that provides high school students and teachers from the rural and isolated areas of Wyoming with an active experience in foreign cultures and languages. For 72 hours at a small college campus, participants communicate only in French, German, or Spanish in activities ranging from soccer and cooking to debates, rap sessions, and picnics. Activities are planned and organized almost entirely by students and conducted with the extensive assistance of native foreign language speakers from the community— housewives, teachers, businessmen, and college professors. Starting as a suggestion in the French club of one Wyoming high school, this "grass-roots" movement has spread through ten school districts, involving a remarkable degree of cooperation between volunteer students, teachers, and community representatives from the entire state. FLIP serves not only as an entertaining and culturally-enriching experience for students, but also as an inservice workshop for foreign language teachers, who, by attending the institute, earn two of the five credits needed every five years to remain certified in the state. A videotape of the institute is presented to community groups and elementary schools to promote interest in foreign languages and recruit for high school language classes.

PROGRAM DEVELOPMENT AND PRESENT STATUS

The idea for FLIP was proposed in the spring of 1971 to the language clubs of Natrona County High School in Casper, Wyoming by Ann Tollefson, Instructor of French. Club members responded enthusiastically and the following September a general organizational meeting was held for all interested students and teachers in the two Casper high schools. Students signed up for seven different committees, elected their own chairmen, and for nine months worked after school and on weekends with the help of teacher advisors. The committees chose topics of discussion, collected materials, rented films, identified and contacted resource people, made arrangements for publicity, scheduling, and room and board, and handled enrollment, budgeting, and registration. The Central Coordinating Committee sent letters describing FLIP to every high school in the state, asking students interested in attending to send for application forms. The Classes and Resources Committees, after recruiting guest speakers and arranging topics for discussion and lectures, appointed competent students to research these topics and prepare vocabulary lists that would help and encourage students to take part in discussions. These lists were distributed to participants at registration and shorter "minimum" vocabulary lists were sent with their letters of acceptance.

The first institute, conducted in June 1972, involved over 100 people: 54 students in French, 15 in Spanish, and 17 in German, as well as 16 teacher-participants and more than 25 instructors and resource personnel. When participants arrived at Casper College, the scene was set for a "mini-trip" to Europe. All signs on campus had been covered with their French, German, and Spanish equivalents, three national flags were flown, dormitory space had been divided according to languages, foreign magazines had been placed in all lounge areas, and taped music from the foreign countries was broadcast in the dormitories and between classes. The Welcoming Committee gave each student a vocabulary list for all three languages, so that French students, for example, could ask directions or say hello to German- or Spanish-speaking students without using English. These words were read aloud to all participants at the introductory assembly to aid in pronunciation. Students were asked not to make phone calls or use radios, televisions, and printed matter in English. No English was spoken for three days except in an evaluative rap session the last morning, and even then participants lapsed into their foreign languages.

Each language group had its own activities and classes; for French and Spanish students, there were often separate activities for two different levels, beginners and intermediate-advanced. Classes were frequently in the form of a short lecture followed by a group discussion. These focused on such topics as travel, art, literature, political and social problems, education, and daily life in a foreign country. A woman born in Algeria discussed the movement for Algerian independence, a native of Chile spoke on life in his country, a native of Germany showed slides and discussed the history of a small German town and the effects of World War II, and a French-speaking resident of Montreal discussed the problems confronting the French citizens of an English-dominated country. The French group also participated in a provocative debate on population control, witnessed the dramatization of an Ionesco play by two professors, and helped a Canadian housewife prepare snails. Spanish students had a seminar in the poetry of their language, took part in a spelling bee and dramatic improvisations, and were taught soccer by a Peruvian native. Students in German saw travelogue films, sang German hymns, and discussed German art with a German artist. Each language had a cooking demonstration and soccer classes, and students were able to test their comprehension skills through such feature-length films as "Les Parapluies de Cherbourg," "Don Quixote," and "Confess Dr. Corda." A picnic for all participants included a soccer match that pitted the French speakers against the German and Spanish students combined, with spectators rooting for their team in the appropriate language. The final evening of the institute was devoted to a banquet and dance.

In written evaluations and the final rap-session, student and teacher participants were unanimously positive in their reactions to the program. A student chairman for each town was chosen, and the institute has been put on an independent, rotating basis, organized by a different school each year. The 1973 FLIP is being planned by students and teachers from the Sheridan, Wyoming schools, and all records and evaluations have been passed on to their Central Coordinating Committee. Several other communities have asked for the responsibility in 1974. It is hoped that "in alternating among the larger towns of the state, we can best utilize the available resource people in it."[1]

TARGET AUDIENCE

Students of all abilities, grades 9–12, from any school district in Wyoming, who have completed at least one year of study in French, German, or Spanish, and any interested foreign language teacher in the state.

MAJOR GOALS FOR PARTICIPANTS

To gain experience in using the foreign language by simulating real-life situations in a foreign country; to develop an appreciation of the cultural heritage, values, and social structures of the people whose language is being studied; to develop an awareness of leisure-time activities in the foreign country.

PROGRAM GOALS

To provide a culturally-enriching experience for students in an isolated, rural area where there are few cultural resources; to promote interest in foreign languages in the state; to develop on the part of teachers a positive attitude toward the teaching of culture and literature and an awareness of a variety of methods in the teaching of culture and literature.

ROLE OF FLIP DIRECTOR

The 1972 FLIP director initiated the program. The director advises the Central Coordinating Committee, attends its meetings, and is responsible for seeing that all work is done and coordinated on schedule. The position of director will rotate each year with the change of districts responsible for planning the annual institute.

ROLE OF TEACHERS

(1) During the formative stages of the program, foreign language teachers from the Casper schools took part in the Central Coordinating Committee and served as advisors to the six other committees. (2) Sixteen teachers from various Wyoming school districts attended the first institute as workshop participants; they went to classes with students and met in informal evening sessions to discuss the application of institute experiences to the classroom. (3) Twenty-five high school and college instructors, as well as three workshop participants, participated as lecturers and discussion leaders. (4) Two teachers from the Casper schools were responsible for videotaping portions of the institute. All teachers were responsible for informal supervision in the dorms and in various campus buildings.

ROLE OF PARAPROFESSIONALS

Eleven native foreign language speakers from the community and state, identified and contacted through letters to state colleges and personal contacts, volunteered their time and services to the institute. They gave lectures and demonstrations and participated in discussions on topics agreed upon with the Classes and Resources Committees.

ROLE OF COMMUNITY REPRESENTATIVES

In addition to using the community as a source of resource personnel, an institute committee arranges for publicity in the local media. For the 1972 institute, the local newspaper published three articles, the television station did a five-minute spot, and the three radio stations each did an interview on the program. The videotape made of the first institute is presented by the language clubs of the Casper schools in the state's elementary schools and community groups to promote the study of foreign languages.

ROLE OF ADMINISTRATORS

(1) The administration of the Casper school district made classrooms and duplicating equipment available for after-school activities of the planning committees and loaned videotaping equipment to the institute; (2) administrators from Casper College cooperated in making arrangements for room and board and the use of classrooms on campus; (3) the Wyoming State Department of Education approved the program of re-certification credit for teachers and supplied mailing labels for sending publicity letters to all state high schools.

TRAINING REQUIREMENTS

No special training is required of participating teachers. Emphasis is placed on the importance of non-professionals as well as trained instructors in conducting the institute. Lecturers and discussion leaders are chosen primarily on the basis of their willingness to volunteer in addition to their expertise or familiarity with topics chosen for discussion.

ROLE OF CONSULTANTS

The foreign language consultant for the state of Wyoming served as liaison with the State Department of Education and prepared the objectives for the program of teacher re-certification credit. He had planned to attend evening discussion sessions with teacher-participants, but was unable to do so.

PROGRAM EVALUATION

At the end of the institute all participating students and teachers completed an evaluation form and took part in an evaluation rap-session in English. All responses were enthusiastic. The most positive reactions were to the debates, discussions, films, cooking and soccer classes, and soccer competition. The Sheridan schools requested the direction of the 1973 FLIP and a strong sense of competition has arisen among the schools to improve the institute each year.

Participating teachers felt that since the students had planned the program, they could see what students found stimulating and how well their ideas worked. Teachers are using several student ideas in their classrooms this year "with excellent results," for example, dramatic improvisations and debates with prepared vocabulary lists on topics of current interest. FLIP was the principal topic of discussion at the 1972 Wyoming Education Association meeting of foreign language teachers. It is expected that this exposure will increase the number of teacher-participants in the future, and more formal workshop sessions for teachers are being planned.

The major criticism of the institute concerned the program for beginners. Only about 20 percent of the participants were in this category in 1972 and stimulating activities at their level were not adequate. Beginners requested more individualized work on pronunciation and vocabulary, and all students desired more active participation in skits, debates, and discussions. A conference was held between the Casper director and the Sheridan teachers working with the 1973 institute in order to re-analyze the evaluations and correct program weaknesses. The program for beginning students will be enlarged, and an effort is being made to find resource people who enjoy working with beginners. The Sheridan group is also planning more participation in such activities as debates and improvisations and hopes to have enough money to distribute vocabulary lists relating to discussions by mail several weeks before the institute.

FUNDING AND COSTS

For the 1972 institute, each participant paid $30 to cover room and board, film rentals, and the cost of publicity and materials. Instruction by native speakers and college and high school instructors was donated, and posters, magazines, and decorative materials were donated by the community and local businesses. The program director works with committees outside of school time, with no released time or financial compensation. The program is independent of any one school district and receives no funding from the schools involved.

The total cost for room and board at Casper College for three days for 100 participants was approximately $2000. The remaining $1000 from the $3000 total tuition fees were spent on film rentals, postage, paper, and duplicating costs for publicity, mailings, application forms, and vocabulary lists, and the purchase and processing of videotape.

ADAPTABILITY OF CONCEPT TO OTHER PLACES

FLIP was developed in a rural area and would be particularly suited to other areas that lack extensive cultural resources. But the concept need not be restricted to such areas. Considerations in organizing a similar program are: (1) student interest and willingness to work extensively on an extracurricular project; (2) availability of resource people (native foreign language speakers, teachers, professors) in the community willing to volunteer their services; (3) inexpensive facilities for lodging and classrooms at a local college campus or other self-contained location; (4) the ability to develop a viable system of recruitment, coordination, and publicity; (5) school administrative support for the use of school facilities for extracurricular planning meetings. The program would necessarily vary according to the resource people available, the topics they would choose to discuss, and the particular interests of the students involved.

PROGRAM INITIATOR AND CONTACT PERSON

Ann Tollefson, Instructor of French, Natrona County High School, 930 South Elm Street, Casper, Wyoming 82601 (307) 234-9121

NOTE
[1] All quotations are from a personal communication to the survey staff.

FOREIGN LANGUAGE WITHOUT FAILURE

ABSTRACT

At Kenston High School in Chagrin Falls, Ohio, a group of foreign language teachers shared some experiences that convinced them that people talk most—and best—when the listener is interested and the talker both knows and cares about his subject, and that people learn best when they achieve success, are interested in the subject and the learning process, and are free from anxiety. At the same time, the teachers looked critically at their classes and decided to create Foreign Language Without Failure.

By 1972 both audiolingual instruction and a system of individualization had been replaced by the "discovery" approach of the CREDIF teaching method, developed at the Centre de Recherche et d'Etude pour la Diffusion du Français in St. Cloud, France. The grading system, based on mastery of skills, ensures that students get many chances to succeed and does not penalize those who fail. And, using techniques developed by psychologists, the teachers have developed personal communication exercises, used in small-group circles, that replace much drillwork with talk-provoking questions and topics.

PROGRAM DEVELOPMENT AND PRESENT STATUS

In 1968 the concern of several foreign language teachers in Kenston High School over the students' lack of involvement and real interest in the foreign language program came to a head. In an attempt to remedy student disinterest, reflected in a 40 percent attrition rate between the first and second year courses, they individualized the French and Spanish classes the next year, letting students work at their own paces with texts, tapes, and other standard materials. At the same time, after reading William Glasser's *Schools without Failure*, the teachers agreed as a group that, rather than grade as they had in the past (A,B,C,D,F), they would give only grades of "Pass," provided that each student met predetermined standards of mastery for every unit and level. Students would not be penalized for taking more than a year to complete a level, and they would also be allowed to drop foreign language courses without penalty.

The teachers' proposal was approved by their principal, and they got temporary permission from the school board to carry out their plan. They then talked with the students, letting them examine both the strengths and weaknesses of the proposed grading system; eventually all the students agreed to try it. The teachers then held a meeting with the students' parents. Chagrin Falls is a town of new suburban areas, several older farming communities, and an aging rural black ghetto. Four hundred parents showed up, the largest number ever to attend a meeting on educational policy at the school. A college professor, who was also a parent, the freshman guidance counselor, the language teachers, and some students presented the proposal in detail, then opened the session to parents' questions. The parents were especially concerned about college entrance requirements, class standing, and student motivation, but the panel was able to put some of their concerns to rest. The guidance department had polled a number of colleges and found them favorable or at least tolerant. By administrative action, foreign languages were removed from the competition for class standing. And the last concern was answered by the students themselves, who persuaded their parents they were willing to work in the program. At the end of the meeting, most parents agreed to the proposal.

But the teachers realized they would have to replace the stimuli of grades and competition with other sources of motivation. Following suggestions in *Schools without Failure*, they instituted class meetings every two weeks to stimulate student involvement. "The students and the teacher sit in a circle, or, if there are too many, a circle within a circle, and they talk (in English) about what the pupils want to discuss, what's happening in the class, a dilemma of society, or a problem with no factual answer. During these meetings, there are no 'right answers.' The teacher makes no prescriptive judgments, and tries to help the other members of the group avoid making any. . . . Some of these meetings were obviously more successful than others. The students were not really very adept at expressing their feelings, and the teachers had very little experience with this type of activity in a learning-teaching situation. Still the classes seemed . . . to work harder and accomplish more following such meetings."[1]

But, overall, the students found that after an initial flurry of excitement they "bogged down in boredom." The problems seemed to arise from the materials and the lack of strong group interaction in the individualized program; the students were "memorizing rather than thinking and mimicking rather than communicating." In the spring of 1969, however, the department chairman heard of the CREDIF approach to language instruction. That summer three of the teachers attended a training institute and learned to use the multi-media materials developed for the approach, and, in the next year, all the school's language teachers began using it. Their experience with the CREDIF approach has been very positive; they feel that students not only learn the language by thinking, but also think in the language. And they have found that it has solved many problems of non-involvement in the language-learning process itself.

The final development of Foreign Language Without Failure came the next year. Several of the teachers attended some weekend workshops of the Human Development Program, discovering techniques for "active listening" as well as learning "more about group dynamics and some techniques that would help students experience positive feelings about themselves and others in the class. By the end of [1970–71, they were having weekly small-group] meetings, of only fifteen minutes' duration, devoted to helping students communicate"[2] in the foreign language.

The combination of the CREDIF approach, mastery testing, and the communication exercises now forms the basis of Foreign Language Without Failure. In 1972–73, there were 92 French, 145 Spanish, and 45 Russian students in the program, and two full-time and three part-time language teachers.

TARGET AUDIENCE

Students in grades 9–12 in levels I–IV of Spanish, French, and Russian.

MAJOR GOALS FOR STUDENTS

"(1) To learn to think critically and develop problem-solving skills; (2) to develop confidence through successful learning experiences; (3) to learn to risk being wrong; (4) to appreciate the abilities of others; (5) to develop proficiency in all four language skills and derive the real joy in learning and the feeling of self-worth that comes with accomplishment."[3]

SCHEDULING ARRANGEMENTS

The students meet for one period a day, five days a week. Communication exercises are held every couple of days and feedback sessions any time a teacher senses that students are dissatisfied.

METHODOLOGY

Language instruction is carried out according to the CREDIF method. Students sit in rows facing each other; a screen and speaker are at one end of the room and a filmstrip projector and tape recorder at the other. There are four major steps to the method: Presentation, Explanation, Repetition, and Transposition. In Presentation, the teacher plays a taped dialogue and shows a filmstrip depicting the dialogue situation. In Explanation, the teacher runs through the tape and filmstrip again, stopping at each sentence in the dialogue, and asks questions that require individual students to separate a sentence into its various structural components and answer with an appropriate sentence. The student then repeats the complete dialogue sentence. The final operation, Transposition, leads students to understand and make new utterances. First, the teacher leads the student in directed dialogues, having them use the parts of each dialogue sentence. Next, the students describe orally the individual frames in the filmstrip and give résumés of the dialogue, using compound sentences, and read both the text materials and their own work.

The final step in Transposition in Foreign Language Without Failure is the use of the language in "personal communication exercises." Although role-playing is used occasionally, the teachers have found that students respond with more enthusiasm when they are encouraged to talk about their own experiences. For instance, when the class has learned the verb "to have," the teacher "sits with the class in a circle asking such questions as: 'How many brothers and sisters do you have?' 'Do you have pets?' 'What are they?' When these questions are well understood and the responses come more easily, the teacher asks each student to choose as a partner the person he knows least in the class. Each pair of students then converses for a few minutes in the foreign language, asking the type of question modeled in the circle and remembering his partner's answers. Finally the entire class returns to the circle to hear each person talk about his partner."[4]

The communication exercises are patterned on techniques developed by such psychologists as Uvaldo Palomares, Thomas

Gordon, and Sidney Simon. The techniques and exercises were translated into the target language by the teachers themselves and placed in a context and progression suitable to different levels. Some examples are:

1. Rank Order—The teacher asks, "Where are you most content? In the street, at home, or at school?" Each student gives complete answers and lists the possibilities in order of preference.
2. Human Development Exercise—The teacher asks each student to tell about a vacation that made him happy. When each student in the group has shared his experience, one or several people tell what each person said.
3. Continuum—The teacher asks each student to place his feelings at a point on a line:
   I prefer being alone_____/_____I prefer being with people.
4. Human Development Exercise—"What do you like to do?"
5. Human Development Exercise—"Think of something that someone tells you to do. Who says it and how does it make you feel?" Or . . . "What did you believe when you were little that you don't now?"
6. Incomplete Sentence—The teacher asks, "If I could change this class, I would . . ." and each student completes the sentence in his own way.

The purpose of these communication exercises is to get students to use the foreign language in a personal way. It is not intended as therapy. The teacher tries to be sensitive to the feelings of the group and redirects exercises if they become threatening to individuals. For instance, if a student responds that his private tennis court is the place that makes him happy, and the teacher sees that other students are intimidated, he might say that his armchair is his favorite place, re-establishing the concept of happiness as the central point of the sharing. Or, in the exercises involving the verb "to like," if the teacher asks each student "Do you like me?" or "Do you like your family?" the question forces a confrontation that may be damaging to the purpose of the exercise and possibly even damaging to some students. So instead the teacher asks, "Do you like red?" or "Where is the place you would like to be right now?" Similarly, the teacher does not pass judgment on students' replies. Whether a student believes that war, for example, is good or bad has no effect on the teacher's reactions or acceptance, and the teacher encourages the group to accept differences of opinion. At the start of the session, the teacher may go through some simple exercises to loosen the group up and then move into more complex ones that depend on the language level of each group and the degree of trust already established. The teacher is both a leader and a participant in the group work; he never asks students to answer questions he would not answer himself. Occasionally native speakers participate in group situations.

In literature analysis, the classes approach the works "through trying to find the values the author portrays and seeing how he develops his literary style and the characterizations from that point of view. Then the classes discuss their feelings about the values."[5] For instance, they may talk about a heroine's problematic situation—or put themselves into the situation and see what they would do.

REPRESENTATIVE CONTENT

All four language skills are studied and used. Short stories, comedies, dialogues, magazines, films, and presentations on the history and everyday life of the foreign cultures are incorporated into the program. Native speakers occasionally present slide shows and talks on their countries.

All courses have "functional" and "linguistic" goals for each unit. In a unit of Spanish I, for example, the goals are: Functional —to be able to discuss likes and preferences, expressed through colors and things in the classroom; Linguistic—to know *ver* and *gustar*, person-number endings of verb forms, and the definite and indefinite article. The goals of the first unit in French I are: Functional—to know and be able to use greetings, introductions, and personal and place names, as well as answer the question "Who are you?"; Linguistic—to know *être* and *habiter*, the conjugation of regular -er verbs, expressions using *c'est*, agreement of adjectives, and the use of the preposition *à* with place names.

Some typical communication exerises and topics are describing photographs and friends, the room in your house you like best and how you feel in it, things you like to buy, neighbors, parts of the day you like best, embarrassing moments you have had, a phone call that would make you happy, vacation trips, likes and dislikes in the class or school, or what made you sad or happy as a child.

MATERIALS

The French, Spanish, and Russian classes use materials developed by the Center for Curriculum Development, as well as films, filmstrips, tapes, magazines, and books from local libraries and other sources. In developing the personal communication exercises, the Kenston High teachers used: Harold Bessel and Uvaldo Palomares, *Method in Human Development* (San Diego: Human Development Training Institute, P.O. Box 20233, San Diego, Calif. 92320, 1969); and Louis E. Raths, Merril Harmin, and Sidney B. Simon, *Values and Teaching: Working with Values in the Classroom* (Columbus, Ohio: Charles E. Merril, 1966). In developing the system of mastery testing, the teachers used William Glasser's *Schools without Failure* (New York: Harper and Row, 1969) and a speech by Glasser, "Language in a School without Failure," presented at the 1970 meeting of the American Council on the Teaching of Foreign Languages. The speech is available on tape from F. André Paquette, Sunderland Hall, Middlebury College, Middlebury, Vermont 05753. The teachers were trained in the CREDIF method by the Center for Curriculum Development and used the book: Colette Renard and Charles H. Heinle, *Implementing* Voix et Images de France (Philadelphia: Chilton Books, 1969).

CREDIT, GRADING, AND ARTICULATION

Unit tests are given every two weeks. Students must complete all units at an 80 percent level of mastery to receive credit for a course; if a student does not, he receives no credit, and no mark of his attendance is entered in his permanent record. Each student's progress is reported to parents every nine weeks as a "pass" if satisfactory or "incomplete" if not. If the report is "incomplete," the teacher prepares a narrative description of the student's difficulties and makes recommendations for remedial work. Some self-evaluation techniques have been tried successfully, but only on an experimental basis.

"Generally an incomplete status can be corrected with an hour or so of individual work under the tutelage of a teacher or advanced student, and renewed effort by the student."[6] If the student cannot complete all the units successfully, he has three options: he can repeat, drop the course with no penalty, or complete the level working with another student, the teacher, or by himself in the summer or the next school year. With teacher permission, a student may complete an unfinished level at the same time he continues into the next.

ROLE OF ADMINISTRATORS

The principal supports the program and now encourages mastery testing in other departments. The Board of Education gave permanent approval to the program in 1971.

ROLE OF CONSULTANTS

Two teachers attended a weekend workshop conducted by William Glasser and several have attended workshops conducted by the Human Development Program. The Ohio Supervisor of Foreign Languages has helped in the program's development, evaluation, and promotion.

ROLE OF COMMUNITY

The initial meeting with parents has been followed by others to discuss mastery testing. Parents participated in an evaluation of the program after its second year and are invited to attend the classes at any time. Local newspapers and a bulletin published by the local board of education have carried stories on the program. And, on and off in the first two years, several native Spanish-speakers from Chagrin Falls worked with the program for half of each school day, learning English at the same time.

TRAINING REQUIREMENTS

Intensive training in the CREDIF method was provided in a two-week workshop, in which the teachers made a close study of the methodological theory, wrote lesson plans, practice-taught and critiqued themselves and others, and learned a new language in "shock" classes using the CREDIF approach. All the teachers participated, and continue to participate, in group sessions and workshops run by the Human Development Institute and other organizations to learn new techniques for promoting group inter-action.

The teachers meet as a group every two weeks to discuss the effectiveness of some techniques and possible alternatives. They frequently attend each other's classes and offer suggestions on improving the exercises and language learning; the department chairman attended Russian classes for a semester to learn Russian and help the Russian teacher adapt the format of Foreign Language Without Failure to his classes. The two Spanish teachers and the two French teachers work closely with each other in developing lesson plans and exercises. Students are asked for suggestions on improving the classes.

PROGRAM EVALUATION

Proficiency tests have not been administered because the staff does not consider them to be reliable. But the teachers report they and the students are much more satisfied with student proficiency now than in the past. Enrollment in foreign language classes has increased by 10% since 1968, even though language requirements at the school were abolished in 1970—a move the language staff supported. The drop-out rate between first- and second-year courses has decreased from 40% to 30%, and discipline problems have diminished significantly. In a questionnaire sent to parents in 1970, ten times as many parents approved the program as did not. And in a "survey of factors involved in succeeding in a non-graded program Mr. William O'Neil found that 73% of the students interviewed answered affirmatively the question, 'Do you like the idea of not having grades in foreign language study?' In spite of the fact that the no-grade program is an island and that students are working for grades in all other classes, 67% thought they would not learn more if grades were given."[7]

FUNDING AND COSTS

The program is funded through the regular school budget. In 1972–73, the average annual expenditure per pupil in the district was $812. Teachers pay for their own workshops. Costs:

$100 Workshops and materials of William Glasser (total for two teachers)
120 Training in the CREDIF method (per teacher)
80 One weekend workshop with the Human Development Institute (per teacher)
5 Workbook (per student)
9 Re-usable student materials (per student)
12 Teacher's guide (one)
26 Filmstrip projector
30 Screen
40 Speaker
160 Tape recorder
130 Tapes (per language)
144 Filmstrips (per language)

ADAPTABILITY OF CONCEPT TO OTHER PLACES

The implementation of Foreign Language Without Failure was greatly aided by the personalities of the teachers; the cooperation of the principal; the encouragement of the state supervisor and other advisors; the support of the students and later their parents; the spirit of cooperation in the foreign language department; the availability of training in group processes; and, finally, imagination and work. The chairman of the department made herself fully accountable for the success or failure of the program at the outset, a factor that proved valuable in gaining acceptance of the proposal.

Several Kenston High teachers have compiled some of their communication exercises into a workbook, *REAL Communication in Foreign Language*, available from the contact person for $3.50. And the teachers are available for consultation and workshops.

AVAILABLE DESCRIPTIONS

Three short descriptions of the program are available from the contact person: "Teaching Foreign Language without Failure: A Thinking and Personalized Method That Works"; "A Report to the National Conference on Grading Alternatives: A No-Grade Island That Couldn't Work but Did" (mimeographed); and "Teaching Foreign Language without Failure" (mimeographed).

CONTACT PERSON

Beverly Wattenmaker, Chairman, Foreign Language Department, Kenston High School, 17425 Snyder Road, Chagrin Falls, Ohio 44022 (216) 543-9281

NOTES
1 Beverly Wattenmaker and Virginia Wilson, "Teaching Foreign Language without Failure" (Chagrin Falls, Ohio: Kenston High School), pp. 6–7.
2 Wattenmaker, "Without Failure," p. 7.
3 Derived from goals stated in the pamphlet "Teaching Foreign Language without Failure," p. 1.

[4] Wattenmaker, "Without Failure," p. 5.
[5] Personal communication to the survey staff.
[6] Wattenmaker, "Without Failure," p. 6.
[7] Beverly Wattenmaker and Virginia Wilson, "A No-Grade Island That Couldn't Work but Did," mimeographed sheet, p. 3.

THE
FRENCH
IN
DELAWARE

ABSTRACT

Foreign language teachers do not always have to depend solely on resources in their own field to make their subject exciting and relevant. "The French in Delaware" is a program designed for upper-level French classes that draws on local historical archives to unite the study of foreign language with the study of local history and the efforts of foreign language teachers with those of a private research library. A study unit, researched and prepared at the Eleutherian Mills Historical Library in Greenville, Delaware enables students with a sound background in French to investigate the contributions of the French to the life and institutions of their state. Using the published memoirs of famous French visitors to America as well as the records of vital statistics, letters, and business accounts of little-known French immigrants of the 18th and 19th centuries, students work in the classroom and in the archives

78

to get a picture of the people who came to Delaware—their lives, their thoughts, and their place in history. In addition to using French in their research, reports, and discussions, students gain insights into the changes of the French language and learn the research procedures needed when using primary sources.

PROGRAM DEVELOPMENT AND PRESENT STATUS

The idea for The French in Delaware grew out of a series of seminars offered by the Supervisor of Foreign Language Education in conjunction with the University of Delaware. Each participant was required to develop a foreign language study unit of some kind. Betty-Bright Low, one of these participants, was working part-time for Eleutherian Mills Historical Library, and, with so many original sources at hand, chose "The French in Delaware" as her research topic. In cooperation with the library director, who provided time for research and Xeroxed copies of the unit, she created a curriculum sourcebook available to French teachers for classroom use. A pilot program was set up in 1970 with three teachers in three schools using the unit as a three-week classroom project in their level V French classes. There are, however, "only a handful" of fifth-level classes in the state, and the participating schools have not spread beyond the pilot group. In two of the three pilot programs, the unit is used in conjunction with independent studies; in the third it is still being presented as a three-week class project. It is hoped that the program will be refined and adapted to other levels of language study in order to include a larger audience.

PROGRAM GOALS

(1) To relate local history to French literature through the journals and commentaries of prominent litterateurs and journalists who wrote on America; (2) to reinforce students' understanding of Franco-American relations; (3) to serve "as an object lesson in cross-cultural understanding"; (4) to provide students

with experience in methods of historical research; (5) to provide enjoyable learning activities, as a "change of pace from pre-college or senior year pressures"; (6) to encourage students to relate their study of foreign language to their immediate surroundings as well as to long-range goals.[1]

METHODOLOGY AND REPRESENTATIVE CONTENT

The unit begins with a tour of the Eleutherian Mills Historical Library, which presents a slide show and a special exhibit of rare books, manuscripts, and pictures on the history of French immigration to Delaware. In class, students study the patterns of immigration, "from the Huguenot era through the great influx which created a sort of Wilmington French 'colony' in the early 1800s."[2] They discuss the historical events in France and America that triggered French emigration, identify the people who emigrated, their characteristics, and their impact on the state, and relate this immigration to the larger immigration picture in the United States.

Since there is no textbook available on this specific subject, the researcher compiled copies of original manuscripts, letters, and records that would shed light on the story of French immigration and would allow students to study the individuals whose lives flourished or failed in their new country. Some general historical works on French refugees in America and the history of Delaware are used, and students are assigned specific portions of the writings of Crèvecoeur and de Tocqueville. They are also given copies of paragraphs from various diarists, such as Madame de la Tour du Pin, Moreau de St. Méry, and Gilbert Chinard's essay, "Le Mirage américain," and are asked to read selections from other diarists of their own choice. The remaining reading is from original manuscripts, some of which are transcriptions, others photocopies of the original handwriting and language. Students examine the reaction of Wilmington to the newcomers, the social relationships within the French "colony," and the immigrants' lasting effects on the community's architecture, occupations, sports, and street names. One family's correspondence is examined in detail to see how letters reflect the attitudes and problems of the immigrant, the French character, signs of Americanization or nostalgia, and the extent to which the French stayed together or were assimilated. The "melting pot" concept and its pitfalls are discussed, as well as the dispersion of the French colony and the customs and families which remain in Delaware to this day.

Teachers are free to emphasize certain readings over others, allow the field trips to replace some classroom discussions, or assign various research projects to individuals or student teams. There are certain required activities outlined in the curriculum in the form of performance objectives. For example, a student should be able: (1) "to demonstrate by transcription his ability to read a short-length, fairly legible early document in French . . . and point out the difference between the French in the document and the French which he is learning; (2) to write in French . . . how the writings of two French travellers during the late 1700s reflect the opinions characteristic of the French idea of the U.S. and its people as related by Chinard in "Le Mirage américain," and discuss in class American attitudes toward the French in terms of the possible existence of a mirage; (3) to trace on a genealogical chart the history of one French family immigrating to Delaware and relate in French . . . the adjustment or lack of adjustment of this family to the general commentaries of at least two French visitors to the U.S.; (4) to revise his writing by correcting errors pointed out by the teacher, practice proper use of structural items in oral and/or written exercises, and take an oral and written test on their use with a minimum of 90 percent correct responses."[3]

Partway through the unit, students take a field trip through the library, the Hagley Museum, the Delaware Historical Society, or the State Archives in Dover, where they are told the procedures for using the collections and historical research. Tax, census, church, and customs records, account books, vital statistics files, old newspapers, shipping papers, and correspondence all provide the fragments from which the students may reconstruct the lives of the French immigrants. Each student is assigned to report on one of the French family names up to 1840 and to trace and discuss the genealogy and lives of the family. Alternatively, students may interview someone of French descent or report on French contributions to the area in fashion, furniture, sports, architecture, technology, or horticulture. They are evaluated on the basis of the reports they write, and graded "pass" or "fail" for this section of their French V course.

ROLES OF TEACHERS, LIBRARY STAFF, AND STATE SUPERVISOR

French teachers involved in the program meet with the research librarian before beginning the unit for at least six hours of seminar work dealing with the sources used, methods of presentation, goals, and major ideas of the unit, and they meet at the end of the program to evaluate student performance. The research specialist of the Eleutherian Mills Historical Library identified source materials, assembled the major ideas and goals of the unit, and prepared the curriculum guide. She conducts seminar training sessions for teachers, and, with the library director, conducts the exhibit, tour, and instructional session on research methods. The library director agreed to cooperate with the schools piloting the program and granted students access to the card catalogue and printed materials, even though the library is noncirculating and does not encourage direct access to the collections by high school students. Students may not handle original manuscripts, but the director has authorized these to be photocopied along with the unit materials and secondary sources. The library also arranges for loans of imprints necessary for the unit. The State Supervisor originally proposed the idea of the study unit and worked with the researcher to organize the materials for use in the classroom.

PROGRAM EVALUATION

The writers of the 1971 Northeast Conference report, in which the program was described, commended the use of a variety of topics and approaches, the integration of the study of grammar into the cultural material, and the use of performance objectives to make clear to the student the manner in which he must show his achievement. They commended the program for making "abstract concepts and ideas, embodied in concrete evidence, reach a high level of crispness and credibility. . . . The manner in which the unit was developed and this type of research topic can be used in other states or regions with similar benefits."[4]

Low notes that student reaction to certain topics was mixed, but all students were surprised at the change of pace in a generally literary course of study, fascinated by linguistic changes from 1800 to 1970, and interested in the parallels between assimilation problems then and now. "From the library point of view, we were very pleased with the general level and research behavior of the students. . . . They were persistent in their research efforts . . . [and] were not content to use only the imprints on the reserve shelf set up for them. They used the card catalogue . . . sought research advice . . . [and] were unafraid of the tedium of scanning many aging newspapers. . . . It delighted the archivist in me to see the gusto with which the students tackled 19th-century French handwriting."[5]

FUNDING AND COSTS

The cost of research was absorbed by the library, which also donates the training of teachers in the use of the unit, the slide presentation and exhibit, and the reproduction of the basic unit materials, curriculum guide, and sourcebook. Some secondary sources and texts were obtained through the State Department of Public Instruction by the individual schools, and portions of these were Xeroxed at the schools' expense.

ADAPTABILITY OF CONCEPT TO OTHER PLACES

Low recommends that teachers take advantage of the rich ethnic history of America and the present "age of photocopy" to bring local history into the foreign language classroom. The first consideration in creating such a program is that there be an appropriate ethnic group that migrated to the locality some time in the past. Low makes several suggestions for beginning the research unit. (1) There should be material available on America, the foreign country, and the locality at the time of the immigration, and information on individual immigrants who may be researched further. (2) All archival repositories in the area should be surveyed to find out what materials are available and what restrictions exist on student use. (3) It is particularly advantageous to have a library or other institution cooperate, to contribute copies of documents, arrange interlibrary loans, set up exhibits, or in any other way help defray a portion of the costs. Otherwise a language teacher (perhaps with a social studies teacher) could carry out the necessary research and assemblage of materials with school funds. (4) Among suggested materials are: those that would bridge the gap between a literary curriculum and a cross-cultural, historical study; commentaries showing the image of America in the foreign country (like Chinard's "Le Mirage américain"); archival materials that shed light on events that affected immigration to the area; materials that emphasize particular local problems facing immigrants and reflect different tastes and skills of individual immigrants; a group of letters showing an individual's opinion of both the native and adopted country over a period of time; a manuscript that is legible and brief enough to be transcribed by students; and documents suggesting situations in some ways relevant to the present. The study could be approached as part of an advanced course or as a mini-course. It could be adapted for lower-level students, deemphasizing original student research and placing most responsibility with the teacher, who could bring in reproductions and transcriptions of relevant documents to be read and discussed in terms of ethnic immigration, contributions, problems, assimilation, and language within the historical framework. More recent immigrations (for example, of Hispanic peoples) could be approached through interviews with the immigrants themselves.

AVAILABLE DESCRIPTIONS

The French in Delaware, published by the State Department of Public Instruction, Dover, Delware, is a pamphlet describing the specific recommended topics, methods, and materials used in the program and is available from the contact person. "The French in Delaware: A Case Study" is a short description of the unit, its history, goals, and typical performance objectives, in *Leadership for Continuing Development*, Reports of the Working Committees: 1971 Northeast Conference Report, pp. 123–27. Low is preparing an article for *History News* on "how the local historical agency can work with educators to develop ethnic study programs appropriate to community needs."

CONTACT PERSON

Betty-Bright Low, Research and Reference Librarian, Eleutherian Mills Historical Library, Greenville, Delaware 19807 (302) 658-2401

NOTES

[1] Genelle Caldwell, "The French in Delaware: A Unit of Study," Prospectus (Delaware Department of Public Instruction, 1970).

[2] Betty-Bright P. Low, Speech presented at a workshop of the 1971 Northeast Conference on the Teaching of Foreign Languages, Boston, Mass., April 1971.

[3] Caldwell, Prospectus.

[4] James W. Dodge, ed., *Leadership for Continuing Development*, Reports of the Working Committees: 1971 Northeast Conference on the Teaching of Foreign Languages (New York: Northeast Conference, 1971), pp. 123–27.

[5] Low, Speech.

GERMAN
LANGUAGE
SUMMER
CAMP

ABSTRACT

A joint effort by German instructors from the Seattle, Washington area and a German-American ethnic organization has led to the development of the German Language Summer Camp, which provides instruction in German and outdoor recreation for 10- to 18-year-olds. For a $100 fee that covers two weeks of room and board and the use of all recreational facilities, students live "family style" with German-speaking adults at the Berghaus ski lodge in the Cascade Mountains. In addition to group and individualized German instruction at the beginning, intermediate, and advanced levels, the campers are offered a program of hiking, swimming, horseback riding, special campouts, picnics, and a variety of evening entertainment. Through the determination and hard work of the program staff, this small-scale camp, operated on a budget derived entirely from student fees, has successfully completed its first season with an enrollment of 27 students from the Seattle area.

PROGRAM DEVELOPMENT AND PRESENT STATUS

The initial proposal for the German Language Summer Camp was drawn up by Willi Fischer of the University of Washington in conjunction with the Continental Club of Seattle, an organization including over 5000 German-Americans. Fischer presented the proposal to William Walker of the University of Illinois in March 1972. Walker and Jytte Bischofberger, a high school German teacher who is a board member of the Continental Club and had conducted previous youth camps at the Berghaus, expanded the idea and developed an outline for a workable program. They hired a German-speaking recreation director, who had received his training while living and studying in the mountains of Austria, and the Continental Club agreed to rent its ski lodge to the camp under group rental regulations. The Berghaus is near swimming areas and hiking terrain, has the necessary physical conveniences, and is decorated and furnished in Alpine style, creating a German atmosphere.

To enhance the "credibility and prestige" of the camp, support was gained from the University of Washington's German department and the Washington chapter of the American Association of Teachers of German, in addition to the Continental Club, which aided in advertising. For publicity, circulars were sent to local foreign language teachers and left in ethnic restaurants and shopping areas. The local newspapers printed announcements for the camp, and articles appeared in the publications of ethnic organizations. By the time camp began on 2 July, the staff had brought instructional and recreational material (mostly lent by the program directors) to the Berghaus, added their own decorations, planned menus, and gone on a shopping expedition for food. Camp was conducted for three weeks; in evaluating the program at the end of that time, both students and adults agreed that the venture was a success. In 1973 the Continental Club is adding to the Berghaus a dormitory for 100 persons; the next camp program is being planned for 1974, with 100 students in two-week sessions.

TARGET AUDIENCE

Students of all abilities, ages 12 to 18 (with some younger students the first year). Twenty of the first-year participants had parents of German background. Eleven had had no previous German language study, while the others had had from one semester to five years.

STUDENT GROUPING AND SCHEDULING ARRANGEMENTS

In 1972 the camp was held for one three-week session. Intermediate and advanced campers attended for the full three weeks, while beginners entered camp at the end of the first week. Most activities involved the entire group, except the small-group and individualized language instruction sessions. A typical day began with breakfast and chores, then full-group instruction, lunch, small-group and individualized instruction, horseback riding and swimming (or a special activity), dinner, and an evening program. Advanced, intermediate, and beginning students had their afternoon instruction at different times, and while one group was "in class," the others had free time.

PROGRAM GOALS

(1) To provide a well-rounded recreational program for students, keeping in mind their particular interests and capabilities; (2) to provide individualized and group instruction in German, emphasizing speaking and reading skills; (3) to look upon camp language instruction as an important supplement to—but not a substitute for—normal classroom instruction; (4) to provide maximum exposure to German culture by immersion in a German

language environment; (5) to create a family atmosphere by encouraging a mixed-age grouping of students and the presence of German-speaking adults; (6) to allow enough free time for campers to develop social relationships with one another; (7) to encourage positive attitudes toward foreign cultures; (8) to provide partial scholarships to students from low-income families; (9) to encourage the participation of students with motivational or learning difficulties.

METHODOLOGY AND REPRESENTATIVE CONTENT

The first evening of camp is devoted to orientation: students are introduced to each other and the staff in German, go on a tour of the Berghaus facilities, and discuss the camp rules in both German and English. They also take an oral inventory of the items in their backpacks—from *der Schlafsack* to *der Badeanzug* —as the first session of informal language instruction. Posters of well-known mottoes are hung around the camp to pique the students' curiosity and add atmosphere, and small placards with German words are placed wherever possible—on faucets, windows, electrical outlets, at the corral, in the kitchen—so that students associate the words with the objects they represent. All menus and chore assignments are posted daily in German.

Group instruction in the morning covers such topics as the beach, sports, parts of the body (in connection with grooming and injuries), and camping gear. The first session is on horses and horseback riding; related vocabulary is presented with the overhead projector and, after some drills, the students are brought to the corral to see the horses for the first time. After a lesson on the rooms of the house, the students tour the Berghaus, identifying the pieces of furniture and other items; similarly, after a lesson on the outdoors, students take a "vocabulary tour" around the grounds. Students also learn songs and play word games during these sessions.

In the afternoon language sessions, advanced students read articles and stories from their text, pamphlets or magazines, read and discuss poetry, and have occasional free-conversation sessions. The intermediate students keep a daily journal in German, which is read and corrected by the instructor each day. Sometimes students read aloud from their journals (provoking nostalgia on occasion, and more often debates—in German—on what really happened). They also study vocabulary, sing songs, review the morning's lesson, and practice common conversational expressions. The beginners work mostly with lessons in their textbook, review the morning's vocabulary, and sing or play games. At both the intermediate and beginning levels, the topics include the months, seasons, weather, colors, and family, as well as such aspects of daily life in Germany as greetings, patterns of politeness, festivals and holidays, transportation, invitations and dates, sports, letter-writing, vacation and resort areas, camping, hiking, and careers. Troublesome grammar structures are reviewed with intensive drills, and most lessons are illustrated with overhead transparencies.

The first evening of camp, students learn the steps for the polka and *Walzertanz* and sing songs in German to "break the ice." The next evening is spent on a "polar-bear walk" through the mountains, where students sing German wandering songs. Other evening activities include charades (on topics like "famous movies and television shows"), ice-cream socials, German scrabble, games in German such as "Welche Buchstabe habe ich" for vocabulary review, and games in English, like "Password," for relief. There are frequent Monday, Thursday, or Saturday Nights at the Movies, parties in honor of guests or just for fun, folk dancing, and pop-music festivals. There are evenings set aside for campers to do what they want—visit each other, dance, listen to records, read, or play games they brought from home. One evening a native of Switzerland who makes and repairs violins in Seattle gave an hour-long talk on the tools, procedures, and problems of his craft and also presented a film on the subject. And toward the end of camp a gala *Abschiedsparty* was held and the students presented some of the songs, games, and dances they had learned during the previous three weeks.

Special activities in 1972 included a group hike through the Alpental ski area, kayaking, and a visit from the German Consul and his staff. One day during group instruction time a German-born miner spoke to the campers about gold-mining in the area, the local geological conditions, and gold-mining equipment used by the early pioneers, then took them on a field trip to the Liberty Mines. The following day, group instruction centered on mining and the types of minerals in Washington, using the appropriate German vocabulary, and a field trip was made to the Hyak Rock Museum shortly thereafter. Another special activity was an all-day, seven-mile hike to Gold Creek in the mountains, where students identified more stones and minerals. The recreation director stressed survival techniques in the forest, introducing students to the use of equipment for climbing, trail-marking, and river-crossing. A campout one weekend was begun with a vocabulary lesson on *Camping und Ubernachten* at the Berghaus, and then the students went on a two-hour backpack hike to the Wenatchee National Forest where they pitched their tents for the night. One Sunday was devoted to a picnic with parents and guests; campers and parents learned the fundamentals of *Handball* and *Fussball*, caught up on each others' news, and enjoyed a simple barbecue lunch. The campers also took a trip to a nearby European candy factory and were given a guided tour through the kitchens—and free samples—by the German-speaking owner. Finally, the last day of camp coincided with the Continental Club's German Picnic, where students met with over 500 German-speaking "neighbors."

ROLES OF STUDENTS, TEACHERS, AND DIRECTORS

Students are expected to speak German as much as possible, but they are also permitted to speak English during some activities and on their free time. Each participant is assigned to do various camp chores, including cooking and cleaning, on a rotating basis, and is asked to bring games and reading material to use in his free time. Teachers participate in most activities with the campers, live with the students, share their chores, and try to make the atmosphere relaxed. They conduct language instruction sessions and supervise other activities. The camp directors are also camp teachers and are responsible for publicity, contact with parents, overall supervision, scheduling, and making arrangements for guest speakers, special events, and field trips. The recreation director conducts all weekend outings and provides leadership in a variety of other activities when the teachers are not available or need a "breather." The recreation director is a native speaker of German.

ROLE OF PARENTS AND COMMUNITY

Parents of students interested in participating in the camp are sent a description of the program, a release form for their children, and a list of items the students should bring. They are invited to one or two picnic events at camp. Several of the parents of the 1972 campers were members of the Continental Club of Seattle. The Continental Club of Seattle cooperated in developing the program, provides the Berghaus camp site, and invites the campers to attend its German Picnic. The community is also the "vehicle" for publicizing the program and recruiting students.

TRAINING REQUIREMENTS

All staff members speak German fluently, and the teachers have had previous experience with different age groups. The camp director has had experience coordinating academic and recreational activities.

PROGRAM EVALUATION

At the end of the camp session, students were asked to fill out a questionnaire evaluating their camp experience. They listed their favorite aspects of the program, in order of preference, as swimming, hiking, free time, and horseback riding. Their least favorite, in order of negative preference, were separation of boys from girls, classwork, curfew, chores, and "the little kids." The directors drew several conclusions from the students' question-naires:

1. Students prefer individualized instruction over group sessions.
2. Students do not enjoy a tightly organized camp, but prefer a situation in which they can assume a greater share in decision-making.
3. Recreation is the most enjoyable part of any summer camp.
4. The majority of students enjoyed a mixed-age grouping over sharply defined age groups.
5. The majority of students had few criticisms of the camp.
6. The majority felt some improvement in their understanding of German language and culture. Reading and comprehension were the areas in which they felt the most progress.
7. The vast majority of participants stated they would attend the camp were it offered again. In a sense the camp must have satisfied their objectives.
8. The overall evaluation of the camp program was "good," with only a small majority of "bad" responses. The majority of "bad" responses were about the group classes.[1]

The director notes that "the statistical validity of this evaluation is far from conclusive or decisive" but that the evaluation contains useful "insights . . . into the nature and organization of the camp."

FUNDING AND COSTS

All camp expenses are funded by the student fees, $50 per week. Most students stayed for two or three weeks. Expenditures for 1972 were:

Food	$780
Promotion	41
Materials	22
Transportation	21
Salaries	830
Rental Deposit	100

The student fees also covered the rental of the Berghaus at the rates of $.75 per night for students who are members of the Continental Club and $1.50 for non-members. Most instructional materials were borrowed from area schools, while most recreational material was provided by the Berghaus.

ADAPTABILITY OF CONCEPT TO OTHER PLACES

Walker states: "Based upon my experiences and observations, . . . such an endeavor is awesome in detail, financially uncertain, physically and emotionally tiring, and, above all, intensely satisfying and gratifying for the teachers and participants." He makes a number of suggestions for developing a similar program. (1) Staff: A camp director should speak the foreign language fluently, have teaching experience in the language, relate well to young people, and have either previous camp experience or the necessary skills to coordinate academic and recreational activities. The teachers should have experience at the pre-secondary levels; there should be one teacher for every 10-12 students and a recreation director to lead outings and supervise some activities. If there is money, a cook and housekeeper could be hired or parent volunteers and university students could be recruited to assist in chores. (2) Camp site: The camp site should have an atmosphere in keeping with the language; easy access to recreational areas; as many conveniences as possible; sufficient storage room and freezer facilities (since food should be bought in bulk); a room large enough for all participants to gather at one time; and a central location, so that transportation is not difficult to arrange. (3) Budget: The budget should provide for salaries, recreational activities, transportation, materials, promotional activities, rent, security deposits, and insurance. (4) Affiliation: The director suggests that affiliation be secured with a school district, ethnic organization, private industry, or other civic group. "Publicity, advertising, and other promotional considerations are enhanced by affiliation. It will also be necessary, if enrollment is slow, to purchase much of the necessary materials and food with your own funds. Affiliation can help to lessen the financial burden on the director if the supporting organization can 'guarantee' funds for advance usage. Often civic organizations own property which is suitable for camp use." (5) Advertising and Publicity: "If a school district is sponsoring the camp, . . . [it] will have the necessary facilities, funds, and mailing lists. Advertising in the newspapers of ethnic organizations is highly effective. Circulars should be colorful and attractive, explaining concisely the major points of the program," and should be sent to individual foreign language teachers. Professional journals and local newspapers will usually carry announcements. (6) Purchasing and Transportation: Menus should be prepared in advance, and, with 25 students, $1000 should be available for initial expenditures. Buy in bulk at wholesale stores and wholesale meatpackers. If it is difficult to anticipate what youngsters like to eat, the director suggests "taking along a mother of a large family to aid you in food purchasing. . . . Plan on a variety in menu selections, as youngsters know when they are getting excessive amounts of hot dogs and hamburgers." If a teacher at the camp is affiliated with a school district, instructional materials might be available without purchase or rental costs. There should be a camper, van, or small truck for special outings and a car available in camp at all times in case of emergency.

AVAILABLE DESCRIPTIONS

"A Manual for the Operation of a German Language Summer Camp," by William Walker and Jytte Bischofberger, is available from the contact person. It contains many suggestions for implementing a camp program, details on publicity, staffing, activities, methods, and topics, and suggested texts, booklets, pamphlets, and hardware. There is also a log of all activities of the 1972 German Language Summer Camp.

CONTACT PERSON

Jytte Bischofberger, 1314 East John Street, Seattle, Washington 98102

NOTE

[1] All quotations are from William Walker and Jytte Bischofberger, "A Manual for the Operation of a German Language Summer Camp" (unpublished, 1972).

GUIDED INDIVIDUALIZED STUDY IN FOREIGN LANGUAGES

ABSTRACT

Guided Individualized Study in Foreign Languages is a program of self-instruction in Garden City High School in Garden City, New York. Using a study guide, students work on their own or in small groups with standard texts and tapes and meet on a regular and frequent basis with tutors who are native speakers of the language. The director of the program, who does not speak the languages offered, meets with each student once a week to discuss the student's progress, and several times a year the students are given examinations by professors from nearby colleges. The annual cost of the program is approximately $125 per student.

PROGRAM DEVELOPMENT AND PRESENT STATUS

Guided Individualized Study in Foreign Languages was started through the Critical Language Program, a developmental

97

and coordinating agency for programs of self-instruction in the aural-oral skills of critical or neglected languages (Thai, Japanese, Chinese, and 22 others). In 1969, the director of the Critical Language Program contacted the Garden City School District about implementing an experimental program of self-instruction in Japanese in the high school. The chairman of the school's foreign language department was appointed director of the program; he recruited students, contacted two Japanese to act as tutors, and with the help of the Critical Language Program organized materials and contacted a director at the Foreign Service Institute to act as an examiner. The cost of the materials and the wages of the examiner and tutors were borne by the Critical Language Program, but the school's program director donated his time and energy.

The program began in the fall of 1969 with 12 selected students, and it proved so successful that the Board of Education assumed partial and then full funding of the program in the following years. In 1972–73, the director included Chinese in the program, changed the teaching format and the course content recommended by the Critical Language Program so as to include reading and writing, and also developed self-instruction programs to replace the regular German and Latin programs which were "going under" because of low enrollments. Enough students enrolled in German and Latin at the start of 1972–73, however, to support regular classes, and these self-instructional programs have not yet been used. At present 11 students are enrolled in Japanese and five in Chinese.

TARGET AUDIENCE

Students in grades 11 and 12 who have had previous language study. An aptitude test is used to help students determine their probable success in the program.

MAJOR GOALS FOR STUDENTS

To develop proficiency in all four skills—but primarily listening and speaking—in Chinese or Japanese.

PROJECT GOAL

To provide courses at low cost in languages for which there is only low student demand.

STUDENT GROUPING AND
SCHEDULING ARRANGEMENTS

Students are expected to work approximately seven and a half hours a week in the program; of this time at least one and a half hours must be spent in the school itself and one hour more must be spent with the tutors in dialogue practice. There are no classes per se, but each month students meet with a tutor for eight 30-minute dialogue practice sessions that may include up to four students.

ORIENTATION

In the first session of the year, the director distributes a sheet of study hints, explains the location of the language lab equipment and its use, explains the procedures and requirements of the program, introduces the native speakers and the students to each other, and carefully explains the roles and relationship they could most profitably hold with each other. Students examine the texts and other materials with the director, who explains some general principles of language learning; as the students have already studied a language, these explanations are quite simple. The director meets with the students weekly throughout the program, and helps them overcome any difficulties they may be having. And, especially in the first months, he attends many of the tutorial sessions, both to observe student progress and to correct any faulty or inefficient learning situations.

Last year the Japanese examiner, who has worked with similar self-instructional programs at the college level, asked each student to record one tutorial session on tape and send it to her. After listening to the sessions, she recorded critiques on the same tapes and returned them to the students and tutors to help them work out the best format for practicing dialogues.

REPRESENTATIVE CONTENT

All four language skills are studied; reading and writing of Japanese characters is introduced in the second year, and reading and writing of Chinese characters is introduced in the sixth month of the first year. Basic information on geography, customs, and culture is introduced through independent projects in which students use library reference materials, periodicals, and newspapers. All students in the program are required to enroll in a one-quarter course in Asian Studies offered by the social studies department, and an extensive "humanities" program in the school occasionally offers activities of special interest. At least once a year, the director organizes an extracurricular activity or a field trip to Japanese or Chinese restaurants and cultural centers in New York City.

METHODOLOGY

The language exercises involve dialogue memorization and various pattern drills; the methodological framework of the program itself is primarily self-instruction. The director supervises each student's study regime and attends many of the tutorial sessions, but each student is free, within limits, to structure his own work and set his own pace. Grammar is explained in English in the textbook, and vocabulary words are spelled in the roman alphabet. Students work either in small groups or alone, as they choose, with the texts, tapes, and other materials, and they memorize dialogues to the "point of automaticity" before going into the practice dialogue sessions with the tutors. In the dialogue practice, the tutor is encouraged to see his role as that of a fellow student and friend, rather than teacher. Students are encouraged not to rely on the native speaker to teach them the language, but rather to use the tutor for practicing proper intonation, accent, and gesture. The tutor is encouraged to use only the standard spoken form of his language, to correct and drill the students, to review only previously learned material, and to use only the target language. The student is told to mimic the native speaker at all times, whether sub-vocally or aloud. Occasionally the tutor explains points of grammar or talks about his country. The tutor assumes a more active role in sessions with second-year Japanese students and students in the last half of the first-year Chinese course, for he then becomes responsible for helping students complete exercises in their character workbooks and helping them make the shift to reading and writing.

CREDIT, GRADING, AND ARTICULATION

At the end of each unit, students are given quizzes prepared by the tutor and the director, and twice a year are given oral examinations by the examiner. The examiner determines students' grades. Students who receive grades of C or lower must do supplementary work and review the original material until they can satisfy the criteria for a B or A; there is a time limit of one quarter for this review. Credit is given as in any other course; however, some students do not take any credit because of a district policy which prohibits students' receiving more than six credits per year. Articulation within the program is not a problem, since students work on their own or in small groups that work at the same pace.

ROLES OF PROGRAM DIRECTOR AND
BOARD OF EDUCATION

The director is also the chairman of the foreign language department, and works only part-time on the program. In addition to duties previously described, he transports several of the tutors to and from the school, promotes the program in the school and district, administers the budget, coordinates all teaching and evaluation, organizes the materials, draws up tests and duplicates tapes with the help of the native speakers, and selects students for the program. The board of education has supported the program and increased its budget each year, in spite of the director's insistence that it be the first program to go in case of budget cuts.

PROGRAM EVALUATION

Guided Individualized Study in Foreign Languages has not undergone extensive evaluation. The attrition rate is low, and the students who do drop out usually do so for reasons other than the program itself (involvement in school plays, etc.). Students are graded on college standards by qualified professors; evaluation by the examiners of students and the program have been very favorable, and a good many visitors have gone to see the program on their recommendations.

FUNDING AND COSTS

Guided Individualized Study in Foreign Languages was funded, in the first year, by a $1000 grant from the Critical Language Program. In the second year, the grant was reduced to $500 and the school district provided another $500. In the third year, the district assumed total support of the program. In 1972–73, the budget for the program was $2000, but not all of this money was used. Texts, tapes, and some tape recorders are provided through the program's budget; several students use cassette recorders and tapes they purchase themselves. Tutors are paid $3 an hour, and examiners receive $150 annually plus travel expenses. (The Critical Language Program no longer funds any programs. It now is a membership organization that simply develops, distributes, and coordinates information on self-instruction programs in critical languages.)

ADAPTABILITY OF CONCEPT TO OTHER PLACES

At least three high schools have used Guided Individualized Study in Foreign Languages as a model for developing their own programs. Adaptation of this program might be limited by several factors: the degree of interest among capable students; the funds available for organization and implementation; the effect on existing language programs and department staffing; the availability of suitable native speakers to act as tutors (many native speakers of foreign languages are in the U.S. on student visas and by law cannot work); and the availability of a qualified examiner (some self-instructional programs circumvent this limitation by contracting with examiners for telephone examinations).

The Critical Language Program has assembled information on tapes and materials in Amharic, Arabic, Chinese, Danish, Dutch, Erse, Modern Greek, Modern Hebrew, Hindi, Hungarian, Italian, Japanese, Korean, Norwegian, Persian, Afghan, Polish, Portuguese, Russian, Serbo-Croatian, Swahili, Thai, Ukranian, Vietnamese, Yiddish, and Yoruba. In addition the CLP has developed a guide for the implementation of programs of self-instruction, available from ERIC (ERIC ED 036 792), as well as a videotape showing a model tutorial session. Over 1000 students in 50 colleges and five high schools are now involved in self-instructional language programs established with the help of the Critical Language Program.

One of these high schools, Calasanctius Preparatory School in Buffalo, New York, used the format recommended by the Critical Language Program for two years in Hindi and Japanese, but revised and finally dropped it. The director and headmaster of the school felt that the Calasanctius Prep students, some of whom were as young as 12, did not have the necessary self-discipline and needed a high degree of interaction with a teacher to remain interested in their work and the language. Furthermore, the staff felt that, as the Critical Language Program approach deals only with oral-aural skills and does not attempt to introduce culture at all, the format limited students to an unacceptable degree in their understanding of the language and people. Calasanctius Prep therefore dropped its self-instruction programs, and replaced them with courses taught by full-time teachers, who also teach other subjects, and part-time paraprofessionals and teachers. The school now offers courses in Arabic, Hindi, Japanese, Hungarian, Chinese, Hebrew, French, German, and Spanish.

Guided Individualized Study in Foreign Languages ran into some of the same problems with the CLP approach, but adopted different solutions. The self-instructional format has been retained, and motivation does not appear to be a problem; however, the Garden City students are a few years older. Reading and writing have been introduced through the use of workbooks as well as a more active teaching role for the tutors in the later stages of the course. In addition, culture has been included through the Asian Studies course and the students' independent research.

AVAILABLE DESCRIPTIONS

The Critical Language Program is described in Peter Boyd-Bowman, "National Self-Instructional Program in Critical Languages," *Modern Language Journal*, 56 (1972), 163–67.

CONTACT PEOPLE

Daniel N. Perkins, Director, Guided Individualized Study in Foreign Languages, Garden City High School, Rockaway Road, Garden City, New York 11530 (516) 747-1800

Peter Boyd-Bowman, Executive Director, Critical Language Program, 209 Crosby Hall, State University of New York at Buffalo, Buffalo, New York 14214 (716) 831-2306

INDIVIDUALIZED GERMAN INSTRUCTION

ABSTRACT

During any one class period in the German Learning Center in Live Oak High School in Morgan Hill, California, 50 students, from beginners to those in their sixth year of German study, may be doing as many as 50 different things at the same time. Live Oak's program of Individualized German Instruction offers 350 students the opportunity to work at their own rate, to receive individual assistance from a staff of teachers, paraprofessionals, and student aides, and to choose from over 40 courses designed to develop proficiency in the four skills and cover a wide range of interests—from basic skill-building, scientific, and commerical German, to German drama, philosophy, and speed reading. Advanced students may also initiate their own "tailor-made" courses to suit their particular interests. Accompanying each course is a graduated sequence of teacher-prepared learning activity packets

(LAPs) that contain specific performance objectives, step-by-step guides for the study of texts and tapes, oral and written drills, and guides for testing procedures. At all levels the student is required only to report to the learning center at the beginning of his daily assigned German period and to attend a weekly 40-minute conversation session with four to six students of similar proficiency. Beyond that, he is responsible for structuring his own time. He may work independently or with a partner, using LAPs and print or recorded materials, and asks for teacher assistance and testing when necessary.

PROGRAM DEVELOPMENT AND PRESENT STATUS

The program began in a more basic form in 1968, when a pre-enrollment of 100 students in basic German would have meant four classes at the same level each day for one teacher. To avoid this, self-instructional materials were developed by a team of two teachers, who arranged to have all 100 students assigned to one class. After an initial presentation to the entire class, the students broke up into eight small groups: two worked in the lab, four worked with reading and writing exercises, and the two teachers each worked with one of the remaining groups for more personal help and oral practice. Each group rotated activities every 20 minutes. The following year the degree of individualization was expanded and the format was extended to the entire German sequence, "freeing the teachers completely at all levels and during every period so that they could spend a maximum amount of time with individuals and small groups while the mass of students worked without direct control."[1] Students attended the German Learning Center in classes of 50, and, except for small conversation groups, no other grouping patterns were retained. Gerald Logan, director of the program, developed a new curriculum that extends beyond the usual four-year sequence; on his own time and with no additional pay, he wrote behavioral objectives, learning activity packets, and tests for over 40 different courses over a three-year period. Another German teacher built the physical environment in the learning center. The program has grown to include over 350 students in all levels in Live Oak High School and two "feeder" junior high schools, as well as three teachers, about 20 student aides, and one native German paraprofessional. And, in a special introductory course offered in the district's elementary schools in 1973, 350 students at the sixth-grade level were involved in the program for ten weeks.

MAJOR GOALS FOR STUDENTS

"To provide the students with the ability to communicate in the second language; to give . . . insight and understanding of the people, culture, and civilization" of German-speaking countries; to provide students with the opportunity to study at their own pace and to concentrate on aspects of the language and subject area that most interest them.[2]

STUDENT GROUPING AND SCHEDULING ARRANGEMENTS

All German courses are available every period every day on an individualized basis; students register for "German" and their choice of course is determined and recorded in the German department. After completing beginning courses, students may take two or more courses simultaneously and register for more than one German period a day. At their assigned period, students at all levels report first to Room 1 of the German Learning Center for a large group vocabulary presentation, and may then remain in Room 1 or go on to Room 2. In Room 1, staffed by one teacher and several student aides, there are audio-visual materials, progress charts, and printed material. Students go to this room for testing and tutoring or to study individually and in pairs. In Room 2 are two small conversation groups, the department office, a German "store," and an "intensive-care" group of students who opt for a more structured class situation at the beginning level and work under the supervision of a student aide.

Each student is also assigned to one weekly 40-minute conversation group of four to six students. These groups are formed according to proficiency level; students can move into more advanced groups when their progress warrants it.

METHODOLOGY

The method is primarily individualized study; behavioral objectives are established for each course and the student works at his own pace with learning activity packets, tapes, audio-flashcard readers, and reference materials. Students take individual tests or quizzes, based on the performance objectives, when they choose, and may be retested indefinitely until at least 90 percent of the material is mastered. About two-thirds of all testing is done orally, and all tests are administered by a teacher or a teacher aide.

At the beginning of each German class period, all students at all levels are given five vocabulary words or phrases, presented by the teacher over a small loudspeaker with a "cultural" representation on a slide projection. Students repeat each word and the teacher gives examples of its use in context and asks questions. Each week 20 words are learned; on Fridays the words are reviewed in a sound-and-light show accompanied by music.

In the weekly conversation groups the teacher or teacher aide engages students at the first two levels in directed dialogue based on the vocabulary introduced daily throughout the preceding week. Students do not see the dialogue sheets and the accompanying vocabulary and German keys until they report to the conversation session. Dialogues are directed in English in order to minimize the time spent in problems of listening comprehension; emphasis is placed instead on speaking in German. At advanced levels there is free rather than directed dialogue, which also incorporates the new vocabulary and may consist of role-playing, retelling of stories, or discussion of particular themes.

REPRESENTATIVE CONTENT

Over 40 courses are offered at five levels. At the Beginning level there are courses covering the four skills of basic German, geared toward high school or college entrance credit, a one-semester introductory course for students wishing to sample the language, conversational German, and a course emphasizing listening and reading. At the Intermediate level are courses in standard college-preparatory German, reading, and vocabulary building. At the Lower and High Advanced levels there are courses in commercial German, specialized vocabulary building, literature, home economics, fine arts, speed reading, creative writing, history, current events, scientific German, short stories, and preparation for college board examinations. College-level courses are offered in composition, linguistics, philosophy, drama, and in-depth study of literature by author or period. Students may initiate their own courses, for which teachers design the objectives and evaluation points and recommend materials.

Some advanced courses and their subject matter are: Everyday Life Situations, for students expecting to visit Germany, involves oral and written work with "computer" sheets, felt-board charts, posters, texts, the German store, and taped dramatized episodes in such situations as traffic, shopping, family, school, and travel; German Philosophy is an introduction to philosophy in German followed by the study of Freud, Nietzsche, Marx, Einstein, or others chosen by the student; Children's Literature, "for those interested in the world in which the German child is raised," includes selections from nursery rhymes, fairy tales, and elementary school books; Secretarial German covers commercial vocabulary, typing on German typewriters, filling out orders and forms in German, and writing business letters.

In the directed conversation at the first two levels, practical, everyday situations are simulated in an attempt to put the student in positions he would face abroad. For example, students might be asked to have a conversation between a salesman and a shopper, between a waiter and a restaurant client, or between two friends deciding whether to attend a soccer match or a concert. At levels beyond the first two, students may play similar roles without explicit direction, retell stories they have read or movies they have seen, talk about current events or their personal interests, create stories, describe pictures, or put themselves in hypothetical situations.

The German program also offers several special services. The resource center and some of the staff are available one hour before and after school and at lunch for students needing extra help or time for doing their work. Information and assistance are provided for students wishing to travel or work in Germany. The department subscribes to over 15 different German magazines and newspapers, and helps students order their own subscriptions or goods from the German mail-order catalogues on display. A German club, open to all students enrolled in German, has organized parties, ski trips, a *Faschingball*, and a German band, choir, and film festival. The staff also assists small groups of students interested in particular activities, such as German folk dancing, music, or lunchtime conversation groups.

CREDIT AND ARTICULATION

Credit for German courses is variable and awarded according to units of work completed. Each unit is divided in 16 assignments, or "hours" of work, consisting of "an amount of work determined by the experience of teachers as to what can reasonably be expected of the average student if he applies himself diligently for one hour." Students take quizzes and tests when they feel they are ready—quizzes at the completion of an assignment and tests at the end of a unit. A student may retake a test or quiz indefinitely until he achieves at least 90 percent mastery of the material, based on the learner objectives. He then goes on to the next assignment or unit. When he has completed all units of a course, he may begin another course.

A course may be worth up to ten units of credit. For example, a "semester course" may consist of five units. A student who completes four units during one actual school semester receives four units of credit toward graduation and then continues the course the next semester, beginning a second course whenever he has successfully finished the first. Another student may complete the same "semester course" before the end of the semester and begin a new course, earning, for example, six units of credit for the amount of work he completes in one semester's time. On report cards, students receive either an A (for average mastery of

95-100 percent) or B (90-94 percent). The number of credits earned is also indicated, accompanied by the letters H.S. (units that count towards high school graduation) or C.P. (courses that count toward college admission requirements as well as high school graduation). If a student earns no credit at all, he receives neither grade nor credit on his report card.

Courses at the Intermediate level require a beginning course as a prerequisite and courses at the Advanced level require completion of certain intermediate courses. There are also sequences of courses, at increasing levels of difficulty, for students preparing for college, for students interested in developing one particular skill, or for those desiring to study German literature in increasing depth. Students who transfer into the program from other schools are given a placement test and advised, on the basis of test results, as to what course would be best for them. This advice is not binding; a student may choose to begin where he feels most comfortable.

MATERIALS

Basic materials are: (1) teacher-prepared text booklets containing reading selections, directions for readings in outside sources, conversation sheets, vocabulary lists, and learning activity packets; (2) teacher-prepared cassette tapes; (3) cassette recorders; and (4) audio-flashcard readers from Electronics Futures, Inc. These readers use five-by-nine inch cards with strips of two-track recording tape at the bottom. A card is inserted into the reader, the teacher records an exercise on the master track, and students record responses on the second track. The surface of the card can be used for a pictorial or printed stimulus. "The advantage of such a machine lies in the single item drill feature. . . . Students can pick the individual drills thay need, . . . go through a series and put aside the cards on which they make mistakes, then feed these through the machine for extra drill." The department also has a carousel projector, a record player, and several sets of earphones.

For specialized, advanced courses there are supplementary

materials: German books on science, business, linguistics, history, philosophy, and literature; periodicals for current events; cookbooks, fashion magazines, and texts for home economics courses in German; German typewriters; posters, theater programs, feltboard charts, supplies and displays for the German store; and "computer" sheets, adapted from a game, in which a light goes on when the words are properly matched or questions correctly answered.

ROLE OF STUDENTS

Each student is responsible for structuring his own time, deciding how much work he will complete, and completing it. He takes tests when ready and does work at home or at school as he sees fit. He is obliged to report for roll call and his conversation group at the assigned times. He may take more than one German course at a time.

ROLES OF TEACHERS, TEACHER AIDES, AND PARAPROFESSIONALS

Teachers counsel students in their choice of courses. They give audio-visual presentations of new vocabulary at the beginning of each class period, and for the remainder of class time attend to individual problems and administer individual tests and quizzes. Teachers are prepared to assist students at all levels of study during any one period. One teacher conducts a conversation group each period. Beyond these specific responsibilities, each teacher helps maintain a smooth flow in the activities of the class and individuals, trying to keep each student interested and foreseeing possible trouble or friction spots. Teacher aides are advanced students who have taken, with teacher permission, a special course training them in administering tests, keeping records, tutoring, and conducting conversation groups. In some years there have been as many as 25 aides. One native German speaker works three full days a week in the German program. She corrects written tests, gives oral tests, helps students, leads conversation groups, assembles materials, records some tapes, and makes presentations to advanced conversation groups.

ROLE OF PROGRAM DIRECTOR

The program director establishes goals and objectives for the program, writes learning activity packets and tests, develops new courses, assigns teachers and aides to specific duties, groups students for conversation, leads advanced conversation groups, makes slide presentations, meets visitors and explains the program, handles the program's budget, gives periodic pep talks to students, and advises the German club.

PROGRAM EVALUATION

Enrollment in beginning German increased by 35% from 1968 to 1971. The number of students choosing to continue into the fourth year of German study tripled between 1968 and 1971. The school's Spanish department, suffering a 50% decline in enrollment over this same three-year period, began a similar program of individualization in 1971–72; since then, enrollment in Spanish has increased and enrollment in German has stabilized.

Most evaluations of student progress have been criterion-referenced tests constructed locally to test the program's performance objectives. Standardized tests with national norms have been considered inappropriate. Members of the department agree that students' skills in German are steadily improving and are superior to what they were in general four years ago. Another indication of student success has been the average number of units of work completed by students each year within the criteria of 90 to 100 percent mastery:

1969–70	6.5 units
1970–71	7.9 units
1971–72	8.4 units

In 1970–71 Howard Altman and Robert Morrey conducted a survey of student attitudes toward individualized instruction. Twelve hundred students in five northern California high schools, including over 200 in Live Oak's German program, participated in the survey. The results, published in the proceedings of the 1971 Stanford Conference on Individualized Foreign Language Instruction, indicated that individualization was preferred by a majority of students who had been in both individualized and non-individualized programs. The features they most liked were self-pacing, the opportunity to study certain aspects of the language or culture in depth, the chance to retake tests, and increased classroom freedom. All of these are major features of the Live Oak program. Students identified as problems their own lack of self-discipline, the lack of suitable materials (particularly for oral work), and the pressure to complete a certain amount of work within a certain amount of time. The Live Oak program has eliminated this latter form of pressure entirely, has developed extensive materials for oral and written work, and has initiated a procedure of periodic pep talks to help students persevere in the self-discipline necessary to work steadily on their own.

FUNDING AND COSTS

The program is financed through the regular school budget allowance for each department, approximately $4 per pupil per year for books and other materials. For 250 pupils enrolled in German, the department would be given $1000 for the year.

Tapes, text booklets, and learning activity packets are locally prepared. The only cost is the paper and tapes on which they are produced. There is no cost allowance for the time teachers spend in preparing these materials or developing the curriculum. German typewriters used in the commercial German course were donated to the program. German books and reference works have been contributed by the director or purchased by the school over a period of many years; the director estimates their total worth at $500. Other specific costs are:

4 audio-flashcard readers	$1000
3 cassette tape recorders	90
Computer sheets	3
Periodicals	150
Slide projector	150

ADAPTABILITY OF CONCEPT TO OTHER PLACES

Considerations in adapting the Live Oak concept of individualized instruction would be: (1) the availability of personnel for developing curriculum and writing LAPs (at Live Oak this was done by the department chairman, working without released time or financial compensation); (2) classroom space and material resources to accommodate large numbers of students working independently at one time; (3) the availability of enough advanced students and/or native speakers to permit a high proportion of tutorial contact and frequent individual testing; (4) administrative support for a variable credit system based on portions of courses completed; (5) individual teachers' ability to direct and manage large groups of students working independently. No special scheduling is required, as students can take any German course whenever their schedules are open. Use of student aides makes individualization possible for large numbers of students with limited professional staff. Types of audio-visual materials, texts, and courses offered can be adjusted to correspond to available resources and student interests. The program could be applied to any language.

AVAILABLE DESCRIPTIONS

Gerald Logan, "Curricula for Individualizing Instruction," in *Britannica Review of Foreign Language Education,* Vol. II, ed. Dale Lange (Chicago: Encyclopaedia Britannica, Inc., 1970).

CONTACT PERSON

Gerald Logan, Chairman, Foreign Language Department, Live Oak High School, Box 827, Morgan Hill, California 95037 (408) 779-3151

NOTES

[1] Personal communication to the survey staff.

[2] Unless otherwise indicated, all other quotations are from "1972–73 German Curriculum Guide and Catalogue of Courses" (Morgan Hill, California: Live Oak High School, 1972).

INDIVIDUALIZED INSTRUCTION IN FOREIGN LANGUAGES

ABSTRACT

The program of Individualized Instruction in Foreign Languages in West Bend, Wisconsin involves more than 900 students at all levels of foreign language study in the district's two junior and two senior high schools. A differentiated staff of 15 teachers, teaching interns, paraprofessionals, and native-speaker aides is the key to a ten-to-one student-teacher ratio allowing for frequent individual tutoring and testing. An extensive group phase at the first level of Spanish, French, or German that introduces students to the basic features of the target language and the methods of individual study leads into a program of nongraded "continuous progress." Locally-prepared "unipacs" that accompany the *A-LM* text series provide explicit performance objectives, directions, and exercises for each concept, replacing the usual teacher presentation; and students receive their initial practice by working individually with tape and cassette recordings of all dialogues, drills, and pronunciation exercises. The teacher acts as a guide, diagnostician, and supervisor, clarifying and reinforcing what has been learned through the texts and tapes. A checklist in each unipac provides a sequence of activities, both required and optional, that lead to the attainment of the stated goals, and students are checked at the end of each "step" before moving on to the next unit division. Several different activity groupings, options in the materials used, and a system of evaluation based on mastery of skills have enabled the West Bend program to attract and satisfy students of varied abilities and learning styles.

PROGRAM DEVELOPMENT AND PRESENT STATUS

Individualization at West Bend began in 1968 as a pilot program, initiated by the district's foreign language teachers and funded by a Title III grant, as an attempt to solve some common and critical problems in foreign language instruction. Enrollment was dropping sharply after the first two levels, students at all levels were frustrated by having to learn a language at a predetermined and uniform rate, and those who were not considered "college-bound" generally avoided foreign languages altogether. The West Bend teachers hoped to create a program that would provide realistic individual goals and stimulation for students of all abilities, offer maximum flexibility of scheduling, and measure progress in language learning on the basis of mastery of skills rather than on time spent in class. The program began with first-level Spanish students in three schools: 33 in grade 7, 40 in grade 9, and 32 in senior high school. The original staff of two teachers was increased to include two intern teachers, two teacher aides from the Amity Institute, and a full-time secretary; this staff also taught 170 non-project students. (Adding five non-certified members to the staff cost only $4800 more than would have been needed to add just one certified first-year teacher.) It was hoped that the school would begin a system of modular scheduling, but this proved impossible.

An introductory phase kept students at each grade level grouped together for background work in pronunciation and audio-comprehension skills and training in the procedures needed for individualized study. The seventh-graders completed four units in 18 weeks as a group, the ninth-graders completed the same number of units in 10 weeks, and the senior high students worked through three units in five weeks. At the end of each introductory phase, the continuous progress phase was begun. Students were given the option of working (1) independently with the unipac activities, remedial or enrichment exercises; (2) in small groups directed by a staff member for conversation practice; (3) in large groups for cultural presentations and work in the language laboratory; (4) in one-to-one contact with a staff member for testing, tutoring, and informal drills and conversation; and (5) in independent group study, in which students chose informally to work in pairs or small groups, quizzing and helping one another. Some students chose to study completely independently with texts, cassette and tape recordings, records, and slides, while others avoided the individual use of audio-visual equipment and worked almost exclusively with staff members and fellow students. Students were given as much time as needed to master each unit or subunit.

The following year the same students began in full-group work, but by the end of the second week all students were ready to return to the continuous progress format. Since flexible scheduling was still not used, all classes were scheduled into 55-minute periods, as they had been the previous year; some flexibility of movement was possible, however, within the language room and available study areas. Meanwhile, the new level I group in Spanish began its initiation into individualized study, and by the spring of 1970 all first- and second-year Spanish students, as well as all first-year French and German students, were in the continuous progress program, and new school facilities made modular scheduling possible. Funds were granted through Title III for program expansion through the third year, but, after that, funding was assumed entirely by the local school district. At present, all levels of all three languages are involved in the individualized continuous progress program.

TARGET AUDIENCE

Students of all abilities, grades 7–12, in the West Bend Joint School District No. 1, in all six years of language study in French, German, and Spanish.

GOALS FOR STUDENTS

To develop proficiency in the four skills of the target language; to gain some understanding of the related foreign cultures; to develop the attitudes and self-discipline needed to work independently; to enjoy and desire to continue the study of a foreign language beyond the usual two years.

STUDENT GROUPING AND
SCHEDULING ARRANGEMENTS

The West Bend schools now operate on a schedule of 21 20-minute modules each day in a six-day cycle. First-level language students meet for two modules daily, while from level II on, students meet for three modules every other day. One additional three-module block per cycle is devoted to cultural presentations, talks by native speakers, and films; attendance at these sessions is optional. Beyond the beginning level, students at all levels in one language are mixed in any one class period and no grade distinctions are made. Conversation sessions are scheduled for each student for one module each week, usually during the regularly scheduled study time.

METHODOLOGY AND REPRESENTATIVE CONTENT

At present, courses center around the *A-LM* series, first edition in Spanish and second edition in French and German (Harcourt, Brace, Jovanovich), and are divided into units, which, in turn, are divided into subunits focusing on specific concepts. For each unit there is a unipac with a checklist identifying the basic unit objectives, the level of proficiency the student is expected to achieve, pretest exercises that permit the student to evaluate his own progress before taking a quiz or unit test, and exercises to supplement the *A-LM* materials. Activities for the unit are listed on the right side of the checklist; on the left are two columns, the first referring to work that must be checked by a staff member, the second to work that can be completed without supervision. The checklist might direct students to read certain selections, work on a structure drill in the lab, complete a written exercise using certain conjugations or vocabulary, or listen to a taped narration. In one unit there may be 30 activities listed, of which the student is required to do only ten, and these must be checked by a teacher. From the 20 others the student is free to select those he feels will help him attain the unit objectives; he may decide to do only two or all 20. When the student feels he is ready, and when his pretest assures him he is, he asks to take a subunit quiz or unit test from a staff member. The tests, oral or written (and more frequently both), are based directly on the objectives; the checklist gives explicit instructions, indicating that for a quiz, for example, the teacher "will dictate a paragraph and you will be expected to write it exactly as it appears in your book." Meanwhile, the teacher's own checklist provides instructions for giving dictation and specific criteria for evaluating each quiz exercise. If the student meets the success criterion (generally 90 percent or better), he may go on to the next subunit or unit. If he fails, he and the teacher decide which exercises he should repeat or which supplementary exercises he should do, and the student re-takes the test when he and the teacher agree he is ready.

Students may work alone, in pairs, or in small groups of three or four, as they choose. More advanced students very often choose to help those at the intermediate stage. The teacher is always available for consultation, and "roams" the classroom, talking with students informally, identifying errors, offering encouragement, or giving tests. After the first year of language study, classroom instructions and all teacher-student communication are in the target language. It has been observed, however, that student-to-student exchanges are frequently in English.[1] In general, beginning students are restricted to work in the unipacs and *A-LM* text, and their classes are frequently conducted in a more structured way. While more advanced students work with unipacs and texts, they may also choose areas for individual readings. There are no "mini-courses" or specialized courses per se; courses are simply labeled "Intermediate" or "Advanced." In advanced Spanish, for example, a student might choose to concentrate on Latin American history or Spanish poetry. In French, students might do some reading and experimenting in French cuisine.

In one module per cycle, students are temporarily grouped for conversation sessions. The assignment to groups is done quickly and informally; a member of the staff goes from student to student, sees which units each has completed, and assembles about 12 students at about the same unit. Topics of conversation vary and depend to a large extent on the unit recently completed. Generally students know the topic beforehand and are prepared to speak on it. For example, beginning students who have just finished a unit related to the family will discuss their own families during the conversation module; more advanced students might share their opinions on a selection from *Don Quixote*.

FACILITIES AND MATERIALS

The foreign language classrooms are equipped with movable curtains, tables, and chairs, and are easily divided into sections for different activities. There are language laboratories in both high schools; the original central console units were dismantled and replaced by individual booths, each equipped with cassette and reel-to-reel tape recorders and a record player with headset. The laboratory also has an "audio notebook," a 22-channel battery-powered tape recorder with headset and microphone which holds 22 15-minute programs stored on one-inch tape, on which students may record and play back their own voices. Multiple copies of all commercially prepared tapes for the *A-LM* series are available, as well as supplementary grammar and pronunciation exercises, prepared on tape by the teaching staff, which form part of the unipac activities. There are also a cassette duplicator to convert programs from open reel to cassettes, portable cassette recorders, a library of records which students may sign out to use in school or at home, and supplementary print and visual materials. A full-time lab aide is responsible for copying, filing, and supervision. There is free movement between classrooms and the language laboratory, and the student schedules his own time in the lab.

The unipacs were prepared locally by the teaching staff, and are now being expanded in order to phase out the *A-LM* texts completely. The new materials will include not only exercises, readings, and explanations like those found in the textbooks (but put in a sequence better suited to the program goals), but also many additional cultural materials and sections geared specifically to conversation sessions.

CREDIT, GRADING, AND ARTICULATION

Students receive traditional letter grades based on the results of *A-LM* unit tests and criterion-referenced tests prepared by the teachers. A student must get a C before moving on to the next unit. The number of units completed does not influence a grade unless a "faster" student does significantly less work than he could. A slow student, however, doing the same amount of work yet working to his ability, may get an A. Progress is recorded on weekly individual progress forms, unit progress charts, and a unit progress wall chart for the entire class, on which names are not identified. Students receive one credit for each year of study, regardless of the number of units completed, as long as passing grades are received.

Articulation from junior to senior high school is accomplished by the use of the same text series and materials and the overlapping of teaching staff in both. Students who begin continuous progress language study in junior high simply pick up where they left off when entering senior high.

ROLES OF TEACHERS, INTERN TEACHERS, AND PARAPROFESSIONALS

Teachers help students on a one-to-one basis, administer tests and quizzes, assess student progress, prepare appropriate remedial or enrichment work, and act as general consultants. They engage students in informal dialogues whenever possible. There is a total of six certified teachers in the three languages. Two intern teachers in each language work each semester as part of the Wisconsin Improvement Program based at the University of Wisconsin at Madison. They are responsible for working in all learning situations, administering tests, and using audio-visual equipment. Some intern teachers are native speakers; in the past there have been interns from Cuba, Colombia, and Nicaragua. For the first two years, two native-speaker teacher aides in each language worked in the program through the Amity Institute. Aides are now found from other sources and are sometimes not native speakers. Those who are native speakers spend most of their time tutoring and presenting cultural materials. All the aides share the duties of the intern teachers and supervise in the lab.

ROLES OF PROGRAM SECRETARIES AND DIRECTOR

Program secretaries act as laboratory aides, keep progress records and charts, prepare all mimeographed material, reproduce tapes, and maintain files. There is one foreign language secretary in each of the three schools. The program director is responsible for the management and supervision of the program and personnel, for curriculum planning and writing, for the placement and selection of paraprofessionals, and for the selection of equipment and materials. He is also a teacher of Spanish at the high school level.

ROLE OF CONSULTANTS

Foreign language consultants were employed during the project stage of the program to help develop materials, make recommendations for methods and organization, and conduct evaluation.

TRAINING REQUIREMENTS

The first year, the staff members participated in a summer inservice training session in individualized instruction. Since then, a brief program of preservice training acquaints new staff members with materials, procedures, and program philosophy, and inservice training is carried out on an unscheduled basis, as needed.

FUNDING AND COSTS

During the first year of the program, 1968–69, a federal grant of $27,445 under the Elementary and Secondary Education Act, Title III, covered additional staff costs, equipment, and materials, payments to consultants, and reimbursement to staff members for summer inservice education. A second Title III grant for $47,520 funded the expansion of the program through the second year. Since September 1970, the program, including the current expansion of materials, has been funded by the school district itself. In the fourth year, all major costs for equipment, materials, and program development had been incurred, the total foreign language program was nongraded, and the per pupil cost for the language program had dropped from approximately $170 the first year to $77. Teachers are currently paid on an hourly basis for materials development.

PROGRAM EVALUATION

During the first two years, an extensive battery of proficiency tests, attitude and self-concept surveys, and observations by outside investigators was carried out. Only a sampling of the test results can be given here. Complete results can be found in the End-of-Project Report, written by Frank Grittner.[2] All data and conclusions that follow are taken from this investigator's report unless otherwise indicated.

Attrition studies showed that for project classes the dropout rate from the first to second year was 14%, as compared to 24% in previous years. From the second to third year, the rate dropped dramatically from the usual 65% to 38%. After the project's first two years, enrollments in the district's Spanish program increased, in contrast to the falling enrollments throughout the country at that time. Seventy-five percent of the students at the end of the first year of the project and 85% at the end of the second year said they would prefer to continue in the individualized program rather than return to lockstep instruction.

Student achievement was measured by the A form of the Pimsleur tests in reading and listening comprehension at the end of the first year and the C form at the end of the second. Although the project students completed, on the average, less than half the first-level course of study by the end of the first year, the mean percentile scores for all three groups were at or near the fiftieth percentile in both skills. In the distribution of scores on the nine-point stanine scale, 12% of the project students fell into the "poor" and "below average" categories in listening comprehension, as compared with 23% of the norm group, but only 13% of the project group scored in the "above average" to "superior" range, as compared to 23% of the norm group. This left 75% in the three middle stanines designated "average." Scores in reading comprehension were similarly distributed, with 81% in the "average" stanines.

At the end of the second year, the stanine distribution of listening scores ran fairly close to that of the norm group, with a slight tendency toward the low-achievement end. In reading comprehension, there was a "distinct shift" toward the lower end in stanine scores; the "average" range scores dropped to 52%, with 38% in the "poor" to "below average" ranges. The investigator notes that the tendency toward lower reading achievement scores by the end of the second year might be a result, in part, of the reduced dropout rate: "it appears reasonable to suspect that the students who tend to score at the low end of standardized tests are the same students who would have been eliminated from a traditional program long before the end of the school year."

On the basis of local achievement standards, using a final exam that had been given to a high school group taught the previous year by the same teacher with the same materials in lockstep fashion, the senior high project students scored slightly higher than the non-project students. The investigator concluded that under the conditions of individualized study, the mean achievement of the project students at the end of the first year was comparable to the achievement of traditionally-taught students, as measured by conventional testing procedures.

One major project objective was to change from a program based on time criteria to one based on performance criteria. This objective "appears to have been fulfilled, as evidenced by the wide variety in the number of units completed. . . . Not only had many of the students in the original pilot group progressed more than twice as fast as their fellow students, but . . . [some] students in the new first-year group had overtaken students in the original group. . . . Four students completed the equivalent of three years' work by the end of the second year." Staff members felt, however, that many of the low-achieving students might be taking unfair advantage of the freedom allowed by the program. One "remedy" for this situation would have been to require that students complete a minimum amount of work before receiving credit, but this seemed to run counter to the purpose of the program. It was decided instead to measure success or failure by taking both aptitude, as measured by the Pimsleur Aptitude Battery, and actual achievement into account. Students who performed significantly below their ability level would be evaluated accordingly.

Another problem was that high-achieving students tended to monopolize staff time because they were more often ready for testing. The "slower" students tended, therefore, to receive less personal attention from the staff, who were kept busy with testing, prescribing remedial activities, and recording grades. In the third year of the program this situation was improved by the completion of a new high school and the introduction of modular scheduling, which made it possible to schedule faster students into the teachers' open hours and avoid the pile-up of students during the regular study periods.

The investigator notes that a general lack of correlation between I.Q. and student achievement strongly suggests that, under these conditions of individualization, foreign language achievement is not a function of I.Q. "as it is conventionally measured." One student had an I.Q. of 97, but he completed three years of work in two years and scored in the upper quartile on all tests. The investigator suggests that "the bright student is not necessarily a better potential student of language but merely . . . more capable of surviving academically when the instructional pace . . . style . . . and content are externally imposed. The results of the study further suggest that I.Q. is not a good criterion for placing students into individualized foreign language programs or for excluding them from such programs."

Among the various attitude surveys administered was the "Critical Incident Technique," which studied student attitudes toward teacher-pupil and peer-group relationships, methodology, administrative factors, and satisfaction in accomplishment. This survey was given to both project and non-project students, the latter working with the same materials and general audiolingual approach but in lockstep fashion. Some project students felt that teachers often pressured them to speed up even though they were told to go at their own rate, but negative comments about the teacher as "authority figure" did not turn up. Comments about the lack of personal help were found only in the non-project classes. Project students, in naming "good features" of the individualized program, referred most often to matters related to methodology; they felt the approach reduced psychological pressures and improved overall performance. Many saw the approach as being adapted to their individual characteristics ("I'm dumb and I like working slow." "You get a second chance."). Many project students felt that there were too many tests and that they often had to wait too long to take tests for which they were ready. But negative factors cited by non-project students were much more specific and numerous. Even though both groups were using audiolingual methods and materials, only the non-project group cited specific audiolingual techniques as being negative and frustrating, or were disappointed about their grades or the manner in which tests showed their achievement.

The investigator concluded that "the feasibility of establishing a continuous progress, nongraded foreign language program within a traditionally-scheduled junior or senior high school has been demonstrated by the West Bend project. That is, it appears that a majority of students are capable . . . of determining their own instructional pace and learning style within a clearly-defined body of content without adversely affecting language achievement."

In a comparative study of three successful programs of individualization, Jean-Pierre Berwald noted that "the West Bend students indicated greater satisfaction with their program" than did students in the others.[3] In the Foreign Language Attitude Questionnaire, administered in conjunction with this study in 1970, only 9% of the West Bend students said that they found the study of foreign language "not enjoyable," only 14% said they could have accomplished more if instruction had been organized in a different way, and 90% or more of all students were satisfied with the type of skills taught, the textbooks, the use of the language lab, the homework, the teacher's helpfulness, and the amount of time allotted for study.

ADAPTABILITY OF CONCEPT TO OTHER PLACES

The writer of the end-of-project report notes several factors to consider in establishing a district-wide program of nongraded continuous progress. (1) At West Bend the program was initiated by the teaching staff, and it is recommended that any similar program "permit a high level of decision-making on the part of the staff members." (2) In a program that demands individual testing at each step of the learning process, it is doubtful whether success can be achieved by one teacher working alone with the usual class load. "It appears that a pupil-staff ratio of approximately ten to one is manageable from the standpoint of avoiding a pile-up of students who demand to be tested." (3) To provide this ratio at reasonable cost, it is suggested that native-speaker aides, teacher interns, and paraprofessionals be employed. (4) "Even with the use of lower-cost staff members, there is a strong question regarding the ability or willingness of most school districts to fund a program which is expensive to implement and, perhaps, to sustain." Once the program has been nongraded, students in the second through sixth level can be scheduled together, and the problem of "justifying" small classes no longer exists. By the fourth year of the West Bend program, when the entire sequence had been nongraded and all major expenditures had been made, the per pupil expenditure was reduced by more than one-half. (5) Finally, "successful implementation . . . requires that staff members accept the role of diagnostician and evaluator in place of the traditional teaching roles."[4]

Berwald notes that by making all step-by-step evaluation self-testing, with self-tests built into the unipac sequence as in a program at McCluer High School in Florissant, Missouri, the teacher is relieved of continuous testing and "secretarial" duties.[5] In the McCluer program, the instructor is more completely free to circulate and offer help, and the "entire classroom operation can be controlled and directed by one person." Teachers and intern teachers have class loads of 20–25 each, while paraprofessional aides are employed only in the language laboratory. Students work in groups of four or five, rather than individually or in pairs, and the self-tests are used only for students to gauge their own progress rather than for grades. "If students failed tests, they were still permitted to continue their work since they were sure to cover the same material in other contexts—so, mastery was not an issue. It was during the [periodic] performance 'check-outs' that students were asked to recite dialogues, pose questions to each other, take dictation, and do a variety of activities for a grade. Each instructor in the program was free to assign grades in his own way." As in West Bend, the language lab is used to provide students with basic information, and the student is free to decide how much time he must spend in it.

AVAILABLE DESCRIPTIONS

A 137-page summary of the objectives, procedures, and evaluation for the first two years of the program, the proposals for the third year, and extensive samples of instructional materials used in German, French, and Spanish in the West Bend program is available from ERIC (ERIC ED 047 574). A videotape, "Student Reaction to Individualization," produced at West Bend, is available from the contact person. A short description of the initial program proposals can be found in "Nongraded Foreign Language Classrooms," *Foreign Language Annals*, 2 (1969), 343–47. Finally, Fred LaLeike and Frank Grittner are preparing a book on individualization, based on the West Bend program, that will be published by the National Textbook Company.

CONTACT PERSON

Fred LaLeike, West Bend Joint School District No. 1, 1305 East Decorah Road, West Bend, Wisconsin 53095 (414) 338-0661

NOTES

[1] Jean-Pierre Berwald, "Three Innovative Programs: Comparisons and Conclusions," to appear in *Foreign Language Annals*, vol. 7.

[2] Frank Grittner, "Individualized Foreign Language Program," End-of-Project Report (Madison: Department of Public Instruction, 1972).

[3] Berwald, "Three Innovative Programs."

[4] Grittner, "Individualized Foreign Language Program."

[5] Berwald, "Three Innovative Programs."

JOHN DEWEY HIGH SCHOOL FOREIGN LANGUAGE PROGRAM

ABSTRACT

In Brooklyn, New York individualized, continuous progress is not just an experiment in a foreign language department, but the philosophy of a whole school. In John Dewey High School every subject area has created performance objectives and independent study programs and has its own resource center and classroom complex. Abolition of grade levels, a system of evaluation based on mastery of skills, and flexibility of scheduling in terms of both the school year and the school day are just some of the features that allow students to follow the course of study most suited to their needs and interests at the rate most suited to their abilities.

PROGRAM DEVELOPMENT AND PRESENT STATUS

John Dewey High School first opened in September 1969. A group of high school principals had been commissioned by the

132

New York City Board of Education to plan an experimental school that "would provide young people with an education to meet the challenges of modern life."[1] The guiding principle of their plan was that "every student should be required to achieve a reasonable mastery of an area of knowledge before he may advance"; the two "cornerstones" of this plan were independent study and individual progress. By abolishing grade levels, the five-period-per-week lockstep pattern, and traditional letter or numerical grades, it was hoped to encourage acceleration and enrichment, to reduce the penalty of failure, and to enable students to advance at their own rates. Some students can graduate in two or three years, others in the usual four, and others in a longer period of time. The school year was divided into five seven-week cycles, with curriculum and scheduling changes each cycle, and the day was divided into 20-minute modules, enabling students to take a wider variety of courses and have ample "self-directed" independent study time. In addition, provisions were made for instruction in practical arts for college-bound as well as work-oriented students, and extra-class activities were incorporated into the curriculum by lengthening the school day to eight hours. Each subject area was assigned a resource center containing reference materials, audio-visual aids, study carrels, and, in the case of foreign languages, a language laboratory. Each of these "satellite libraries" is surrounded by five classrooms, and movable walls of folding wood panels permit classes to be enlarged or broken up into small groups. Students can use their independent study time to go to the resource center and receive assistance from a teacher or paraprofessional, do homework, or explore the available materials on their own.

In 1969 there were 1000 students in the school; another 1000 were added each year for the next two years, bringing enrollment to its maximum of 3000. All 3000 students take at least one level of foreign language. In 1972–73 there were over 1900 students enrolled in programs in French, German, Hebrew, Italian, and Spanish at five levels of study; and there are Independent Study programs in Latin and Russian, languages that are not offered as classes because of low student demand. The department has a total of 16 foreign language teachers.

TARGET AUDIENCE

All students who attend the school are given a foreign language for at least one level. If a student has opted to take no language and his reading score is poor, he is placed in a pre-level I conversation course.

STUDENT GROUPING AND SCHEDULING ARRANGEMENTS

The school year is divided into five seven-week cycles, with an optional sixth cycle during the summer, and students and teachers have new programs each cycle. The eight-hour day is divided into 22 20-minute modules; language classes are generally scheduled for a combination of two consecutive modules twice a week and three consecutive modules twice a week. Each class is also scheduled into the language laboratory at least once every two weeks. The school-wide scheduling configuration provides for a regular pattern of independent study time, during which students can establish meeting times with teachers in the resource centers.

In class meetings, students are grouped according to general proficiency level. Homogeneity of grouping is achieved as the cycles move along during the year: students who fail to master a cycle's work are placed in "retention" classes, while others move ahead. Students on Independent Study in foreign languages, usually those who are learning a second foreign language, are not grouped at all, but work during their open modules on their own or receive assistance from a teacher in the resource center or from the Independent Study coordinators.

CREDIT, GRADING, AND ARTICULATION

At the end of each seven-week cycle, the student's work is evaluated for that period of time. The grading system is neither numerical nor letter equivalent; instead, students are given a rating of "Mastery" (M), "Mastery with Condition" (MC), or "Retention for Reinforcement" (R). The student who is rated M moves ahead into the next phase of work. The MC student also moves ahead, but the teacher writes a "prescription," or "Supportive DISK" (Dewey Independent Study Kit), that directs the student to certain objectives and exercises for mastering the phase of work in which he was weak. He is given a specified amount of time, negotiable with his new language teacher, to complete the topics listed. The student does this work in the resource center, with help from a teacher on duty, while proceeding into the next phase of work in his regular class. The R student also receives a prescription form, but is not moved ahead; the prescription serves as the basis of the next seven weeks' work. Since he has not mastered the objectives of a cycle's work, he is not asked to move on to the more complex tasks of the next phase. Retention is only for seven weeks, rather than for a semester or year.

Articulation is built into the system of continuous progress, the mastery system of evaluation, and the provisions for acceleration, retention, and ability grouping. Students who began their study of foreign language in intermediate or junior high schools are placed in classes on the basis of their previous experience when they enter John Dewey. Articulation is also achieved by the sequences of courses, which were prepared by the teachers in the department, as well as by frequent teacher conferences.

METHODOLOGY AND REPRESENTATIVE CONTENT

Each teacher is free to use the methods he feels will most effectively help his students develop all four language skills. Activities are usually teacher-directed. Teachers can break up the time blocks into a variety of activities, and team teaching is often used. When two classes of the same level and phase are programmed for the same time slot and placed in adjoining classrooms, the teachers can plan their lessons together and unite their classes for some activities. For example, while one teacher works with a large group, the other may either move around the room offering individual help or work in the adjoining room with selected students from both classes on a specific objective.

Individualized instruction with learning activity packets is also used in an "open-classroom" approach; the number of classes and teachers using this approach varies from cycle to cycle. Students work with instruction sheets and packets (LAPs) for each topic; these include an objective for each part of each lesson, several model sentences illustrating the objectives, a generalization that explains the concept of the objective, drills that test the student's understanding and application of the objective, and a pattern drill to practice orally with a classmate. At the end of the lesson, the student is usually directed to do an exercise "to see how well [he] can put everything together": for example, to make up original sentences that illustrate each of the lesson's objectives or create a brief dialogue incorporating the new structure mastered in the lesson. Students work with texts and written exercises and are encouraged to use the audio-visual equipment available in the classroom, such as the tape recorder or phonograph. However, it is the written work, answering questions and writing out drills, "that provides the student with a very clear picture of his mastery of the topic." The student may work alone or with one or several classmates who are on the same topic. The groups form spontaneously, and the teacher circulates among the individuals and groups offering "explanations, oral use of the foreign language, and encouragement." Other students may serve as tutors, and within each group there is usually one student who naturally assumes leadership. The teacher, too, helps students find the right group to work with and "creates situations for peer teaching, thereby meeting the need of the weaker student and reaffirming the degree of mastery of the more advanced student." Students take tests on a given topic when they feel ready and may retake tests until achieving a Mastery rating. Periodically the entire class is reassembled for activities such as auditory comprehension and dialogue practice.

In most Level I courses, a multi-media approach is used: for example, the French and Spanish texts are accompanied by films, filmstrips, and tapes. Beginning students with low reading scores are offered a "conversation" course that gives them instruction in the basic sound system of the target language and teaches much of the vocabulary and idiomatic expressions of Level I. The student who successfully completes the five phases of this pre-Level I course goes into Level I, where he can concentrate on reading and writing. Some five-cycle courses are lengthened to seven cycles for students who demonstrate, in the first cycle of a course, the need for a longer period of time to master the work. As described earlier, there are one-cycle "retention" classes for students who fail to master one phase of a course; they work either independently with their prescription forms and teacher assistance or in groups reviewing the same phase of work. A system of "Student-Created DISKs" has recently been introduced for individualized projects. Students sign contracts on which they write their own objectives, specify materials and evaluation techniques, and "assign" themselves readings and exercises in areas of particular interest. Finally, Independent Study programs in Latin and Russian allow students who would like to study a second foreign language to do so without scheduled classes. The students receive self-instructional Dewey Independent Study Kits and work with the DISKs, texts, and tapes in the resource center during their free modules. At all levels, in all languages, and in all types of courses, the primary emphasis is on developing all four skills, with an opportunity for specialized readings and projects at advanced levels.

In order to offer students "an alternative educational experience and a means to put into practice the skills they have mastered during the phase," a "Dewey Day" is held the last day of each cycle. Instead of attending regular classes, students register for activities they create themselves. One Dewey Day in the foreign language department was devoted to an International Café, with one café for each language group. Students prepared menus, food, money, decorations, and entertainment, and used the target language in preparing and running the cafés. On another Dewey Day, a 747 flight to Spain, France, Italy, and Israel was simulated by opening the walls between three classrooms to simulate the expanse of the plane. Students "divided the plane into sections for each of the national airlines, decorating the chairs with crepe paper seat belts in the colors of the flags of the country. Safety instructions were given in the foreign language. . . . Prior to the day of the 'flight' the students had to purchase their tickets in the resource center and obtain a facsimile passport in the appropriate language. Highlights of the flight included foreign language films, fashion shows, refreshments, and even dancing in the aisles." Other Dewey Day activities in foreign languages have been a computer-dating service, visits to ethnic restaurants, and a Casino, with games in the target language. Another school-wide program that involves some foreign language students is a "Four and One" arrangement in which the student attends the school for four days a week and on the fifth works at a museum, store, or other cultural or business establishment. One French student, for example, spent the fifth day at the Services Culturels Français in New York City, involved in language-related activities.

FACILITIES AND MATERIALS

The language laboratory has four tape decks and 36 positions; 30 are audio-active and six are equipped with tape recorders. Commerical tapes accompanying the text series, tapes prepared by the Bureau of Foreign Languages of the Board of Education of the City of New York, and teacher-prepared tapes are used. In the resource center, a separate room, there are study carrels, shelves of reference books, and the students' prescription forms. Three classrooms have windows that open into the resource center, which allow teachers to monitor students who work there on special tasks during class time. The resource center also has two positions for a dial access system, where students can "touch dial" tapes located in the building's central tape storage unit.

ROLES OF TEACHERS, STUDENT TEACHERS, AND PARAPROFESSIONALS

Each teacher has five classes and also spends one hour and 40 minutes per day in the resource center. Teachers counsel students to help them determine appropriate courses of study or resolve learning difficulties. Two teachers also have released time to coordinate the independent study program. There are department meetings twice per cycle to discuss the program's procedures and share ideas. There is a faculty conference with the school principal periodically. Student teachers from nearby colleges work in the resource center helping individual students and distributing materials. They also assist teachers in individualized classrooms, assuming the role of "manager" and guide. There is usually one student teacher in the department at any given time. Two para-professionals work in the language resource center and laboratory to provide supervision, distribute and keep track of materials, maintain files of student records, worksheets, and prescription forms, and, if they have training in the foreign language, help students with their work.

ROLE OF PROGRAM DIRECTOR

The program director teaches one class per cycle and is responsible for determining teacher assignments, coordinating the use of the classroom and the resource center, conducting departmental meetings, supervising teachers, selecting materials, making changes in the curriculum, and, as Assistant Principal for Foreign Languages, serving as a liaison with the school administration.

ROLE OF COMMUNITY

The University Applications Processing Center, a computer center affiliated with the City University of New York, is used by the school to work out scheduling patterns; it can, for example, program two Level I Spanish classes of the same phase into the same block of time to facilitate team-teaching.

Each year a general orientation meeting acquaints the parents of incoming students with the principles and procedures of the school, and a school newsletter is sent to parents periodically.

TRAINING REQUIREMENTS

All teachers were required to attend a summer orientation workshop during the first three years of the program to familiarize them with the new school organization, techniques for individualized instruction, and the use of the resource center. In addition, teachers in the workshops were given time to prepare the objectives for each course and write curriculum materials. Teachers who have entered the school since then are given a standard orientation at the beginning of the year.

FUNDING AND COSTS

The three summer teacher workshops and curriculum writing were funded by a State Urban Education grant under Title I. Title III library grants funded some materials in the "satellite library" resource center. The New York City Board of Education agreed to fund computer services for four years. Salaries for paraprofessional aides in the resource center have been provided by the New York State Department of Education. Other costs are financed through tax-levied funds administered through the city's Board of Education; these include salaries, commercial materials, administrative costs, and overtime payment for teachers for the extended school day (eight hours as compared to the six hours and 20 minutes per day required of teachers in other New York City public schools). Specific costs were not available.

PROGRAM EVALUATION

Although there has been no formal evaluation of the foreign language program at John Dewey High School, a stream of visitors to the school have, by their very presence and by their reports, indicated strong interest and approval of the system of organization in general. A teacher from another New York City school noted after his visit: "Enthusiasm for the program has been transmitted to the kids, and I didn't meet a single student who was unhappy or seemed bored. In fact, each youngster was a walking press agent for the school." "All of us were enormously impressed with the vitality of the faculty, students, and administration," wrote Daniel Tanner, Professor of Education at Rutgers University. Charles Leftwich, from the Institute for Learning and

Teaching of the University of Massachusetts, Boston, wrote that "It was most refreshing to be able to see and enjoy a climate of cooperation and mutual commitment of learning involving students, staff, and parents of an urban high school. . . ." And Yigal Allon, Assistant Prime Minister of Israel, wrote: "since I returned from the U.S. I have been singing the praises of your school. . . . I have decided to open an experimental school on similar lines and have appointed a committee of experts to draw up the program."[2] Elements of the program have also been adapted by other New York City schools: for example, a system of cycles in at least two schools, nongradedness in senior elective courses in another, and "WISK" study kits at Wingate High School.

Students volunteer to attend John Dewey High School; although those from the local district have priority, students from throughout the borough of Brooklyn may apply for admission. The first year of the program when, in essence, the idea was first being "sold," there were 3000 applicants for 1000 places, and applications have continued to outnumber available places, indicating student endorsement of the school's philosophy.

ADAPTABILITY OF CONCEPT TO OTHER PLACES

Obviously, "whole cloth" adaptation of the John Dewey Foreign Language Program would require complete reorganization of a school—if not a new school altogether. The program does, however, offer a number of ways to combine and recombine new and existing resources, and different features of the program could be used in different schools. For example, schools currently operating on modular scheduling, with a foreign language resource center or the possibility of creating one, could schedule large- and small-group sessions in classrooms along with individualized work in the resource center. With personnel and time to develop study packets and the possibility of implementing flexible grouping, short-term "retention"-type classes could be used in school systems that operate on cycles. Movable walls could just as easily be movable curtains, and curtain divisions could more easily be furniture rearrangements to divide a class into groups. And growing numbers of schools are willing to accept evaluation systems based on mastery of skills.

AVAILABLE DESCRIPTIONS

A description of the John Dewey High School Foreign Language Program by Stephen L. Levy, program director, appears in Ronald L. Gougher, ed., *Individualization of Instruction in Foreign Languages: A Practical Guide* (Chicago: Rand McNally, Inc., 1972), pp. 130–48. Aspects of the program are described in "Curricula for New Goals," by Gladys Lipton, in *Foreign Language Education: A Reappraisal*, Vol. 4 of *ACTFL Annual Review of Foreign Language Education*, ed. Dale Lange and Charles James. A paper presented by the program director at a colloquium sponsored by the New York State Education Department and the New York State Federation of Foreign Language Teachers in 1970 is available from ERIC (ERIC ED 043 266).

CONTACT PERSON

Stephen L. Levy, Assistant Principal (Supervision), Foreign Language Department, John Dewey High School, 50 Avenue X, Brooklyn, New York 11223 (212) 373-6400

NOTES

[1] Unless otherwise indicated, all quotations are from Stephen L. Levy, "Foreign Languages in John Dewey High School: An Individualized Approach," in *Individualization of Instruction in Foreign Languages: A Practical Guide*, ed. Ronald L. Gougher (Chicago: Rand McNally, Inc., 1972), pp. 130–48.

[2] Personal communications to administrators at John Dewey High School reproduced in a John Dewey High School student publication.

LATIN
FLES PROGRAM

ABSTRACT

The Latin FLES program in the Washington, D.C. Public Schools provides an approach to the study of classical language and culture geared toward fifth- and sixth-graders from the inner city. Over 2400 students receive Latin instruction for 20 minutes each day from "itinerant" teachers who travel from school to school. Audiolingual dialogues and drills are situated in the context of Roman life and mythology, and students also study English vocabulary and structures derived from Latin. Teachers try to avoid grammatical jargon and to make their sessions as varied and lively as possible. The study of Latin is not meant to be a preparation for high school, college, or even future language study; instead, it is used as a means for students to see language in terms of symbols that can be controlled, to improve their English language

144 - OPTIONS AND PERSPECTIVES

skills, and to understand classical culture as it relates to their own lives.

PROGRAM DEVELOPMENT AND PRESENT STATUS

FLES instruction in modern languages began in the schools of the District of Columbia in 1959, but it was not until 1966 that a new Supervising Director of the Department of Foreign Languages, Judith LeBovit, persuaded the District Superintendent to add Latin to the elementary curriculum. Whereas FLES Spanish and French attracted the most able students, it was hoped that Latin instruction, "recast with reference to modern day requirements, would result in very significant and rapid gains . . . [for] educationally and culturally disadvantaged inner-city students."[1] The text and teachers' manuals were written by Sylvia Gerber and Annette Eaton during the first year of the program. They wrote in haste, often finishing one lesson the night before it was to be used in class, and they hoped that the materials would be tested in the classroom and then revised and published. In the program's first year, four teachers taught some 600 sixth-grade students in 20 classes in 17 schools; the second year, when enthusiasm among elementary principals began to spread, the number of students, schools, and teachers doubled. By 1971–72 the Latin program included 12 teachers and 2213 students in 82 classes in 69 schools. Each year the budget crises that threatened to end the program were resolved, and in 1972 the principals, when asked to list priorities, chose FLES over science and music; Gerber says that the modern language FLES programs "rode in on the toga tails of FLES Latin."[2] After the equalization of per pupil expenditures in 1972, in compliance with a court order, some schools had to give up their Latin classes, while others were allotted double or triple the time for foreign language instruction. This has resulted in an increase in the number of pupils involved in Latin—2458 in 31 schools—because the amount of time teachers spend travelling has been reduced. And in some schools, where there are not enough sixth-grade classes for the amount of teacher time allotted, fifth-grade pupils also receive Latin instruction. But the demand for Latin FLES continues to exceed the supply of teachers budgeted for the program.

TARGET AUDIENCE

Students of all abilities, grades 5 and 6. The program is especially designed for educationally and culturally disadvantaged students.

PROGRAM GOALS

(1) To introduce students to an experience with a foreign language; (2) to widen the students' horizons by contact with a culture different in time and space from their own; (3) to give the students experience with an inflected language and with a word order that requires special attentiveness to the endings of words; (4) to teach basic grammatical relationships in an uncontrived, relevant way, with a minimum of technical grammatical terms; (5) to provide experience in careful silent reading of words that follow a consistent phonetic pattern; (6) to provide daily word study which emphasizes the Latin elements in English words; (7) to provide enrichment material from sources collateral to Latin (mythology, Greek and Roman history, biography, etc.); (8) to teach the reading of Latin without constant translation; and (9) to place strong emphasis on ethical principles as evidenced in the lives of historical Roman personages.

STUDENT GROUPING AND SCHEDULING ARRANGEMENTS

Students are grouped heterogeneously in classes of about 30 and receive FLES Latin instruction for 20 minutes each day, five days a week.

REPRESENTATIVE CONTENT

The study of Latin is designed to be of both humanistic and linguistic value to students. The director notes that the point of the program is "not to cultivate an old tradition for tradition's sake, but to use earlier tradition in terms of its present-day relevance." She hopes the program will give students a feeling for imagination, myth, and poetry by making the language, and the people who once spoke it, come alive through dialogues, pictures, and activities with which the students can identify, as well as short literary selections.

The chief linguistic goal of the program is to improve English language skills. Emphasis is placed on clear pronunciation and enunciation. "Because of the highly inflected endings in Latin, the students are required to sound every syllable, articulating especially the last one clearly. For inner-city students who tend to slur the last syllable of a word, this is of tremendous value." Regular vocabulary study emphasizes the Latin elements in English words, and the silent reading of Latin words that follow a consistent phonetic pattern provides help for many students who have problems reading English.

The student text is divided into nine units that focus on Roman life and culture. Each unit contains a dialogue, oral drills, a song, a poem, and supplementary material like mottoes, words of Latin origin, and stories based on classical mythology. The number of words introduced in the curriculum is limited, but teachers are encouraged to introduce additional vocabulary of their own choosing. Students learn to listen to Latin, and to speak, read, and write it—in that order. The first few lessons are conducted with an oral-aural approach, but dialogues are not memorized; the shift to reading and then writing is made by the end of the first month of instruction. Grammatical terms are used as little as possible, and "no effort is being made to teach the traditional first-level course of secondary school Latin. Only linguistic essentials are taught."[3] The curriculum is designed to be used with a minimum of hardware equipment because of cost, the short duration of classes, and the necessity for the teacher to travel. Overhead transparencies

and pictures are often used to reinforce new material learned orally, and the teachers try to keep the short 20-minute sessions
lively and intense by varying activities as much as possible. Dialogue practice and drills are usually conducted in Latin, word
study in English.

A typical lesson might begin with a quick review in Latin of
words and structures learned previously; for example, students
could be asked to identify objects and say where they are in the
room, and then tell where Rome is, where Italy is, and where
Washington is. The teacher might next read a new dialogue several times and have the students repeat each line, first as a class,
then semichorally, and finally individually. Some drills based on
the dialogue sentences might be introduced, or the teacher might
project transparencies (usually pictures of a Roman family "en-
acting" the dialogue) and have the students repeat a sentence,
often with substitutions inferred from the visual clues. At this
point, to change the type of activity, the class might do some
grammar work in English. They might also work on derivatives:
the teacher could give a sentence in English—"urban life can be
very exciting"—and students define "urban" based on their
knowledge of the Latin word "urbs" from a previous lesson. Or,
the teacher might read a sentence in Latin using the word "habi-
tat" and ask the students to give its English cognates. To end the
lesson, the teacher might run through a review drill in Latin with
pictures or have the students repeat a Latin motto or sing a song.

ROLES OF STUDENTS AND TEACHERS

Students are expected to participate actively in class. FLES
Latin teachers are given a manual containing suggestions for increasing student motivation, presenting the materials, drilling, and
testing. They are visited periodically by a supervisor from the
foreign language department and participate in monthly workshops on methods and curriculum. Orientation in the program and
counseling for students are provided by the teachers, often in
cooperation with the counselors, administrators, and other teachers in the individual schools.

ROLE OF SUPERVISING DIRECTOR

The Supervising Director of the Department of Foreign Languages has final responsibility for curriculum changes, organizes workshops, training sessions, schedules, and observations, and hires new teachers. She arranges schedules and procedures with principals and promotes the program in schools not yet involved and in the community at large. The director discusses the program at foreign language meetings throughout the country and abroad and writes articles about the program for professional journals.

ROLE OF COMMUNITY

Articles about the program appear frequently in local newspapers. The Latin FLES teachers, with the help of the Foreign Language Department staff, are responsible for discussing the program with parents and other interested persons, both individually and at PTA meetings or Open House. Teachers also arrange trips to museums or other places of cultural interest for their own classes.

TRAINING REQUIREMENTS

New teachers have two weeks of orientation prior to the beginning of the school year; they meet with supervisors and "veteran" teachers to discuss the curriculum and the methods to be used. They also have an opportunity to observe veteran teachers in the classroom. Department supervisors work closely with new teachers, giving advice and assistance when needed. Inservice training is provided through the monthly workshops and visits by the Foreign Language Department supervisors.

FUNDING AND COSTS

All aspects of the program, except the publication of materials, are funded by the budget of the District of Columbia Public

Schools. Specific costs for program development, teacher training, salaries, and materials were not available. The publication and distribution of curriculum materials are being conducted under a grant from the National Endowment for the Humanities.

PROGRAM EVALUATION

Support for the program by administrators and students is indicated by the steady growth of enrollment from 600 students in 17 schools in 1966–67 to 2458 students in 31 schools in 1972–73. As many as 69 schools participated in past years, before a court order equalized per-pupil expenditures. The program has also aroused much interest in other large city school systems and has been used as a model for FLES Latin programs developed in such cities as Philadelphia and Cleveland. Over 500 requests have been received from all parts of the U.S. for information and curriculum materials. Many teachers and administrators have come to see the Latin classes in operation, and classes have been videotaped for viewing at foreign language meetings. The Supervising Director has been invited to a number of professional meetings in the U.S.; she has spoken about the program at the Tenth International Congress of Linguists in Bucharest, Rumania, at the Departments of Classics at the University of Heidelberg and the University of Berlin, and at meetings of language instructors in France. Articles on the D.C. Latin program have been published in France and Germany, and inquiries have come from Canada and other countries in Europe, South America, and Africa.

In October 1971, the Division of Planning, Research, and Evaluation of the Public Schools of the District of Columbia released a document entitled *A Study of the Effect of Latin Instruction on English Reading Skills of Sixth Grade Students in the Public Schools of the District of Columbia, School Year, 1970–71.* "The study appraised the impact of one year of FLES Latin study on English reading ability, comprehension, and vocabulary. It showed that at the end of the school year 1970–71: (1) The English reading scores of students who had taken *any* foreign language in the elementary schools were significantly higher than the scores of students who had taken no foreign language. (2) The English reading scores of students who had taken Latin *for only one year* were higher than the scores of students who were in their fourth year of Spanish or French instruction. (3) The students who had taken Latin in 1970–71 not only attained a higher *absolute* level of reading ability than those who had taken French or Spanish, and than those who had taken no foreign language, but also attained a greater *amount of improvement* in the months from October 1970 to May 1971 than did those who had taken French or Spanish, and than those who had taken no foreign language. In addition, the study reached the conclusion that Latin instruction in the elementary school imparts a further educational asset pressingly needed in urban areas. According to the study, 'Latin instruction . . . [besides improving mastery of English] provides opportunity for appreciation of other people's culture.' "[4]

ADAPTABILITY OF CONCEPT TO OTHER PLACES

A school district with funds to hire, train, and coordinate a special teaching staff and school administrators willing to support the program could develop a FLES Latin program aimed at "verbally poor" and other students. The D.C. Department of Foreign Languages has offered to make its curriculum materials and guides available nationwide; these can be obtained from the contact person.

The Latin FLES program of the School District of Philadelphia was begun after Philadelphia administrators visited the Latin FLES program in Washington in conjunction with a conference conducted by the American Classical League in 1967. The Philadelphia program staff underscore the fact that their program is a "self-contained entity and of great value to pupils per se and not necessarily in terms of future work in the language."[5] It involves a two-year sequence for fifth- and sixth-grade students. In the fifth grade, the cultural focus is on everyday life in ancient Rome. The course is called "How the Romans Lived and Spoke" and is divided into nine units on the Roman family, the family's meals, clothes, house, recreation, education, and occupations. The sixth-grade course, "Echoes from Mt. Olympus," focuses on classical mythology; eight units cover such topics as "Jupiter and his Siblings," "The Myths in Nature," and "The Founding of Rome." Units are broken into *lectiones* in the teacher's guide; each *lectio* is a 20-minute segment of instruction incorporating dialogues, drills, games, playlets, and songs in Latin, or exercises from a gamebook on English derivatives. Each of the itinerant FLES Latin teachers has a multimedia *Instructional Kit*. Some items—maps, films, filmstrips, charts, and pictures—are obtained from commercial sources. Others were produced locally: uncaptioned visual cues that are used to explain the dialogues without English, a set of tapes on which songs and playlets are recorded, a supply of fifth- and sixth-grade readers, and teachers' guides. As in the District of Columbia program, reading and writing always follow oral mastery, English vocabulary-building is a major goal, teachers try to make the study of Latin relevant to the students' lives, and "presentation is lively, dramatic, and enthusiastic, fully involving and exciting the child." There is a period of preservice training for new teachers, and monthly inservice sessions for the entire staff provide the opportunity to discuss the curriculum, materials, problems, and techniques with the curriculum specialist or, on occasion, with outside consultants. The "core" materials were written by curriculum specialists hired by the district and published locally. Two grants from the National Endowment for the Humanities helped finance program development and curriculum writing. In 1972–73 the Philadelphia FLES Latin Program included over 6000 students in grades 5 and 6, and Latin has been added to the curriculum in over 20 junior high schools to provide further study for the students (an "overwhelming" majority) who choose to continue.

AVAILABLE DESCRIPTIONS

(1) A film presenting a sample D.C. Latin FLES classroom session and comments by staff members is available from John F. Latimer, American Classical League, Department of Classics,

George Washington University, Washington, D.C. 20006. (2) Published descriptions of the program can be found in James W. Dodge, ed., *Leadership for Continuing Development,* Reports of the Working Committees, 1971 Northeast Conference on the Teaching of Foreign Languages (New York: Northeast Conference, 1971), pp. 119–22; and in Judith LeBovit's "Qui Timide Rogat, Docet Negare," Keynote Address at the 1967 Oxford Conference, reprinted in *Classical World,* 1967.

CONTACT PERSON

Judith LeBovit, 8542 Georgetown Pike, McLean, Virginia 22101

NOTES
[1] Survey questionnaire.
[2] Sylvia Gerber, "The Washington (D.C.) FLES Latin Program," a speech delivered at the ACTFL Annual Meeting, 1972.
[3] Survey questionnaire.
[4] Survey questionnaire.
[5] Rudolph Masciantonio, "The New FLES Latin Program in the School District of Philadelphia," *Modern Language Journal,* 16 (1972), 169.

MANAGED SELF-INSTRUCTION USING PROGRAMMED MATERIALS

ABSTRACT

In Tucson, Arizona over 700 students in the district's junior and senior high schools are enrolled in self-instruction programs in French, German, Spanish, Latin, and Hebrew. Working alone or in small groups, students progress at their own rates through programmed texts and audio-visual materials. "Management teams" of certified teachers and native speakers work with individual students about twice a week. The cost of the program, as projected over the next ten years, is approximately $20 a year for each student.

PROGRAM DEVELOPMENT AND PRESENT STATUS

Programmed self-instruction in foreign languages attracted the Tucson Public Schools for several reasons: small enrollments threatened to eliminate Chinese, Russian, and some Latin classes, and centralizing them in one school had not solved the problem. Furthermore, as "a methodology, programmed [self-] instruction has repeatedly demonstrated that it is: (1) effective in producing learning outcomes of a high order; (2) accurate in developing certain language skills; (3) productive in permitting self-pacing and promoting responsibility of students [for managing their own learning]; and (4) extremely cost efficient."[1]

In 1968, 16 eighth-graders were selected according to high language aptitude, general academic ability, and proven maturity, to take part in a three-month trial program of self-instruction. The students used programmed texts and tapes for one hour each day. Once every ten days, the district coordinator visited with each student to help resolve problems in the use of the materials, but the students were not given any formal opportunity for using the language or any teacher-originated instruction. The results, in both attitude and performance, were positive. The following year, 30 similarly selected students used programmed materials in French, German, or Spanish for eight months. The French students had weekly contact with a native speaker, but the others followed the format of the previous year. Evaluation in the second year was considerably more elaborate and indicated that motivation was a better criterion for selecting students than language aptitude or general ability. Furthermore, the French students found that the contact with a native speaker improved both their performance and motivation.

During the summer, the Tucson Public Schools drew up "management teams" of housewives, college students, librarians, counselors, administrators, and teachers, student teachers, and teacher aides in a variety of subject areas to work with the students in the self-instruction program. Most of the managers were native speakers of a foreign language or reasonably proficient. In 1970–71, about 100 seventh- and eighth-graders enrolled in self-instruction programs in six different schools. Orientation sessions were held for all students, and individuals began the program when they felt they were ready. "Depending on the nature of gradually revealed need, certain students worked almost completely independently, given only infrequent emotional and interactive support. Others studied under considerable supervision, and were given much individualized help. In time, however, most students appeared to develop powers of self-direction, self-reliance, and responsibility for goal-setting, use of time, and goal attainment unusual for this age group under normal school conditions."[2] The results of the third year convinced the Tucson Public Schools that the approach was viable, and program development continued.

In 1972–73, 700 students in grades 7–12 were in self-instructional courses, levels I–IV, in French, German, Spanish, Latin, and Hebrew. Ten junior and five senior high schools were involved in the program. There were four full-time and one part-time certified itinerant "teacher-supervisors" and two non-certified native speakers of Spanish. The German, French, and Hebrew teacher-supervisors are native speakers of the language and fulfill both the native-speaker consultant and teacher-supervisor roles.

TARGET AUDIENCE

Students of almost any degree of language aptitude or general academic ability who want to learn a foreign language in this way and agree to maintain the materials and equipment in good condition.

MAJOR GOALS FOR STUDENTS

To develop proficiency in all four skills in the target language as well as an understanding of the culture.

ORIENTATION

A teacher-supervisor explains the nature, purpose, and use of programmed self-instructional materials in several orientation sessions. The students are encouraged to select the language skills they particularly want to develop. Throughout the program, they are, and are made to feel, responsible for pacing and managing their own learning. If they do not understand certain explanations or feel the need for variety, they are encouraged to use different programmed materials, work with the audio-visual materials, switch to a different group, or change their learning style or pace. Working with the results of the Pimsleur Language Aptitude Battery and the student's grades in the past, the teacher-supervisor and the student work out a schedule for the student's probable progress. The student is not required to maintain this schedule, but it helps prevent his being discouraged (or slacking off) if his pace is different from others. They also work out a tentative schedule of consultations.

STUDENT GROUPING AND
SCHEDULING ARRANGEMENTS

Students are scheduled into five periods a week according to their own schedules, the availability of rooms, and the schedule of the teacher-supervisor. In the experimental phase, students consistently mentioned that they preferred to work around other people, although not necessarily with them. Care is taken, therefore, to schedule students in self-instruction together and place them in areas large enough to accommodate several students who may be working independently.

METHODOLOGY AND REPRESENTATIVE CONTENT

Students use commercially prepared programmed texts and tapes, as well as recordings, films, filmstrips, taped conversations, and other audio-visual materials. They work on their own or with other students in small groups; frequently one student is paired with another, and they decide by themselves how closely they want to cooperate. The teacher-supervisor oversees the use of the materials and keeps a record of each student's progress for the district and the building principal. Depending mostly on students' requests, the teacher-supervisor talks with the students about their learning difficulties, diagnoses problems, recommends remedial or supplementary work, and gives emotional support. Usually these meetings take place twice a week. The teacher-supervisor also arranges extracurricular activities and acts as a liaison with parents.

The native-speaker consultant gives students direct contact with the foreign culture as well as opportunities to use the language. The consultant is asked to "avoid anything approaching a teaching style" and concentrate instead on developing natural conversations with students. The students are encouraged to use the foreign language freely and to speak about anything that interests them. The consultant uses gestures and expressions common in his culture and helps the students use and respond to these "signals." He also tries to communicate—through personal examples if he can—the value that certain art forms, institutions, or cultural patterns have for people of his nationality. Like the teacher-supervisor, the native-speaker consultant understands that students are likely to work toward different objectives at different paces and that some students will not require his help as much as others.

CREDIT, GRADING, AND ARTICULATION

The programmed materials provide self-testing with each step as well as periodic unit tests. The teacher-supervisor checks each student's unit tests. At the end of each level, students undergo a battery of tests to determine whether they can progress to the next. When they complete a level, students receive one full credit, regardless of the time it has taken them. Articulation does not pose a problem, as the programs are self-contained and students can move from one level to another individually.

ROLE OF PARENTS

Parents receive a letter that describes the program, explains the learning variables of pace, rhythm, and attention span, and asks for their support and interest. They are required to sign a form agreeing to their children's participation.

ROLE OF DISTRICT COORDINATOR

The district's Coordinator of Modern and Classical Languages visits the students, native-speaker consultants, and teacher-supervisors from time to time to provide encouragement and assistance. He keeps in close touch with the building principals, allocates materials, and describes the program to principals and teachers of schools not presently involved.

TRAINING REQUIREMENTS

Training for teacher-supervisors and native-speaker consultants is carried out in monthly group sessions with the district coordinator.

FUNDING AND COSTS

In the junior high schools, the program is funded through the schools' regular budgets. In the high schools, the equipment and materials are amortized through a central bookstore fee system. Films, filmstrips, and other audio-visual materials are made available through the budget of the district coordinator. An exact breakdown of costs was not available. Over a ten-year period, the cost of the entire program (materials, teachers' salaries, etc.) is expected to be approximately $20 per student per year.

PROGRAM EVALUATION

In evaluating the program in the first and second years, students were asked questions based on the behavioral objectives established for the program at the outset. In May 1969, 100% of the first-phase students responded; in May 1970, 88% of the first-phase students and 60% of the second-phase students responded. The objectives are outlined below along with the percentages of affirmative answers based on the number of students actually responding.

1. The student will find independent foreign language study using programmed materials usually to be an interesting and satisfying experience.
   > 82% of first-phase respondents affirmed this in May 1969
   > 82% of first-phase respondents affirmed this in May 1970
   > 78% of second-phase respondents affirmed this in May 1970

2. The student will be favorably disposed to study in the future another subject independently using programmed materials.
   > 71% of first-phase students affirmed this in May 1969
   > 53% of first-phase respondents affirmed this in May 1970
   > 56% of second-phase respondents affirmed this in May 1970

3. Despite more or less serious frustrations and boredom, the student will tolerate the relative monotony of programmed learning to gain worthwhile objectives.
   > 82% of first-phase respondents affirmed this in May 1969
   > 93% of first-phase respondents affirmed this in May 1970
   > 78% of second-phase respondents affirmed this in May 1970

4. The student will value the opportunity to set his own learning pace.
   > 94% of first-phase respondents affirmed this in May 1969
   > 100% of first-phase respondents affirmed this in May 1970
   > 89% of second-phase respondents affirmed this in May 1970

5. The student will value independent study over traditional classroom study.
   > 49% of first-phase respondents affirmed this in May 1969
   > 67% of first-phase respondents affirmed this in May 1970
   > 33% of second-phase respondents affirmed this in May 1970

6. The student will value foreign language study more highly after the project than he did before.

> 76% of first-phase respondents affirmed this in May 1969
> 80% of first-phase respondents affirmed this in May 1970
> 67% of second-phase respondents affirmed this in May 1970

In 1971, the achievement of an experimental group of the 12 second-phase French students was compared with that of a control group of 12 eighth-grade students in another school. The control group students were screened for admission into French by an aptitude test and had studied French with a teacher, using standard materials, for 16¾ months in the seventh and eighth grades. The experimental group was also screened for admission by the same aptitude test and had worked with programmed materials, spent one or two sessions a week with a native-speaker consultant, and studied French for 7¼ months. The two groups were given the listening and reading sections of the Pimsleur Proficiency Test, Form A. There proved to be no significant difference in the two groups' mean raw scores, even though the experimental group had studied French only half the time the others had.

As part of the evaluation, the program staff polled the school's three counselors and found that they expressed a "balanced appreciation" of the program's strengths and weaknesses and wished it to continue. In periodic evaluations conducted since the third year, the staff has found the program's main problems arise in the supportive network (distribution of materials, scheduling, etc.). These problems are corrected by the district coordinator to the best of his ability.

ADAPTABILITY OF CONCEPT TO OTHER PLACES

The program staff recommend that students be admitted to similar programs on the basis of interest rather than aptitude or ability; that orientation in the materials and method is essential; that the ratio of pupils to equipment allow self-pacing and regrouping; that students be encouraged to assist in developing subsystems in the program (such as procedures for distribution and storage of materials); that students be given language aptitude tests to establish loose guidelines for their progress; that all people involved in the program understand their roles and responsibilities; and that any disruptions of schools' normal routines be carefully considered in advance to minimize possible antagonism to the program.

AVAILABLE DESCRIPTIONS

Bockman, John F. "Evaluation of a Project: Independent Foreign Language Study by Selected Eighth-Graders at Townsend Junior High School Using Programmed Materials, March 3 to May 23, 1969." Tucson: Tucson Public Schools, 1969. (ERIC ED 033 632)

Bockman, John F. "Townsend Junior High School Independent Foreign Language Study Project; A Second Evaluation and Progress Report." Tucson: Tucson Public Schools, 1970. (ERIC ED 040 642)

Bockman, John F. "A Three-Year Research Project on Individualized Foreign Language Learning Based in Programmed Instruction and in Management by Consultation—Summary of Rationale and Principal Findings." Tucson: Tucson Public Schools, 1971. (ERIC ED 048 813)

CONTACT PERSON

Felizardo L. Valencia, Coordinator of Modern and Classical Languages, Tucson Public Schools, P.O. Box 4040, 1010 East Tenth Street, Tucson, Arizona 85717 (602) 791-6230

NOTES
[1] John F. Bockman and Valerie M. Bockman, *The Management of Foreign Language Learning* (to be published by Newbury House, Rowley, Mass.).
[2] John F. Bockman, "A Three-Year Research Project on Individu-

alized Foreign Language Learning Based in Programmed Instruction and in Management by Consultation—Summary of Rationale and Principal Findings" (Tucson: Tucson Public Schools, 1971), p. 4.

[3] John F. Bockman, "Townsend Junior High School Independent Foreign Language Study Project: A Second Evaluation and Progress Report" (Tucson: Tucson Public Schools, 1970), pp. 9–13.

MINI-COURSE CURRICULUM

ABSTRACT

For students in advanced German at Ridgefield High School in Ridgefield, Connecticut, the beginning of every marking period is also the beginning of a new German course. The Mini-Course Curriculum, developed and conducted by one teacher, gives students the opportunity to choose four out of six ten-week courses offered each year. Through seminar classroom discussions and independent projects, the 30 students enrolled in German IV and V pursue special interest areas ranging from German for Travelers and Scientific German to Recent German Literature. The program involves close cooperation with the science, English, art, and social studies departments in the school, extensive use of materials collected by the director in America and abroad, and frequent lectures and discussions with guest speakers from the community.

The first few weeks of each course are conducted in a formal class situation and are devoted to background vocabulary, grammar, and an overview of the course. Midway through the marking period students select specialized areas for individual projects and readings, and meet for brief individual conferences with the teacher each day. Increased enrollment in advanced German since the start of the program indicates a very positive student response to the variety of subjects offered and the opportunity to explore them in depth.

PROGRAM DEVELOPMENT AND PRESENT STATUS

The mini-course program was initiated in response to general disinterest among students in continuing into advanced German courses. In developing the program, the director first established the policy, enthusiastically welcomed by the guidance department, of accepting average students into advanced language courses— not just the "cream of the crop"—and of offering a program more attractive to these students than the traditional Advanced Placement course. Using topics suggested by the students themselves, and taking advantage of free materials available from organizations in German-speaking countries and the U.S., she prepared a curriculum of six courses, working with no released time or additional pay. She then secured administrative approval to conduct mini-courses two periods a day, rather than the one period usually allotted to both levels of advanced German, to allow for the division of students into smaller groups as well as a choice of two different courses each marking period. When the program was first put into operation in September 1971, this scheduling arrangement proved impossible because of budgetary problems, and the 30 students in both levels were grouped in one class and took the same sequence of four mini-courses. The following year the initial scheduling arrangement was approved, and six courses were offered, with students choosing between two alternative courses during two of the four marking periods. A seventh German mini-course will go into effect next year, and several more are now being planned, including one on film-making and another on ecology. This year the Spanish department in the school began a more modest but similar program involving two advanced level mini-courses in Latin American civilization.

MAJOR GOALS FOR STUDENTS

To continue to develop all four language skills in advanced classes; to read German for pleasure; to be able to study specific interest areas, and to choose these areas from among several options.

STUDENT GROUPING AND
SCHEDULING ARRANGEMENTS

Each course is given for one ten-week marking period. A combined level IV–V class meets during the second hour of the school day and another combined level IV–V class during the third; each decides which mini-courses to take. Individual students who do not wish to study the mini-course chosen by their class often complete a different mini-course on an independent study basis. During the first five weeks of the marking period, students meet in class daily. During the remaining five weeks, class meetings are held two or three times a week for discussions and presentations of reports. The remaining time is used for independent readings, research, and preparation of reports. Individual conferences in German are held with the teacher each day.

METHODOLOGY AND REPRESENTATIVE CONTENT

All courses are conducted in German and devote some time to German language study as well as to the course's special area of concentration. Students are provided with a German grammar text and review language exercises formally in the laboratory and informally in class discussions. In most courses readings beyond the background selections are individualized. Students write frequent short critiques, summaries, and essays.

In "German for Travelers," topics include the geography of German-speaking countries, methods of transportation and their specialized vocabulary, lodging, food, shopping, sightseeing, sports, newspapers and magazines, train schedules, and German, Swiss, and Austrian currency. Students memorize several basic "travel dialogues" and simulate situations such as checking into a hotel, arranging transportation, and ordering meals. Each student specializes in one city or area of a German-speaking country and reports orally and in writing on that area. A field trip to the German-speaking district of New York City gives students practice in travel situations.

In "The German-Speaking Lands and America" students consider the mutual influences of the German and American languages on each other, patterns of German immigration in America, famous German-Americans, the impact of American youth culture and the presence of American military forces on German-speaking countries, the German image in American television and literature, and America as viewed in German literature. Assignments include watching television shows like "Hogan's Heroes" that deal with German stereotypes and writing critiques of these programs. Each student is "teacher" for a day on the topic of his choice. Field trips are made to the German Consulate and Goethe Haus in New York or to the German Center in Boston.

"Scientific German" entails readings in German in biology, math, physics, psychology, chemistry, medicine, and engineering; translating scientific German into English; reading biographies of German scientists; and the study of special grammar and vocabulary typical of scientific German. Worksheets are prepared by the teacher for individual work, and there are frequent oral and written reports by the students, as well as guest speakers from the New England Institute for Medical Research.

"The German-Speaking World—Its History and Culture" is

a survey of the history of Germany, Austria, and Switzerland from the ninth century to the present. The customs, art, architecture, and music of the three countries are discussed, films are correlated with each unit, and wide readings are required. Students prepare brief lectures in German, and German-speaking people from the Ridgefield area are invited to talk to the class about everyday customs in their native countries.

"Survey of German Literature" includes readings from the classical, romantic, and expressionist periods. Authors included are Vogelweide, Strassburg, Kant, Lessing, Goethe, Schiller, Nietzsche, and Mann. *Wilhelm Tell* and *Tonio Kroger* are read in their entirety. Students see slides and filmstrips from areas of Germany which provide the setting for works they read, review grammar in context, and take a field trip to lecture programs at Yale or the Goethe Institute in Boston.

"Recent Swiss, German, and Austrian Literature" is devoted to the study of representative modern writers from these countries. The basic text, *Im Stil unserer Zeit*, provides a framework for surveying recent writings, grammar review, and vocabulary building. From a list of several books, students choose two or three to read in their entirety. Close contact is maintained with staff members teaching English courses in modern literature, and speakers from nearby universities are invited to address the class. One guest speaker led a discussion on Hermann Hesse and his impact on American youth.

Students select their own topics for independent projects within the context of each mini-course. A student might, for example, do a study of airline brochures and advertising in German periodicals for the German for Travelers course. Or he might study German script, read material in old German type, and practice German handwriting and use it to write letters and compositions. One student built his own printing press with German type; another wrote a composition on propaganda in a neo-Nazi newspaper. Other projects have included the construction of a kiosk, complete with theater announcements and advertisements written by students, and a German newspaper edited by one student with contributions from other members of the class.

CREDIT AND ARTICULATION

Each mini-course carries one-fourth credit toward graduation; students are expected to take four mini-courses each year in levels IV and V for one full credit each year. They may, during marking periods in which two different mini-courses are offered, elect to take an extra mini-course for one-fourth extra credit. German III students who have teacher permission may elect one of these courses in addition to the regular German III course and receive one-fourth extra credit. Close cooperation with the English and social studies teachers permits students, in some cases, to prepare papers and reports on the same topic for both German and social studies or English. The student writes the report in English for the non-language course and in German for the German mini-course, and receives credit for the work in both subjects.

The curriculum outline for level IV and level V mini-courses is distributed to all level III students and their parents so that interest may be developed in advance. Several of the activities used in mini-courses are also used as extra-credit projects at the first three levels, for example, the study of a German newspaper or practice in writing German script. To stimulate interest in language study among younger students, many high school students in advanced language classes act as "teachers" in the district's elementary schools, where there is no formal FLES instruction. After one year of this informal instruction in German in the sixth grade, the seventh-grade German enrollment increased from 75 to 135.

MATERIALS

A wide selection of textbooks, anthologies, novels, and reference works is available for individual reading assignments and projects. Supplementary materials include wall maps of German-speaking countries, city maps, mail-order catalogues, railroad timetables, filmstrips and tapes, sets of foreign currency, records, and cassettes of current German popular music. The program director has made use of free periodicals, posters, travel folders, booklets, films, and other materials available from such sources as the German Consulate, Goethe Institute, and Lufthansa Airlines, and strongly recommends these channels for obtaining materials without cost. The program also uses an audio laboratory; overhead, filmstrip, opaque, and 16mm projectors; tape recorders available for use in the classroom; and a media center with one section devoted to foreign language books, filmstrips, tapes, and periodicals.

ROLE OF STUDENTS

Students select four out of the six mini-courses offered each year and are responsible for completing individual written and oral reports. Students often act as "teacher" in the classroom discussions, giving short lectures on topics of their choice. They make suggestions for subjects to be covered in the mini-courses, choose topics for their individual projects, and help evaluate the courses at the end of the year.

ROLE OF TEACHERS

The program director is the department supervisor for foreign languages in two schools as well as the teacher of the mini-courses and one other class. She selects topics for mini-courses from student suggestions, arranges for scheduling in cooperation with the school principal, writes the curriculum and goals for each course, assembles materials, prepares worksheets for individualized readings and vocabulary work, advises students in their choice of projects, evaluates all student work, conducts classroom discussions, arranges for guest speakers and field trips, and meets frequently with each student. Cooperating teachers in science, social studies, English, music, and art supply reference materials and information for the related German courses, speak occasionally in the German classes, and accept student projects done both in German and English for credit in the non-language areas.

ROLE OF GUEST SPEAKERS

German-speaking people from the Ridgefield area are invited regularly to the German classes to speak about their work or about customs, travel, and daily life in their native countries. Guest speakers from the New England Institute for Medical Research, Yale University, and Bridgeport University are invited to speak to classes (in German and English) on scientific German, literature, and the fine arts.

ROLE OF PARENTS

The curriculum is explained to parents during Parents' Night at the school, and the printed course outlines are sent to them each year. Information is supplied to the local PTA and the press to promote the idea of mini-courses in the local school system and community. Parents have responded favorably to the program.

TRAINING REQUIREMENTS

No special training is required. The program director was granted a Fulbright-Hays project grant for the summer of 1969 to "assemble and develop authentic supplementary instruction materials for secondary school German classes."

FUNDING AND COSTS

The program is funded primarily through the regular school budget expenditure of $1100 per pupil annually. A grant of $150 from the Literary Society Foundation of New York was also used to pay for program materials. The program director estimates the cost of the program to be a total of $4500: $3000 towards the teacher's salary for the two daily class periods of teaching time devoted to the mini-course program and $1500 for books and materials. Curriculum writing is done by the director without additional pay or released time.

PROGRAM EVALUATION

Informal attrition studies since the mini-course program began indicate that 75% of the German III students in the school, including many "C" or average students, continue into German IV, and 75% of these continue into German V. Results of the Foreign Language Attitude Questionnaire administered at the end of the 1971–72 school year were inconclusive, but in general students displayed a positive attitude toward German-speaking countries and toward the United States. Individual interviews with students were held by the program director; students felt "in general that much more material was covered [in the mini-courses] than in the usual advanced German course. They particularly liked the idea of dealing with one topic for one quarter, then taking up a completely different topic." The Spanish department in the school, noting the students' enthusiasm in German, began its own program of mini-courses in 1972–73.

ADAPTABILITY OF CONCEPT TO OTHER PLACES

Considerations in adapting a mini-course program would be: (1) school administrative support for a fractional credit system, for example, four one-quarter credits each year; (2) the ability and willingness on the part of a teacher or administrator to write a curriculum for several different courses and to solicit student suggestions; (3) the availability of resource materials and texts for several different subjects, or access to channels such as those recommended by the program director for obtaining free materials; (4) administrative cooperation in scheduling advanced courses in such a way that students have a real option; (5) the willingness of teachers in other departments to share information or participate in the mini-courses.

AVAILABLE DESCRIPTION

"Mini-Course Curriculum for German IV and German V," a description of the mini-courses, is available from ERIC (ERIC ED 050 633).

CONTACT PERSON

Merriam Moore, Chairman for Foreign Languages, Ridgefield High School, Ridgefield, Connecticut 06877 (203) 438-3785

MINORITY STUDIES IN FOREIGN LANGUAGES

ABSTRACT

Why are there more Puerto Ricans in New York City than in San Juan? Does Black American English have any relationship to French? Why did Indians seize Wounded Knee in 1973? Should Mexican Americans have bilingual schools? These are some of the questions asked in the foreign language classes of the public schools in Prince George's County, Maryland, where the study of ethnic and cultural minorities has become an important part of the foreign language program. Methods and areas of investigation usually used in social studies are being integrated into the cultural activities in lower-level language courses and into six-week units in "student-centered" classes at levels IV and V. In the latter, students choose research topics in such areas as "Puerto Rico and the Puerto Ricans" and "Mexican Americans," and while the reference sources they use may be in any language, their class presentations are in only the target language—orally or in writing, individually or in groups, in formal debates and interviews, or with skits, music, and food. The interdisciplinary activities and guides for these units were prepared by teachers and consultants from the district and throughout Maryland.

PROGRAM DEVELOPMENT AND PRESENT STATUS

The Prince George's County Public Schools are cooperating in both a state and local endeavor to integrate minority studies into all areas of the public school curriculum. The local school administrators, for example, have urged all departments to include in their courses appropriate aspects of Black Studies. And the schools are participating in a state-wide project, initiated when the Maryland State Board of Education adopted a bylaw in 1970 calling for programs "developing understanding and appreciation of ethnic and cultural minorities."[1] The offshoot of this resolution was the creation of a curriculum sourcebook, "New Perspectives in Intergroup Education," which is intended as "an initial step toward integrating intergroup education into the total curriculum" in accordance with the principle that "the schools of Maryland should be committed to the elimination of prejudice."[2] During the summers of 1970 and 1971, committees of teachers and consultants from all over the state developed interdisciplinary instructional activities that emphasize the contributions of ethnic and cultural minorities to American society. The activities in the sourcebook are designed for students from kindergarten through grade 12. Schools in Prince George's County are among those in which the activities have been tested. A federal desegregation order that went into effect in the county's schools in January 1973, involving the reassignment of over 33,000 students, has made the need for this "new perspective" all the more immediate.

The integration of minority studies into the foreign language program of the Prince George's County schools has been part of this total effort. It has also been part of a series of measures to make foreign language instruction more relevant to students of differing abilities and interests. Within the broad objectives established by the county's division of foreign languages for each level of each language, the departments of the 59 junior and senior high schools are free to develop their own variations of organization, methodology, and course content. Any school may pilot a new course, and, after a year, present it in syllabus form to the Instructional Council, Board of Education, and Superintendent of the Prince George's County schools for possible approval. This built-in structure for change has made possible several innovative foreign language programs. One is multi-level grouping in such schools as Oxon Hill Senior High, where there are regular "on-level" courses and slower-paced "off-level" courses throughout the sequence of each language. Other schools have introduced courses with a cultural emphasis—Spanish, German, or French for Travelers—for students who generally would not choose to study a language. And a "student-centered" approach has been started at the upper levels of French and Spanish in many schools; students in these courses participate in defining objectives for the study of "sociocultural/literary" topics and do both individual and group research projects. The student-centered classes have provided a good framework for ethnic studies.

The following description refers primarily to the classes of Milagros Carrero, a teacher at Bowie Senior High School in Prince George's County who participated in one of the committees that developed "New Perspectives in Intergroup Education." In her student-centered Spanish classes she has used many activities from "New Perspectives" as well as a comparative study of race relations. She also developed a resource unit on "Puerto Rico and the Puerto Ricans." A unit on Mexican Americans was written by Dora Kennedy, Supervisor of Foreign Languages, as part of a course at the University of Maryland, "Language and Cultural Minorities."

TARGET AUDIENCE AND METHODOLOGY

The target audience is students in levels IV and V of Spanish. In the student-centered approach, the student is guided into different learning activities by the teacher, but the teacher is never the center of attention. Together, teacher and students choose a general topic to investigate and decide how the class will be organized for the unit. To motivate the class, the teacher might ask a set of leading questions. For example, on a unit on Puerto Ricans she might ask, "Who are the Puerto Ricans? Do you know any Puerto Ricans? What is a favorable comment you have heard about Puerto Ricans? An unfavorable comment? Do you agree or disagree with these comments?" and so on. The questions can be grouped under the topics the students find most interesting, and the teacher may organize the class into small groups to research each topic. The teacher might next present a short unit on letter writing so that the students can write to Spanish organizations to get information. Part of each period is then set aside for gathering information; reference resources may be in English or Spanish, but discussions and projects must be carried out in Spanish. After the information is gathered, the students present it to the class in various ways: panel discussions, debates, skits, student-led class discussions, written group reports, or individual oral or written reports—in Spanish. Students might also have individual long-range research projects to complete by the end of the unit. A student-centered unit such as "Puerto Rico and the Puerto Ricans" or "Mexican Americans" is expected to last about five or six weeks.

REPRESENTATIVE CONTENT

The district encourages all foreign language teachers to develop units or learning activity packets on Black American culture. The Afro-French cultures of Western Africa and the Caribbean and the African elements of the Spanish-speaking islands of the Caribbean have been used as a "natural bridge" to the subject of Black American cultures in French and Spanish classes. In a unit on race relations, Carrero has her Spanish classes investigate the interracial relationships among Latin Americans and contrast them with those among North Americans. Students investigate such topics as integration and discrimination in Hispanic countries and the U.S., the status of each racial group—black, white, mestizo, and Indian—in the U.S. and Latin America, and the status of European minorities in Latin America.

Carrero has also used several activities suggested in "New Perspectives in Intergroup Education" either as part of a larger unit of study or as short-term projects. One activity is "Walking in the Shoes of the Spanish-Americans." Students research the relations between the U.S. and Mexico, Cuba, or Puerto Rico and might role-play a Puerto Rican giving his reaction to the debate over the political status of Puerto Rico, interview Cuban immigrants to see how they feel about U.S.-Cuban relations, or imagine they are Spanish-speaking Americans and try to portray how they would feel. Another activity is the "Foreign Language Survey," the goal of which is "to explore barriers to communication and effects they have on the feelings of individuals."[3] Students conduct a survey in the school and community to find out how many people speak a foreign language, how many learned a foreign language as a first language, how they learned English, what difficulties they had, and how they felt when they were unable to understand English. The students listen to a recording of a language totally unfamiliar to the class, like Swedish, report on how they feel when they don't understand what is being said, and then discuss how immigrants have probably felt and reacted. They might try to become more familiar with the language by studying its major features and listening to stories, poems, or songs in the language.

Another "New Perspectives" exercise is "Solving Problems in Human Relations," designed "to examine problems faced by American Indians as [the Indians] see them and to become familiar with proposals for solutions which they suggest."[4] Students do research to identify the problems and the Indian perspective on them. They might invite an Indian to class and compare his ideas with the ideas found in reference books, or assume the roles of members of the Bureau of Indian Affairs and plan strategies for helping Indians participate more directly in decision-making which affects their daily lives. In an exercise on Indian Culture, students read about the life of the Indians and such customs as the Sun Dance, Swinging at the Pole, or the Wu-Wun ordeal. They compare the Wu-Wun, for instance, with a camping trip, and find additional similarities between Indian life and other cultures in America.

"Analyzing Stereotypes" is an activity in which students search for newspaper, magazine, and television ads that misrepresent ethnic groups. They try to identify the purpose of the ads and revise them in a way that the ethnic groups are portrayed more accurately. Carrero has also used debate topics from "New Perspectives" that include: Do the New Mexico land grants belong to the U.S. or to the Hispanos? Was the takeover of Alcatraz by the Indians justified? Support or refute arguments for the new militancy of Mexican Americans.

"Puerto Rico and the Puerto Ricans," a unit for upper-level Spanish students, is used by teachers in whole or in part. The unit has three main themes: Puerto Rican culture, the history of Puerto Rico, and the present condition of the Puerto Ricans. The major objectives for the last are to find out which Puerto Ricans come to the United States, why they come, and to what cities they come; identify situations in which prejudice and discrimination have played a part in slowing many Puerto Ricans' social advancement; compare the education Puerto Ricans receive with that of other Americans; analyze the present political status of Puerto Rico and understand the rights of the Puerto Ricans as American citizens; examine actions taken by some militant groups in light of their demands; and evaluate those demands.[5] Students might study a list of demands made by Herman Badillo, Congressman from the Bronx, New York, or write an essay on whether there should be bilingual education for Puerto Ricans. They might discuss the status of the young Puerto Ricans who return to the island from the mainland (the "Pitiyankis"), or debate the pros and cons of the plan of the United States to mine copper in Puerto Rico. Other debate topics are: "The Puerto Ricans should *not* have to go to wars declared by the U.S. since they cannot vote in federal elections" and "Puerto Rico should never gain independence because it cannot support itself."

In the study of Puerto Rican culture, the class might invite a Puerto Rican from the community to answer questions about family relationships, the roles of men and women, and the meaning of *machismo*, and discuss possible solutions to problems Puerto

Rican teen-agers face in the U.S. because of cultural differences. Students can compare the Spanish spoken in Puerto Rico with that in other Hispanic countries and the Spanish spoken by Puerto Ricans in New York City, and do some research on "Spanglish," making a list of words and their meanings. They might read and discuss the book, *Down These Mean Streets*, by Piri Thomas, or articles from the magazine *The Rican* to find expressions of the feelings of Puerto Ricans on the mainland. There are recipes in the unit for such foods as *pasteles* and *sancocho*, which the students prepare with the help of the home economics department. Or they might listen to recordings of Puerto Rican music, see dances, and study Puerto Ricans who have made their mark in music, art, science, sports, and philosophy.

In the study of Puerto Rican history, topics include the comparison of the Taino Indians with Indians from North, South, and Central America, Indian words in Puerto Rican language, and why there are no Indians on the island today; the mixture of races in Puerto Rico; the U.S. takeover in 1898 ("Was it fair? Who was getting more benefits then? Today? What privileges do the Puerto Ricans enjoy by being American citizens?" etc.); and the movement for independence. Students stage a mock election with campaigners for the three major parties representing Statehood, Commonwealth, or Independence.

Another unit designed for student-centered classes in Prince George's County is "Mexican Americans." Some of the topics in the unit are: who the Chicanos are, where they live, their lifestyles and customs; reasons for the increasing political activism; leaders and martyrs; rallying causes (grape and lettuce boycotts, pressures for bilingual education); the rejection of the "Tío Taco" or "tanned Anglo" concept; the Chicano variety of Spanish; racial and cultural discrimination in the Southwest; the "melting pot" concept vs. cultural pluralism; political organizations (GI Forum, Brown Berets, etc.); the role of the federal government; migrant workers and the struggle for unionization; poverty; underachievement in school, its causes and solutions; the difference between Chicanos' problems and those of Puerto Ricans, Cubans, or other immigrants; and emerging Chicano literature and theater. Also, the history of Mexico is studied and there are required readings such as *La raza* (Samora), *South by Southwest* (Tebbel & Ruiz), and the bilingual poem, "I am Juaquín" (Gonzales).

There are many suggested topics for panel discussions and debates. Some are:

–Why should we have bilingual education for Chicano children? Shouldn't they learn English and be assimilated?
–Is it possible to maintain ethnic identity and yet be a part of the mainstream in the U.S.?
–Is the U.S.-Mexican War now judged to have been an imperialistic war by most historians? Discuss from both the Anglo and Chicano perspectives.
–Is it fair for migrant workers to refuse to pick the crops and let them spoil? Refute or support the position of Cesar Chavez.

There are also many topics for individual or small group projects; the following are some examples.

–Write for a copy of a Chicano newspaper; prepare a comparison between this newspaper and a Black newspaper as to format and content.
–Investigate the lives and contributions of Cesar Chavez; Rudolfo Gonzales (why is he called the "Poet of the Boxing Ring?"); and Luiz Valdez and the "teatro campesino" in Delano, California.
–Study the Aztec calendar and prepare an explanatory report.
–Investigate Calo, a variety of Chicano Spanish.
–Prepare an illustrated Chicano dictionary, with both contemporary and historical terms.
–Prepare and present short skits on the Mexican Revolution; the Grape Boycott; a day in the life of a migrant worker; Chavez conducting a meeting of Chicano farm workers; or an Anglo family whose daughter is dating a Chicano youth.
–Investigate a local Chicano organization, its activities and purposes.[6]

MATERIALS

Reference books, supplementary texts, newspapers and magazines in both English and the foreign language are used in all cultural units, as well as films, filmstrips, records, slides, tapes, and transparencies. Students are encouraged to write to Spanish-American organizations and publishers to obtain information, additional newspapers, or pamphlets. Curriculum guides in English for the ethnic studies units are distributed to all foreign language teachers. Teachers and students are currently translating these guides into each of the foreign languages taught in the county.

ROLE OF TEACHERS

Each foreign language teacher determines in what form and to what extent the ethnic studies units will be incorporated in his classes. Teachers are in continuous contact with the district's foreign language supervisor to request materials and report on their implementation of the ethnic studies units.

ROLE OF SUPERVISOR OF FOREIGN LANGUAGES

The district's supervisor of foreign languages conducts training workshops and staff meetings and sends periodic bulletins to the schools' departments on materials and instructional methods. She is responsible for coordinating activities and distributing information among the departments of the 59 secondary schools, for initiating evaluation of new programs, for overall supervision of teachers, and for changes in the curriculum. She prepared the unit on Mexican Americans.

TRAINING REQUIREMENTS

New teachers in the Prince George's County schools have a pre-school workshop for three to five days. There is one day each year for county-wide inservice training, and each June the supervisor of foreign languages conducts a one- or two-day workshop for upper-level foreign language teachers. There are monthly staff meetings at each school coordinated by the supervisory staff, and articulation meetings are held between senior high schools and their feeder schools several times per year. Specialists of the Maryland State Department of Education offered three one-month workshops in the summers of 1969, 1970, and 1971 for teachers developing and implementing "New Perspectives in Intergroup Education."

FUNDING AND COSTS

The district supervisor of foreign languages estimates the annual expenditure for texts and other materials in foreign languages to be $1.50 to $2.00 per pupil, not including equipment costs. The district also spends about $200 per year for foreign language consultants, but inservice meetings are conducted "on school time" and add no extra costs. Specific costs for printing and distributing curriculum guides were not available. "New Perspectives in Intergroup Education" was funded by state and federal funds, amounting to about $23,000 (1969–71) for curriculum writing, workshops, consultants, testing, printing, and evaluation.

PROGRAM EVALUATION

Studies of the whole foreign language program in Prince George's County indicate that there has been some increase in enrollments from 1969 to 1972 and that the largest dropout rate is between levels III and IV. (Students have responded on surveys that foreign language classes interfere with other senior elective courses.) Evaluations of the system's senior high schools by the Middle States Association of Colleges and Secondary Schools "have resulted in very high ratings for the language program in each school evaluated, and there have always been more commendations than recommendations."[7] The MLA Cooperative Tests (Level M) are administered each year to level III students throughout the system. "Our schools are diverse; test scores reflect this. Medians range from 72 to the 88th percentile each year."[8] Formal research of new foreign language programs is initiated by the supervisor under the direct guidance of the district's Department of Testing and Research.

"New Perspectives in Intergroup Education" is currently being revised after one year's use in pilot classes, and testing and evaluation by the Maryland State Department of Education are ongoing.

ADAPTABILITY OF CONCEPT TO OTHER PLACES

The extent to which minority and ethnic studies could be integrated into a foreign language program would depend on (1) the availability of personnel qualified to research and develop activities that would meaningfully relate the study of minority cultures to both foreign language instruction and the needs and conditions of the community; (2) the availability of consultants for program development and/or teacher training; (3) the support given by the administration, within one school or system-wide; (4) the interest on the part of students, parents, and teachers; and (5) funds for curriculum development and teacher training. Implementation of such a program would require that a teacher have a broad understanding and sensitivity to the values, conditions, and perspective of the cultural groups under discussion as well as to the values, conditions, and perspectives of his students.

CONTACT PEOPLE

For information about the Prince George's County Public Schools' foreign language program, contact: Dora Kennedy, Prince George's County Public Schools, Upper Marlboro, Maryland 20870 (301) 627-4800. For information on "New Perspectives in Intergroup Education," contact: Ann Beusch, Specialist in Foreign Languages and ESOL, Maryland State Department of Education, Box 8717, Friendship International Airport, Baltimore, Maryland 21240 (301) 296-8300 Ext. 416

NOTES

[1] "New Perspectives in Intergroup Education," working copy (Baltimore: Division of Instruction, Maryland State Department of Education, Fall 1971), p. ii.

[2] "New Perspectives," p. i.

[3] "New Perspectives," p. 178.

[4] "New Perspectives," p. 183.

[5] Milagros Carrero, "Puerto Rico and the Puerto Ricans: A Teaching and Resource Unit for Upper Level Spanish Students or Social Studies Classes" (Prince George's County Public Schools), p. 6.

[6] Dora F. Kennedy, "Mexican Americans: A Teaching and Resource Unit for Upper Level Spanish Students" (Prince George's County Public Schools).

[7] Survey questionnaire.

[8] Survey questionnaire.

QUINMESTER PROGRAM IN FOREIGN LANGUAGES

ABSTRACT

In many schools in Dade County (Miami), Florida, the school year now includes all 12 months and is divided into five nine-week blocks called quinmesters. Students attend the four "quins" of their choice to make a year's attendance. Self-contained nine-week courses with specific, short-term objectives have been developed in every subject area. In foreign languages, this has meant the creation of a number of options and more relevant courses for students, a de-emphasis of the "college-preparatory" aspect of foreign language courses, and an opportunity for teachers to write, with pay, some of the courses they teach according to their own skills and their students' interests.

PROGRAM DEVELOPMENT AND PRESENT STATUS

The creation of the quinmester system arose out of economic and logistic needs. There were too many students for the school buildings during the academic year, and many buildings were vacant during the summer. A team of administrators and consultants from Dade County studied other school systems with similar problems, as well as the special needs and trends of Dade County itself. The result was the quinmester, which, it was hoped, would offer a solution to crowded conditions and provide a greater variety of course offerings. Year-long courses would be replaced by courses lasting nine weeks, and some students would attend regular school sessions during the summer. Much publicity and explanation were needed to gain acceptance of the system in the community. "During the 1971 summer session many families considered the course a nice place for students to go until their vacation began. It was their first experience with a full school in the summer, and some thought it only a fun thing."[1] Many parents, however, have started taking vacations at other times of the year, and, surprisingly, there have been very few negative reactions. Also, the Greater Miami Coalition, a local unit of United Fund, made a study of the new curriculum and accepted the program's philosophy, indicating community endorsement.

In the summer of 1971 there were five pilot schools. These were joined by two more in the fall of 1971 and 12 more in June 1972. In each subject area, teachers and administrators were asked "to rethink the curriculum and design a richer program with broader appeal. It was everyone's desire to create courses with more relevance to the needs and interests of a greater number of students." One teacher in each subject was selected and trained to work full-time on planning, organizing, and editing quin courses. The teacher was helped by a consultant in the subject and, in the case of foreign languages, by an advisory committee of teachers for each language. By the summer of 1972 there were 205 quin courses listed in French, German, Hebrew, Latin, Italian, Russian, and Spanish. More than 40 of these have been completed and sent to the district's duplicating department for dissemination. Each year more courses will be introduced as they are written and as the schools' annual budgets allow for the purchase of new materials. At present, 19 of the 59 Dade County secondary schools are on the quinmester system, with 4770 students enrolled in foreign languages and 46 foreign language teachers. More of the district's secondary schools will enter the quinmester system each year, and several are already using the quinmester materials.

TARGET AUDIENCE

Students of all abilities, grades 7–12. The grade level at which students begin language study varies from school to school and from language to language.

STUDENT GROUPING AND SCHEDULING ARRANGEMENTS

Some quinmester schools are on 20-minute modules in varying patterns; others have daily 50-minute periods. Students are grouped in the usual language levels, I-V.

REPRESENTATIVE CONTENT

Each language provides a sequence in the "standard" program based on state-adopted texts. There are also "alternate" courses, which are usually based on the course writers' own experiences and knowledge. At the beginning levels, there are several different courses designed to attract various types of students. For example, in first-year Spanish there are five courses from which a student can choose his initial course. Three of these are standard courses, each using a different text and a course outline written by teachers. The other two courses were written entirely by the writing staff and do not use a text. At the upper levels there are even more alternatives: in French V there are nine choices and 17 in Spanish V. The only requirement made of course writers is "to supply a course organized for the development of the multiple skills, attitudes, and cultural insights, and with a lexical and structural control that will make the transfer of a student from an alternate to a regular course a fairly simple procedure." All courses concentrate on a limited area of information or skills. Students are free to take different types of courses, mixing "standard" with "alternate," for example, or moving from a conversation course to one geared towards developing all four skills. They are also free to leave foreign language altogether at the end of any quinmester.

A teacher's manual is prepared for each course. The manual contains a course description, performance objectives, a sample evaluation for an objective in each skill (including culture and student attitude), suggested teaching procedures, suggested supplementary materials, and a bibliography. The objectives serve as a guide and help the teacher fit the material into the nine-week block of time. Examples of some courses are Say It in French, Bon Voyage, En France, German for Fun, Advanced German Refresher, Fun at the Kibbutz, Classical Myths in Today's World, A Traveler's Bag, A Taste of Spanish, and Great Writers of Spain. A Taste of Spanish, for example, is an introductory conversation course giving an overview of Spanish language and Hispanic culture designed for "the student who would like to learn some Spanish but is uncertain about his desire to continue its formal study. The course content includes: greetings, number 0-100, days of the week, months of the year, weather, time, the family, colors, games, dances and songs, plus sufficient grammar to facilitate meaningful learning of the material." Survive a Russian Party is an introductory Russian course stressing pronunciation and the Cyrillic alphabet. Introductory Spanish I develops conversational skills through dialogues based on typical school activities. Facts and People—Where to Find Them uses Spanish to develop research skills using the library. Progressing in Spanish, Part III centers on a city in Spain, a city in South America, and a visit to a railroad station. A two-quin course in advanced Latin, A Revolutionary: His Life and Trials, focuses on the background of the Catilinarian Conspiracy and Cicero's orations against Catiline. There are also interdisciplinary courses which offer students the choice of credit in one or two areas, for example, Recreational Sports in Spanish, Spanish Shorthand-Theory, Spanish Shorthand-Speedbuilding, and a few Spanish literary quins that also carry credit for language arts.

METHODOLOGY

In almost all schools, an audiolingual approach is used in full-class or small-group arrangements. There is an increasing, but so far scattered, use of individualized instruction to permit students to profit from the variety of available courses when scheduling does not allow a student to enroll in the class itself.

CREDIT AND ARTICULATION

Each quin course is worth one-quarter credit. Students are graded A,B,C,D, or E. Final grades are recorded five times a year, once for each quin, and not only at the end of the year. Evaluation is based directly on the accomplishment of learner objectives.

Each course is designated by a state code number; a series of numbers indicates a sequence of instruction. Each course description includes a statement such as "This course is designed for students who have controlled 7505.02 or equivalent material," the number relating both to the course and the text used. Similarly, most course descriptions indicate which courses would be acceptable continuations. The texts, too, follow a sequence, and teacher-written courses are constructed with a view toward easy re-entry into "standard" courses. The language teachers work closely with the guidance department in helping students determine which of the options would best fit the student's own goals, and often a "package" of quins is planned with a student at the beginning of the year, designating a suitable series of quin courses. Students are not required to take any sequence and may simply enroll in one quin course, discontinue language study after that, and receive one quarter credit.

MATERIALS

For the "standard" program in most schools, the *A-LM* series, second edition, is the basic text. Tapes and any other materials which individual schools can purchase are also used. The Reference List in each quin course outline suggests relevant materials and their sources. For "alternate" courses, materials are teacher-prepared and assembled into booklets, which, like the course outlines accompanying the "standard" courses, are distributed through the district's duplicating department.

FUNDING AND COSTS

Over a four-year period $916,000 has been allotted for all facets of Quinmester in all curriculum areas. This includes writers' workshops and fees to consultants and teachers on special assignments to work on the new curriculum. The average annual expenditure per pupil for the district is $967.

PROGRAM EVALUATION

The Consultant in Foreign Languages notes several advantages in the program: "One is that some students who would never take a language will now 'risk' nine weeks." Another is that a student who does not like the language after nine weeks is not forced to continue it in boredom for a whole year, does not develop a prolonged dislike for the language, and may decide to try it again later. In addition, this type of organization permits a large variety of courses and "each school staff has the opportunity to choose the courses it will offer in order to satisfy the needs and interests of its students." Many teachers feel that the quin courses have led to increased student interest and achievement, but there has not been total acceptance of the philosophy of non-sequential mini-courses by foreign language teachers in the district. Although there has not yet been a formal study of the effect of the quinmester system of foreign languages in terms of enrollment, proficiency, or attitude, the district does compute annual "failure rates." The district's failure rates for 1972 in foreign language high school classes decreased in general from the 1971 rate by

0.7%; this rate was surpassed by the quinmester high schools, with a drop of 2.0%. The junior high schools in general reported an increase in failures, while the quinmester junior high schools showed a decrease.

ADAPTABILITY OF CONCEPT TO OTHER PLACES

Aside from the conversion to a five-part, 12-month school year, or the creation within a traditional school year of a total curriculum based on short-term courses, the concept might be applied solely to the foreign language sequence of a school or school district. While "mini-course" programs have generally been used only in upper-level language classes, the Quinmester Program uses short-term courses in the lower levels as well. It establishes the feasibility of using mini-courses with all levels and ability groups if there are adequate provisions for curriculum overhaul, articulation, and credit.

AVAILABLE DESCRIPTIONS

Alonso, Elizabeth B., and Mirta R. Vega. "Quinmester Courses—What Are They?" *American Foreign Language Teacher* (Summer 1972), pp. 12-13.

Many of the course descriptions and outlines have been accessioned into ERIC, each identified by a different number. Courses and their ERIC numbers are listed in issues 2 and 3 of volume 6 of *Foreign Language Annals* (December 1972 and March 1973).

CONTACT PERSON

Elizabeth B. Alonso, Consultant, Foreign Languages, Dade County Public Schools, 1410 N.E. Second Avenue, Miami, Florida 33132 (305) 350-3600

NOTE

[1] All quotations are from Elizabeth B. Alonso and Mirta R. Vega, "Quinmester Courses—What Are They?" *American Foreign Language Teacher* (Summer 1972), pp. 12–13.

THE SKYLINE CENTER: WORLD LANGUAGE CLUSTER AND CAREER DEVELOPMENT CENTER

ABSTRACT

The Skyline Center is a "magnet" school with intensive programs in 28 vocational and academic subject areas, drawing students from the 20 regular high schools in the Dallas (Texas) Independent School District. In the World Language Cluster (WLC), as the foreign language department is called, 675 students take courses in morning or afternoon sessions in any of ten languages and general linguistics and in another department, the Career Development Center, 103 students are enrolled in 15 language courses oriented toward specific vocations. In addition, the WLC offers students the opportunity to take highly intensive "crash" courses of three hours a day in the more common languages or to enroll in any of three social studies courses that use Spanish-language textbooks and are conducted entirely in Spanish. The

193

advantages of the magnet school are obvious; the courses in linguistics and six of the languages, as well as the CDC courses and the intensive language programs, were not offered in Dallas before the establishment of Skyline because of low student demand for them in individual high schools. In addition, the concentration of students interested in foreign cultures has made it possible to develop a lively program of extracurricular activities.

PROGRAM DEVELOPMENT AND PRESENT STATUS

The Skyline Center began in 1971 as an outgrowth of "Goals for Dallas," a community improvement program initiated after the shock of President Kennedy's assassination. Among other projects, Goals for Dallas called for the improvement of job training and placement in the city and the establishment of a new vocational high school, for which Dallas voters approved a $21 million bond issue in 1967. The following year, a new district superintendent began to expand the definition of Skyline's vocational education program to include a broader spectrum of students as well as "career education" in areas, like foreign language, not usually considered in vocational education. The district contracted with RCA for help in developing some of the CDC courses and running some parts of the school's program. And it involved local businessmen, college professors, unions, and other organizations in developing courses that would be of immediate and long-term value to students in finding jobs. In the foreign language area of the CDC, courses have been developed in which students learn specialized vocabularies, grammatical constructions, and customs along with skills related to vocations ranging from fashion design to secretarial work or ranching. And in the language courses of the WLC, intensive programs have been designed specifically to help students reach "salable" levels of proficiency in the target languages.

An equally important aspect of the Skyline Center is the "magnet" concept. Intensive programs in areas ranging from airframe construction to cosmetology or foreign language are organized as "clusters"; each cluster has some courses that could not normally be filled in individual high schools. At present the World Language Cluster offers courses in Linguistics, Spanish, German, French, Italian, Russian, Hebrew, Mandarin Chinese, Latin, Modern Greek, and Swahili. Fifteen language courses are offered in the CDC. The staff of the WLC intends to add Portuguese, Japanese, and different CDC courses to the department's offerings in the next several years.[1]

TARGET AUDIENCE

Students in grades 9 through 12 in any of the 20 high schools in the Dallas Independent School District who have never received a failing grade in any course, have good study habits and strong interest in foreign language, and are recommended by the principal and at least one teacher from their "home" school. Three personal interviews with the counselors of the student's home school, the advisory committees of the WLC, and the WLC language teacher(s) are used to determine which students should be admitted to the WLC and CDC.

The Skyline Center is really three schools in one: a comprehensive high school for 1429 students who live in the area, as well as another 500 students bused to the school under a court desegregation order; a magnet school for 2301 students, 1471 of whom remain at Skyline for all their courses (the other 830 attend only the cluster courses at Skyline, and return to their home high schools for other courses); and a Center for Community Services, a continuing-education program with over 3000 students enrolled in vocational and academic courses. In 1972–73, 450 people enrolled in continuing-education courses in the WLC and the language area of the CDC. Classes are in session continuously at the Skyline Center from nine in the morning until ten at night.

MAJOR GOALS FOR STUDENTS

In the World Language Cluster, students are expected to develop proficiency in all four language skills in any of ten languages and acquire some understanding of the respective cultures. In the Career Development Center, they are to develop language skills and acquire knowledge of a culture useful in particular vocations. And, in the General Language course, they are expected to develop some understanding of the principles of linguistics. All goals are stated in behavioral terms.

SCHEDULING ARRANGEMENTS

Those students who attend Skyline for only the afternoon or morning cluster sessions are bused or arrange their own transportation from their home schools to Skyline. CDC courses meet one to four times a week for the full academic year. Courses in the World Language Cluster are scheduled for four class meetings a week, from one to three hours long; they meet for a full academic year. In each WLC course, one additional class meeting each week is scheduled as "unstructured time" in which students "engage in self-directed activity based on teacher guidelines." This activity usually entails dialogue, drill, and conversation practice with other students or teacher aides, completing oral exercises in the Listening Center (a portable set of carrels with cassette recorders), or independent research and reading in the Media Center. The Media Center contains a small library, filmstrips, records, tapes, and other materials.

REPRESENTATIVE CONTENT

Five levels of French, German, Spanish, and Latin, two levels of Italian, Russian, Modern Greek, Modern Hebrew, and Swahili, one level of Chinese, and one course in General Language are offered in the World Language Cluster. Advanced language courses are of two types: college-preparatory, which focus on the study of literature and culture; and vocational, focusing on the study of specialized vocabularies and grammatical constructions and foreign customs and culture relevant to specific vocations or activities like traveling. These divisions do not constitute "tracks": students may enroll in either type of course, as they choose. They are, however, required to take General Language, a course in basic linguistics and philology.

The presentation of literature in the college-preparatory courses centers on the analysis of writing styles, modes of conversation, the use of idioms, and the culture of the country as it is reflected in the work of individual writers.

The foreign language vocational courses are offered in the Career Development Center. They include Spanish for Ranch and Farm Workers; Spanish for Education (for prospective bilingual or ESL specialists); Bilingual Secretarial Training in Spanish and English; Typewriting and Shorthand in Spanish; Interpreting and Translating (everything from legal documents to stage plays and jokes); Spanish for Travelers; French for Travelers; French in the World of Fashion; Foreign Language for Music Majors; Chicano Spanish; Spanish Vocabulary for the Construction and Building Trades; and Medical Terminology in Spanish. In Foreign Language for Music Majors, an example of a vocation-oriented course, the students study and practice the phonetic systems of French, German, Italian, and Spanish, and learn the basic music terminology in each of these languages. In Bilingual Secretarial Training, the students not only practice typing in both Spanish and English, but also learn to use appropriate forms of address and such terms as "invoice" and "expedite" in both languages.

In addition, three non-language courses, Law in a Changing Society, Latin American History, and Latin American Studies, are conducted entirely in Spanish using appropriate Spanish texts and materials. Law in a Changing Society is a "problems-of-democracy" course that examines the role of the legal system in the development of the United States.

METHODOLOGY

The approach in the language courses is primarily audiolingual and based on pattern drills. Several unique forms of exercises have been developed: for instance, the students do ballet and dance exercises at a barre once a week to develop gestures and body movements appropriate to the language and culture, use mirrors to study their facial expressions and hand gestures, and practice projecting emotions by voice alone in intonation and mouth position exercises. Students are trained in "diaphragmatic breathing" techniques as an aid to smooth speech production. In some of the WLC classes and the CDC course in Interpretation and Translating, students listen to numerous tapes of "speakers with very unusual voices and styles." All advanced classes are conducted entirely in the foreign language, and language students are expected to use only the target language from the minute they enter the Skyline Center.

WLC classes use the Skyline Center's television studio and auditorium to produce videotaped and live dramatic presentations in the foreign languages, and role playing and skits are an important activity in all classes. In Spanish and French classes, paraprofessionals who are native speakers lead drill and conversation exercises, help individual students with their learning problems, and act as resource consultants in lessons on culture. Foreign tourists and foreigners resident in the Dallas area frequently visit the WLC and CDC classes to speak about their careers, activities, and countries. Conversation groups, foreign language dinners, field trips, guest speakers, movies and dances, clubs, and singing sessions provide students with opportunities for using the target language in informal settings.

CREDIT AND ARTICULATION

Provided their admission into the WLC has been approved, students in grades 9–12 at any level of language learning may enroll in courses in the WLC. All students who enroll in WLC courses are required to participate in the General Language course, until they have met eight behaviorally stated objectives. The WLC courses in French, German, Spanish, and Latin are structured through 18 broad behavioral objectives in each language. Advancement within each sequence depends on students' satisfying the objectives specified for each level. Students must meet at least 12 of the 18 objectives in a WLC language sequence before they can enroll in CDC courses in that language. If they want, students may enroll in courses in more than one language, in more than one course in a language, in more than one CDC course, or in WLC and CDC courses simultaneously. The WLC and CDC follow a credit and grading system that is coordinated with that in the cooperating schools.

ROLES OF TEACHERS AND PARAPROFESSIONALS

The roles of teachers vary widely from course to course. Teachers meet regularly to discuss and evaluate the program and methodology. They prepare most of the materials for the CDC courses and some of the material for the General Language course. Four of the 13 language teachers in the WLC also teach in the CDC courses. Teachers conduct, supervise, or initiate many extracurricular activities, and counsel the students in their choice of courses. Three paraprofessionals, who are native speakers, work with the Spanish and French classes, and help individual students with learning problems. One other paraprofessional supervises the use of the Listening and Media Centers.

ROLE OF PARENTS AND COMMUNITY

Parents regularly sponsor and attend dinners and field trips, help supervise or organize extracurricular activities, and identify speakers for the program. The parents of students enrolled in Modern Hebrew helped secure a teacher for the class and were influential in its initiation and organization.

"Goals for Dallas" was instrumental in gathering community support for a new vocational school, and the community has been very involved in the school since 1968. In fact, the Dallas Chamber of Commerce has a full-time person to coordinate the meetings and activities of the 300 people in the community who serve on committees, develop courses, speak to classes, and work in other ways with the school. The school also serves the community: it runs the apprenticeship programs for the local building-trades and printers unions, and cooperates with local industries in placing students and developing relevant programs. Community involvement in the World Language Cluster has been substantial. A college and a synagogue in Dallas helped search for qualified teachers of Swahili and Modern Hebrew. The Mexican consul and representatives from the PTA and the community serve on the advisory board of the WLC. Local businesses have applied to the WLC for help in utilizing the foreign language skills of employees. Foreigners resident in Dallas speak with the classes in the target language, and professors from local colleges participate in discussions. The WLC has also received gifts of money from a number of people in the community with a special interest in foreign language study.

ROLES OF ADMINISTRATORS, SUPERVISORS, AND SPECIAL CONSULTANTS

Administration of the WLC is shared by the district consultant of foreign languages, the principal of the Skyline Center, the chairman of the WLC, and a standing advisory committee of teachers and representatives from the community and school district. The district consultant teaches one WLC class, interviews students for admission into the program, coordinates requests for supplies and staff, conducts program evaluation, sits on the advisory committee, participates in teachers' meetings, and publicizes the program in the community. The principal of the Skyline Center coordinates the busing and scheduling arrangements, and carries out other usual administrative functions. The department chairman directs the WLC and CDC programs, teaches classes, recruits and interviews students, participates in teachers' meetings, conducts program evaluation, and supervises the program organization and scheduling in cooperation with the Skyline Center administration. The advisory committee assists in publicizing the program, designing and developing the curriculum and materials, recruiting teachers and resource people, interviewing students for admission, locating sources of financial support, and evaluating the programs' activities.

Consultants from the community and local and regional colleges and businesses helped develop the courses in the WLC and the language courses in the CDC.

TRAINING REQUIREMENTS

Although there is no formal training program, teachers involved in the vocation-oriented courses have some experience and/or contact with the vocational areas. They develop their expertise in a variety of ways: living or working in a foreign country, multiple majors in college, experience in industry, family contacts, and others.

FUNDING AND COSTS

The average annual expenditure per pupil in the Dallas Independent School District is $688. The average annual expenditure per pupil in the CDC and WLC programs is $1344, of which $344 is diverted from the budgets of the students' home schools if the students attend Skyline for only one session. Funds from the federal government, the Dallas district, and individual donors make up the difference.

A lower pupil to teacher ratio, special teachers in some languages, consultants, tutors, paraprofessionals, a speaker program, and extracurricular activities in the WLC and the CDC language courses add, for each student in these programs, approximately $1000 in costs over the annual expenditure per pupil in the district.

ADAPTABILITY OF CONCEPT TO OTHER PLACES

Factors to consider in establishing either a magnet school for language study or a vocation-oriented curriculum would be: the size of the district (in Dallas, there are 68,168 students in grades 9–12); the degree of interest students show in languages not offered in individual high schools, in vocation-oriented foreign language courses, or in advanced or intensive foreign language study; the availability of suitable and qualified teachers and/or native speakers to serve as teachers and/or resource consultants; and the compatibility of scheduling practices throughout the district or area. Other considerations might include: designating a school or area within a school which could include classrooms, a resource center, a library, and an audio-visual center; busing and scheduling arrangements among the cooperating schools; publicity and recruiting among teachers and students; curriculum design and development of materials for courses for which commercial texts are not available; and some form of community cooperation, perhaps involving local businesses in the vocational foreign language courses.

School district administrators might welcome a magnet school in foreign languages, for it could either relieve them of the responsibility of maintaining marginal foreign language programs in individual schools or open the way for an expansion of the district's offerings in foreign language. Certainly a magnet school or center for vocation-oriented foreign language study could be established on a smaller scale than the Skyline Center.

AVAILABLE DESCRIPTIONS

Johns, H. H., Jr. "Career Development Becomes F.L. Objective," *Accent on ACTFL*, September 1972, pp. 16–22.

Janssen, Peter A. "Skyline: The School with Something for Everyone," *Saturday Review of Education*, 11 November 1972, pp. 37–40.

CONTACT PERSON

H. H. Johns, Jr., Foreign Language Consultant, Dallas Independent School District, 3700 Ross Avenue, Dallas, Texas 75204 (214) 824-1620

NOTE

    [1] Some of the information in this report was derived from Peter A. Janssen, "Skyline: The School with Something for Everyone," *Saturday Review of Education*, 11 November 1972, pp. 37–40.

SOUTH
CAROLINA
STUDY-TOUR
OF
FRANCE

ABSTRACT

Students studying French in South Carolina not only read Daudet, but can also see the windmills that inspired his best stories; they not only learn about French history, but can see the castles where treachery once vied with glory; can not only hear about French cuisine, but sample it too in some of the best regional restaurants and in the homes of hospitable French families. Students on the South Carolina Study-Tour of France live for three weeks with families in one of several small French cities, explore the monuments, museums, and theaters of Paris for nine days, and then for five weeks take a bus tour around the entire country—from the pottery factories of Quimper and the wine cellars of Champagne to the Roman ruins of Nîmes and the sands of the Côte d'Azur.

204

The beaches and fields, the bus, and the historical sites themselves all serve as classrooms: traveling is integrated with readings and discussions to give students an academic view of French language, history, literature, and arts as well as a basic understanding of daily French life. The program was organized by one teacher in the state, is financed by the participants, and conducted by South Carolina teachers of French. It begins with an exchange of orientation packets between the director and each student during the year preceding the trip, and ends with each student gaining two high school credits—as well as long-lasting memories and a keener interest in French.

PROGRAM DEVELOPMENT AND PRESENT STATUS

From the beginning, the study-tour has been organized and directed by Jeanne Palyok, a French teacher at Dreher High School in Columbia, South Carolina. For several years she had been on the staff of the NDEA Foreign Language Institutes in Toulouse, where one of her duties was to organize tours of southeastern France for institute participants. On one of these tours she met the president of the Annecy chapter of "France-États-Unis," a cultural-exchange group, who told her that several local families who hosted a group of American college students in July would be happy to host other students in June if a group were to come their way. Palyok decided to form that group, drawing on the resources of her state and on her own experience as a tour director. Through letters to all French teachers in South Carolina and announcements in the state's foreign language bulletins and meetings, she recruited 23 students for the first study-tour in 1970. Homestays were provided by the families in Annecy, bus transportation was arranged through the Centre de Coopération Culturelle et Sociale in Paris, and local Syndicats d'Initiative and universities helped arrange lodgings throughout the tour. By the third year there were 82 students—enough for four tour groups—and the director hoped to find families in towns like Annecy that were similar in size to the students' hometowns. Staying in smaller towns helped students adjust to the first shock of French culture before moving on to the second shock of Paris. She wrote to the presidents of France-États-Unis in Kayserberg and Angoulême and to the Mayor of Tours. All agreed to find families and, with permission from her school district, Palyok went to France for a few days that January to talk to the people involved and assure herself and the students' families that the students would be in good hands. Since the first tour, she has arranged for buses and drivers through private companies and has contacted hotels and "foyers" on her own. The South Carolina Department of Education, which had approved the study-tour on a year-to-year basis as an experimental program, approved it in 1972 as a permanent program in good standing.

TARGET AUDIENCE

Any student in the state who has completed at least two years of French is eligible to participate; the director usually accepts from her own school only eleventh- and twelfth-grade students who have had a minimum of three years of French, but she cannot require this on a statewide basis.

STUDENT GROUPING AND SCHEDULING ARRANGEMENTS

Students are divided into groups of 20 to 25; in 1972, one group consisted of students from only one school and the others were a mixture from several. Each group is accompanied by two South Carolina teachers of French and goes to a different town for the homestay. At the end of the homestay, all the groups go to Paris where they stay in the same hotel for nine days. For the five-week tour, each group is assigned to one bus; each busload visits the same areas for the same length of time, but the itineraries do not coincide. Teachers are given detailed itineraries including road numbers, hour-by-hour schedules, maps, guides, pertinent addresses, and directions for finding lodgings, restaurants, and activities. In the summer of 1972 none of the groups got lost or missed a meal, visit, or lodging.

FOOD AND LODGING

Homestay families are selected by the local France-États-Unis or mayor's office. Before departure, students fill out a questionnaire describing their interests and an attempt is made to match students with families most suited to their preferences. On the tour, lodging is found in family-style hotels, "foyers," and college dormitories. During the homestay meals are provided by the families. On tour there are frequent picnic lunches, while dinners are in foyers, cafeterias, hotels, and university restaurants. In each region at least one meal is taken in a first-class restaurant so that students may have a sampling of good regional French cooking. "Each student is strongly encouraged to taste whatever is placed in front of him. . . . With proper preparation, students have not balked at this."[1] As often as possible students are given money and are allowed to shop for their own lunch, forcing them to use French and become acquainted with shopping practices.

REPRESENTATIVE CONTENT

During the year preceding the trip the director sends to each participant monthly information packets on the geography, history, and culture related to the places to be visited. There is a unit, for example, on certain cities, one unit on certain faux pas it would be advisable not to make, another on typical French moral values and family rules, and a packet on French writers who will be studied in conjunction with geography. Students must complete a quiz on each unit and return it to the director; quizzes are not graded and may be completed with books and worksheets in hand, but are used as "proof" that the material has been read. Information packets are also sent to participating teachers. During the homestays, students are given a worksheet indicating certain things to do. For example, they may be asked to go to a store and make a list of things they would buy for a picnic, to ask a policeman for directions, or to call the director in Paris from the local post office. Students are given maps and advised to explore the towns on their own as much as possible.

On the tour, the groups visit the menhirs and dolmens of Brittany and the prehistoric caves of Dordogne, and examine styles of architecture in the cathedrals of Poitiers, Notre Dame de Paris, Reims, and Chartres. At Chartres they spend an afternoon with a university lecturer in a private session. They also study the styles and history of castles such as Haut-Konigsbourg, Versailles, Fontainebleau, Pau, and certain châteaux of the Loire. Students visit the Louvre, the Jeu de Paume Museum, the Toulouse-Lautrec museum in Albi, and Barbizon, where some impressionist painters worked. They are given a list of museums they may visit on their free time. In Paris they go to the opera, see a play at the Comédie Française, and go to a Ionesco play in the Latin Quarter. Last year they were able to see plays at festivals in Lyon and Avignon. Before attending the performances, the plays are read and discussed by the group. Other visits include a glove factory in Millau, a perfume factory in Grasse, a silk museum in Lyon, a champagne cellar in Reims, a Roquefort cheese cave, and a porcelain factory in Limoges. A World War II pilgrimage includes a visit to the Vercors, an important area in the history of the French Resistance, to the American military cemetery in Brittany, and to the Armistice site and museum on concentration camps in Reims. The groups go to Charmette to see the Rousseau museum and read excerpts from his *Confessions* at the site which he described; to the Moulin de Daudet where one of Daudet's stories is read; to the lake where Lamartine wrote one of his best-known poems; and to the fortified cities of Carcassonne and Aigues Mortes, where Saint Louis is discussed. Nature and geography are discussed and admired at the cliffs of Brittany, the Gorges du Tarn, on rides through the Pyrénées, the Alps, Juras, and Vosges, and along the coasts of the Atlantic and Mediterranean. During free time, students are encouraged to go out in groups of three or more and speak with French people to inquire about interesting points.

EVALUATION AND CREDIT

Students are evaluated by the teacher on the basis of periodic oral tests and conversations with individual students during the trip, observation of student participation and progress, scrap-books, and a final exam. This last, intended as a review of all activities in France, is given on the return flight, and students may use their notes and brochures and discuss the questions among themselves. Students are evaluated in terms of their knowledge of French history, literature, art, and architecture in relation to the sites visited, as well as their progress in the language. Two credits are awarded for participation, one in French and one in history.

ARTICULATION

In the years preceding and following the trip, courses or class-room activities related to the tour are left to the individual teach-ers. The director, for example, focuses on Annecy, where some students will have their homestays, in her eleventh-grade cultural presentations. She finds that students returning from the tour want more formal work on grammar, which she provides. Study-tour veterans share their experiences with those in their French class who did not go, describe the tour to lower-level classes, and en-courage others to participate.

ROLE OF STUDENTS

Students attend all functions; read and discuss plays before seeing performances; speak French at supper and at announced periods during the day; keep a personal diary; take pictures and make a scrapbook on returning to the United States; and take the final examination.

ROLE OF TEACHERS

Before departure one teacher is designated the group leader. He handles any financial transactions not taken care of by the director, for example picnic lunches and certain entrance fees, and keeps all receipts and a ledger account of all expenses. Teachers accompany their groups at all planned activities, but student free time is also teacher free time. Teachers must be prepared to discuss the places visited and are expected to take notes during visits and ask questions and conduct discussions afterwards. Teachers act as chaperones and supervisors; they "serve more or less as the parents of the students" and "the attitude of the teacher may make the difference in whether or not the students will suffer culture shock from a sense of insecurity." For the first two summers, any teacher who could gather ten or more students from his or her school went along with the group; in 1972 it was felt that it would be better to select teachers on the basis of experience, language proficiency, recommendations, and interviews instead. In meetings before departure, the director briefs all teachers on the details of the itinerary and the importance of their role as "substitute parents."

ROLE OF STUDENT ASSISTANT

In 1972 a college student who had once been on the study-tour was asked to accompany the group when one of the teachers found just two days before departure that she was unable to go. The assistant was familiar with the lodgings, could take responsibility for room and key distribution, knew the itinerary, assisted in teaching, led students in singing French songs, and served as a liaison between the students and the older teacher. Palyok hopes to have a student assistant for future study-tours.

ROLE OF PROGRAM DIRECTOR

The program director writes and screens all application forms; selects participants and teachers; conducts orientation correspondence and meetings for students, teachers, and parents; prepares readings and materials for orientation and the tour; designs the itinerary and topics to be covered; and arranges all transportation to, from, and in France and all lodging facilities. During the homestay period, she circulates through France on a Eurailpass, seeking tickets for festivals or performances she might not have known about in advance. She also accompanies one group on its tour and takes care of major financial transactions.

ROLE OF PARENTS

Parents of participants sign a release form for their children, agree to the terms of conduct and organization established by the director, certify that their children are in good health, may authorize their children to drink wine or beer at meals, and attend orientation meetings with the director, students, and teachers.

FUNDING AND COSTS

All expenses for the program are paid for by the students. Fees for the first three years were $950 per student, but in 1973 they were increased to $1050 because of the devaluation of the dollar. The fee covers round-trip air fare, insurance, all bus transportation in France, fees to host families (ranging from $5 to $30), all lodging and three meals a day, occasional snacks, entrance fees to museums, plays, the opera, festivals, and tips, as well as the travel expenses of the accompanying teachers and director. One full scholarship or several partial scholarships are provided for students unable to pay the fee; this money is earned by French students through car washes, sales, and other projects.

PROGRAM EVALUATION

Preston L. Musgrove, Modern Foreign Language Consultant for the State of South Carolina, notes that "this summer [1972] it was my pleasure to personally evaluate the program and I feel that it is the best thing to happen to foreign languages in South Carolina in a long, long while. Consequently, in the future it will no longer be considered experimental, requiring special approval by the State Department of Education. It is encouraging to note that the program has been so well accepted that plans are being made to offer a similar experience in Spain next summer for South Carolina Spanish students." The number of students in the program grew from 23 in 1970 to 82 in 1972. Student enthusiasm is indicated not only by their willingness to spend several years working part-time to earn the money for the trip, but also in the participants' tendency, noted by the program director, to dominate the French classes to which they return after the trip. All participants would like to return to France, and their only complaints, besides those related to some restaurants, lodgings, and a few isolated activities, have been that they were not required to speak French more often. There has been no formal evaluation of general student progress following the trip. The director notes, however, that one "fast" first-year student placed into a third-year class after the study-tour and finished at the top of that class, and one "fair" student placed third on the final exam the year after his return. Another student who resisted speaking French even midway into the trip returned home an eager and voluble French student: he had met a non-English-speaking French girl and spent several days with her family.

ADAPTABILITY OF CONCEPT TO OTHER PLACES

Factors to consider in developing a locally-arranged study-tour program are: (1) student willingness and ability to finance the trip; (2) a teacher or administrator familiar with the foreign country and able to design a workable itinerary; (3) approval from local and state education officials; (4) the ability to find host homes, "foyers," hotels, or dormitories, as well as air flight and transportation in the foreign country; (5) and the establishment of living and health standards acceptable to the American parents.

Musgrove notes that the program "has been limited to South Carolina students because it is felt they have much in common, coming from a small, relatively homogeneous state, and therefore fewer personal and social adjustments have to be made. For the same reason it is recommended that the program not be offered as a model except to small areas or school districts." The program director notes other considerations: (1) It is best to locate homestays in towns similar in size to the students' hometowns to minimize culture shock. (2) The first time a program is tried, it is convenient to use an agency such as the Centre de Coopération Culturelle et Sociale to help arrange homestays, bus transportation, itineraries, and lodging; a teacher should become familiar with the itinerary and lodgings before attempting to construct a tour independently. (3) Organizations such as France-États-Unis and local governmental or educational organizations in the foreign country can be contacted to locate host families; many towns have a Syndicat d'Initiative which can help find inexpensive lodgings. (4) Students who have completed three or more years of French get more out of a trip than students with less experience in the language. (5) Students of differing ages, even a year or two, have a hard time functioning as a group and tend to polarize; when possible, students of the same age and grade level should be grouped together. (6) It has been more practical and natural not to insist that students use French at all times. (7) With orientation before and during the trip explaining to students what might be radically different from what they know in terms of food, living quarters, or sanitation conditions, culture shock is greatly reduced and students accept a good deal without complaints. (8) Teachers should be selected on the basis of character rather than their ability to gather a group of students, since so much of their role is parental in nature; also, the director recommends that teachers who have never been to the foreign country be included, as long as they are accompanied by a more experienced tour leader. (9) A student assistant, particularly a college student who is a study-tour veteran, is invaluable. (10) Students are happier in foyers, which have private rooms, than in youth hostels, and are likely to prefer any restaurant or picnic to a university restaurant.

CONTACT PERSON

Jeanne Palyok, Teacher of French, Dreher High School, 701 Adger Road, Columbia, South Carolina 29205 (803) 256-1695

NOTE
[1] All quotations are from personal communications to the survey staff.

STUDENT-CENTERED CLASSROOM

ABSTRACT

In Clarence Central High School in Clarence, New York, the study of French and Spanish is structured through individual and small-group work and periodic large-group instruction. Student interaction is promoted through communication exercises and peer teaching as well as specific teacher behaviors. Students play a large role in determining both the teaching and learning styles and are offered a choice among several modes of learning.

PROGRAM DEVELOPMENT AND PRESENT STATUS

In 1967, Joseph Zampogna, a teacher at Clarence Central High School, was given a two-year leave of absence to work with the Human Relations Education Project of Western New York, a

215

program funded through Title III to help train teachers in more student-centered and affective approaches to teaching. As part of his work, Zampogna was trained in interaction analysis and group dynamics. After he returned to teaching, he applied some techniques recommended by the Project in two foreign language classes in hopes of improving student performance and attitudes. There are now 100 Spanish and 50 French students enrolled in the program; a total of 500 students are enrolled in French and Spanish language classes in the school.

TARGET AUDIENCE AND PROGRAM GOALS

The target audience is students in grades 9–12 in levels III–V of French and I–V of Spanish. The goal of the program is to create a learning and social atmosphere in the classroom that will promote student interest and achievement in all four language skills.

MAJOR GOALS FOR STUDENTS

(1) To interact and cooperate with their peers in learning; (2) to reach higher levels of proficiency in all four language skills than students in textbook-centered classes; (3) to help determine the pacing, teaching style, and curriculum; (4) to continue in language study through all five levels, as a result of satisfaction with language learning.

REPRESENTATIVE CONTENT AND METHODOLOGY

Each class meets five periods a week. At the end of every period, each student writes a checklist of learning tasks for the next day and checks off the activities he completed on the previous day's list. Once a week, the class meets in a standard format;

the teacher gives information to the students as a group on the reading, group assignments, culture, and problems in grammar that are likely to arise.

Two periods a week, the students work on Individual Study activities that include viewing filmstrips and films, listening to tapes or news broadcasts from French-Canadian radio stations, and, in two Spanish courses, working with programmed materials. These materials were prepared by Zampogna and other local teachers in a workshop; they are based on behaviorally stated objectives and include introductory grammar explanations, demonstration exercises in both English and Spanish, and pretests. After doing the pretest, the student works through the program, checking the answers to each step against a key. Programs are occasionally broken up with anagrams and word games to relieve monotony. At the end of a program, the student is tested orally by the teacher and takes a written test. If he scores below 65 percent, he uses the test to analyze his learning problems, usually with the help of another student or the teacher, and may complete supplementary exercises and another quiz built into the second half of the packet. In courses for which programmed materials have not been produced, students do the exercises and drills in their workbooks and textbooks.

In the week's other two periods, the students work in small groups, formed on the basis of interest or ability. They practice dialogues from the textbooks or teacher-prepared flash cards, quiz each other with student-prepared vocabulary cards, play foreign language games, read plays aloud, and work on drills. The teacher moves around the classroom, entering into students' activities unobtrusively, asking and answering questions or clarifying grammar points. He stays only as long as he is needed. In the advanced levels, students are free to create their own projects and groups, but in the beginning levels the teacher groups and regroups students to form better learning situations. Student cooperation is reinforced through peer teaching. In first-year courses, when a student finishes a unit he is assigned to help another individual or group work with a similar unit for at least one period. After the first year, peer teaching is voluntary, but students are told that they can best reinforce their own learning by teaching the material and they are praised and thanked by the teacher and other students for their help.

Students in advanced classes are required to do individual and group readings and projects on specific topics of their choice in broad areas designated by the teacher (for example, 20th-century literature). Several students, for instance, created a slide series and wrote a foreign language script to go with it. One student is practicing the imperfect tense by writing a book of fairy tales. Another gave an explanation and recital of French organ music in a local church; a third gave a ballet demonstration, explaining the dance in the foreign language. Quite a few students have prepared foreign meals, and one did a news analysis for the class. A couple of students painted a "tree" of a family of French immigrants to the United States, with apples representing the individual members, and told the apples' stories to the teacher and some classmates. If students cannot develop their own projects or reports, the director gives them topics they can choose from.

GRADING AND TESTING

About 60 percent of the teacher's classroom time is taken up with evaluation, and he therefore uses testing situations to teach as well. Sometimes several students are tested at once. Two types of tests are used in the program: Formative and Summative. Formative tests are single-concept tests, and most items are information-recall. About one-fifth of each test is oral. Students must score at least 80 percent to move on to the next lesson within the unit. Summative tests are given at the end of units; 80 percent of the items call for comprehension of unfamiliar material. Students must score at least 65 percent to move on to the next unit. There is no penalty for retaking tests.

ORIENTATION

Orientation rap-sessions are held for the first two weeks. The teacher explains the nature and use of programmed materials and mastery testing, as well as relevant information about language learning and learning psychology. Students talk about how they learn best and how they feel about mastery testing, managing their own time and learning, and peer teaching. Some students resist the teacher's taking a different role; others feel languages should be learned in only one way. These feelings and others are explored both at the beginning and throughout the year.

Four communication games, done in English, decrease the students' resistance to interacting in class and peer teaching. In one game, the Wheel, each student is given a sheet of paper with a circle containing 11 "what?" questions (Age? Favorite country? Attitude toward school?) as "spokes." Partners ask each other the questions, remembering and restating their partner's answers. Some questions are then reframed as "why?" questions (Why is . . . your favorite country?). Finally, some others are reframed as "how?" questions (How could you change your attitude toward school?) and the partners talk freely about the question. In Pairing, another exercise, students are paired at random and asked to explain to each other a presentation the teacher makes. Another exercise, Inner-Outer Circle, is used to develop skills in conversation, observation, and listening. Five students sit in a circle, discussing an assigned topic. Five other students sit in a larger circle outside the first, each observing one student in the inner circle. At the end of the exercise, the students talk with their counterparts in the other circle, talking about the original discussion and their part in it. For the fourth exercise, Triads, Quartets, and Quintets, students meet in conversation groups to talk about a predetermined topic, using a list of questions prepared by the teacher. In the first years of the program, the students did these exercises throughout the year and in the target language. In 1972–73, however, Zampogna restricted their use to the orientation sessions.

CREDIT AND ARTICULATION

Since the student-centered approach is not used in all language classes, it has not been possible to implement a continuous progress system; students in the program are required to complete at least six units a year. The other language classes usually complete ten. Faster students are encouraged to take on extra work. To date all students have met the pace and been placed either in a more advanced class in the program or with another teacher who is willing to accept them.

ROLES OF TEACHER, PARENTS, AND COMMUNITY

The teacher is crucial in the development of positive student attitudes and interaction. (See Program Evaluation section.) Parents attend one orientation meeting in August and two Open House meetings during the year to talk with the teacher and students. Native speakers of French and Spanish visit the classes occasionally to show slides and talk about their countries.

TRAINING REQUIREMENTS

Besides the training he received in the Human Relations Education Project, the teacher has received training in interaction analysis and group dynamics in both academic and non-academic programs and has taken a large number of courses in the psychology of learning and behavior modification.

FUNDING AND COSTS

The program is funded through the regular school budget; the average annual expenditure in the district is $1100 per pupil. The following materials are part of the school-wide language program which are used in the Student-Centered Classroom:

Two Ampex tape decks and record players	$2000
Two Wollensack tape recorders	200
One cassette tape recorder	25
Four sets of headphones	100
Two overhead speakers	60

The costs for two jackboxes, textbooks, workbooks, and other materials (maps, magazines, games, etc.) were not available. There are no special costs.

PROGRAM EVALUATION

Four types of evaluation have been applied to the program: a Learning Environment Inventory Scale, to determine how students perceived the class; a Teacher Description Instrument, to determine how they perceived the teacher; the MLA Cooperative Foreign Language Tests, to measure language proficiency; and an attrition survey. Forty-five students in the third year of French took part in the evaluation; they were randomly divided at the start of 1971–72 into a control group and an experimental group. All the students had followed the same course of study in the first two years of French; the grade average in French for the control group was 84.3, for the experimental group 82.1. The average I.Q. of the control group was 120.4, that of the experimental group 117.8. All students received 40 minutes of French instruction a day. The groups were taught by two teachers whose language skills were rated "good" by the Modern Language Proficiency Tests. The teacher of the control group used an eclectic approach with both audiolingual and cognitive code learning techniques, spoke French about 85 percent of the time, and incorporated a standard amount of cultural and audio-visual material into the course. The experimental group was taught with the techniques already described.

A t-test was used to determine the difference between the two groups' means on the Learning Environment Inventory Scale. The experimental group rated its classroom environment significantly higher in the categories of Diversity (class divides efforts among several purposes); Democracy (class decisions made by all); and Student Satisfaction (with classwork). The experimental group rated the class significantly lower in Speed (i.e., they had less difficulty keeping up); Friction (fewer students considered uncooperative); Favoritism (less evidence of special projects going to good students); and Apathy (about classwork).

The two groups were given the French MA Form of the

MLA Cooperative Foreign Language Tests. The experimental group scored significantly higher than the control in all four categories of listening, speaking, reading, and writing.

At the end of the year, 63% of the experimental group and 35% of the control group opted to take French IV. As reasons for their continuing, the experimental group said: like French (95%); classes relaxing and stimulating (91%); want more French study (88%); like structure of classes (85%); can follow own pace (85%); to improve and not forget French (84%); material not dull (82%); learn better when not pressured (81%); to improve speaking (70%); plan to go on in college (65%); to study classic literature (55%). Obviously the methodology and small-group structure played some role in students' continuing.

To discover if the different teaching behaviors played a role in shaping students' attitudes toward the class and French, both groups were given a Teacher Description Instrument to evaluate their teachers' behaviors. The TDI consists of 15 behavior categories that students rate on a frequency scale. Both groups rated their teachers identically in their knowledge of the subject, ability to go beyond the text, and use and design of tests. They saw no significant difference in the way the teachers worked at the board or repeated explanations for slow students. In nine other categories, however, the experimental group students rated their teacher significantly higher. They rated him higher: in encouraging them to think for themselves, presenting problems as challenges, and trying to increase their interest; in courtesy, consideration, friendliness, and openness to different points of view; and in using teaching aids and supplementary materials, explaining grammar at a level they could understand, using constructive criticism, and encouraging students to work together. They felt more strongly than the control group that their teacher put the subject across in a lively way, using humor and personal and practical examples. They rated their classes as having more time for questions and discussions and their teacher as more willing to give individual assistance. They rated him more effective in coordinating lab and class work, encouraging students to use reference books, and supplementing the text. On the other hand, the control group students rated their teacher significantly higher in planning presentations and class periods logically and in detail, keeping to a schedule, and spending time on "important and relevant material." But the control students also felt that he "rehashed" the text and other materials more frequently and assigned an "unreasonable amount of work, very difficult reading, and a lot of burdensome and busy work." From these ratings, Zampogna suggests that the teaching behaviors in the experimental program classes make up a student-centered teaching style that is instrumental in improving student attitudes and performances, as well as alleviating "some general behavioral problems encountered when teaching in a textbook-centered classroom."[1]

ADAPTABILITY OF CONCEPT TO OTHER PLACES

The director recommends that teachers interested in adapting the format have some training in the psychology of learning, inter-action analysis, and group dynamics, and should acquire or develop materials suitable for independent-study activities. In the summer of 1972, Zampogna coordinated a nine-week training session for 50 teachers interested in group work and individualized instruction and a four-week workshop for 20 teachers to develop programmed materials and board games for French, German, and Spanish. Single copies (only) of these materials are available at $20.00 (per language) from Joseph S. Plesur, Coordinator of Instructional Services, District #1 BOCES Service Center, 455 Cayuga Road, Cheektowaga, New York 14225.

AVAILABLE DESCRIPTIONS

The program and some of its evaluation results are described by Anthony Papalia and Joseph Zampogna in "An Experiment in Individualized Instruction through Small-Group Interaction," *Foreign Language Annals*, 5 (1972), 302–06. Another aspect of the evaluation and program is described by the same authors in "An Experimental Study of Teachers' Classroom Behaviors and their

Effect on FL Attrition," *Modern Language Journal*, 56 (1972), 421–24.

CONTACT PERSON

Joseph A. Zampogna, Instructor of French and Spanish, Clarence Central High School, 900 Main Street, Clarence, New York, 14031 (716) 759-8311.

NOTE
    [1] Survey questionnaire.

SUMMER FOREIGN LANGUAGE DAY HOUSE INSTITUTES

ABSTRACT

A joint effort by the city Board of Education, a state university, and the large and diversified community provides students from Chicago's public schools with an eight-week foreign language enrichment program. The Summer Foreign Language Day House Institutes began in 1964; six teachers and an average of 170 students of all abilities from the city's 116 junior and senior high schools participate each summer. They receive intensive instruction in French, German, Spanish, or Latin in the classrooms and on the grounds of the University of Illinois's Chicago Circle Campus, but as much time is spent off-campus or with visitors from the Chicago community as in the more formal study of language and culture. The Day House students take to the streets of their city to visit the ethnic neighborhoods, shops, museums, and factories where they directly confront the cultures and languages—no

225

longer "foreign"—that they have studied, profiting from the human and cultural resources abounding in a large American city.

TARGET AUDIENCE

Any high school student with at least one year of foreign language study and any elementary school graduate with two or more years is accepted upon application. To recruit students, announcements are sent to foreign language teachers in each of Chicago's schools, notices are posted on classroom bulletin boards, and articles appear in the city's daily newspapers. In the summer of 1972, a total of 165 students attended; they represented many ethnic groups and commuted from all parts of Chicago. Because the program is voluntary, neither discipline nor attendance poses a problem.

MAJOR GOALS FOR STUDENTS

(1) To develop proficiency in the target language through real-life encounters with speakers of the language; (2) to pursue their own paths of inquiry into linguistic and cultural subjects of special interest; (3) to compare similarities and differences of life in other countries with their own way of life through varied interactions among all four language groups; (4) to develop an appreciation and understanding of other lifestyles and cultures; (5) to learn about the cultural and political developments of other countries and the extent to which they influence contemporary world events.

STUDENT GROUPING, SCHEDULING ARRANGEMENTS, AND CREDIT

Students attend the Day Houses daily from 9 a.m. to 1 p.m. for eight weeks. Students are grouped according to proficiency level in small- and large-group sessions for 45 minutes of basic language instruction each day. Students receive no credit for participation; they are awarded a certificate at the end of the Institute, and a record of their attendance is put in their school files.

REPRESENTATIVE CONTENT AND METHODOLOGY

The program is activity-oriented with an emphasis on culture, but formal instruction in the four skills is provided in the daily language sessions. Instruction is audiolingual-visual, using textbooks and film series, with teachers from the same language often practicing a team approach. In 1971 the materials of *Dialogues africain contemporains* (Center for Curriculum Development) were introduced to provide a multi-media approach to the study of French in an African setting. Classes are held in the air-conditioned university classrooms or outdoors on the campus grounds; the language laboratory is used for daily practice with taped drills and pronunciation exercises. Some geography, cultural and political history, art, and literature are also presented in these more formal sessions.

Native speakers from the Chicago community, representatives from foreign consulates and travel agencies, and staff members of the foreign language department of the university visit the Day Houses frequently for discussions and lectures. There have been visits by a French architect, a German-born professor, a Spanish poet, a German-American newspaper reporter, a representative from a Spanish-American airline, professional musicians, and even a group of French Boy Scouts. Members of the Department of Classics have given presentations "ranging from an analysis of an Horatian ode to a Latin anatomy lesson."[1] Students of German visited a local Volkswagen showroom and had lunch at a German restaurant; Spanish students have visited Puerto Rican and Mexican-American neighborhoods, a taco factory, and the Migration Division of the Commonwealth of Puerto Rico. Latin students, "turned on" by discussions of Greek heritage, as well as by *souvlaki*, asked for lessons in Greek one year; since then, lessons have been provided at the Latin Day House so that students can now read passages from Plato and Saint Matthew as well as from Cicero and Catullus. Most participants have gone on tours through the Circle Campus, to the city's Art Institute, private art galleries, and the Museum of Natural History, guided by Institute teachers speaking the foreign language. Folk dancing, skits, singing, poetry contests, films, the production of foreign language newspapers, and young people's concerts in the park round out the activities for each language group.

Students and staff members also join in planning cross-cultural activities involving all four language groups. Bastille Day is celebrated by all Institute students, often with the French group presenting a *Théâtre de Guignol* puppet show. In 1972 the celebration was followed by a "cheese-in," where students and parents sampled French foods. Students from all languages also attended a performance by a Brazilian folk singer who sang in many languages. Each session ends with a ceremony during which students receive certificates for participation, musical and dramatic performances are given, and parents accompany their children to a German, Mexican, or French restaurant. In 1971 the culminating activity of the Day Houses consisted of authentic African songs, dances, and poetry in French, as well as a display of flags from the African nations, all in the open air.

ROLES OF TEACHERS AND ADMINISTRATORS

Outstanding teachers are hired for the program. They meet for half a day of training before the Institutes begin, have daily staff meetings for planning activities, and frequently team-teach. The Director of the Division of Foreign Languages for the Board of Education of the City of Chicago serves as a consultant to the program and conducts the preservice training session. The Board of Education sponsors the program, hires teachers, initiates the recruitment of students, and provides books and other materials for the Day Houses. The University of Illinois provides classrooms, a language laboratory, a lecture center, facilities at the student union and library, and equipment.

ROLE OF PARENTS AND COMMUNITY

In addition to drawing on the community for resource people and cultural visits, the program receives favorable coverage from the local newspapers. Two television stations have covered the culminating activities, and the Chicago *Daily Defender* has printed several enthusiastic articles. Parents are invited to attend all events at the Day Houses: fiestas, Bastille Day celebrations, and the culminating activities.

FUNDING AND COSTS

Students pay a $1 registration fee. The cost of the summer program is the teachers' summer salary (provided by the Board of Education), plus the following "hidden" costs: free use of the facilities at the University of Illinois and free services of the language lab staff (estimated at a cost of $1000 to the university); free use of films, available from the Division of Visual Education of the Chicago Public Schools; instructional materials donated by various publishers through the years and used from summer to summer; and consultant services and program management supplied by the professional staff of the Division of Foreign Languages.

PROGRAM EVALUATION

"Chicago foreign language teachers have found that students who attend the Day Houses show marked improvement in such skills as oral comprehension and speaking. In addition they have a more serious attitude toward the study of foreign language."[2] Both students and teachers are enthusiastic about their participation in the program.

In a questionnaire administered to the 1967 Day House participants, students recommended that the Day Houses be continued and indicated that they would urge their fellow students to participate the following summer. In a 1968 questionnaire, 76% of the 64 students responding said they felt that they learned more in the Day Houses than in their regular high school classes. Seventy-eight percent said they would like to have the language laboratory, movies, and filmstrips from the Day Houses used in their regular high school program, and 92% said they would like to have the telephone tapes, which were used at the Institute at that time, also used in their schools. In rating the various activities of the program, they listed in order of preference: tours, special activities, songs and dancing, conversation, the basic culture program, the language laboratory, guest speakers, and the basic language program. At that time teaching assistants were also working with the Day House classes, and 88% of the students said that they thought it was a good idea; they liked the individual help the assistants provided, and some found it easier to relate to an assistant than to the regular teacher.

ADAPTABILITY OF CONCEPT TO OTHER PLACES

A school district, a university, or a combination of the two could provide the professional staff, funding, and setting for an urban summer enrichment program in foreign languages. The main advantages of the Day Houses are that there is virtually no cost to students, students of all abilities and with a minimum background of language study are accepted, and a large audience can be attracted. The Chicago Day Houses do not propose to be a "culture island," but rather a link between the foreign language classroom and the larger community; exploration of a city composed of many ethnic lifestyles and understanding cultural differences on a local level are as important as the use of the language in the classroom several hours a day and the development of language proficiency. In developing a program with similar orientation, care should be taken to search out all cultural aspects of potential interest to students within the city and to find resource people speaking the target language from both the academic and non-academic communities.

AVAILABLE DESCRIPTIONS

The program is described in Hannah W. Choldin, "Foreign Language Day Houses," *Modern Language Journal*, 7 (1968), 88–89; and David J. Plesic, "The Latin Day House," *Classical Outlook*, 49, No.7 (1972), 75–76.

CONTACT PERSON

Edwin Cudecki, Director, Division of Foreign Languages, Board of Education, 228 N. LaSalle St., Chicago, Illinois 60601 (312) 641-4048

NOTES
¹ David J. Plesic, "The Latin Day House," *Classical Outlook*, 49, No. 7 (1972), 76.
² Hannah W. Choldin, "Foreign Language Day Houses," *Modern Language Journal*, 7 (1968), 89.

SUPERVISED MULTI-MEDIA CORRESPONDENCE STUDY

ABSTRACT

The University of Colorado has developed multi-media programs of "correspondence study" in French and Spanish for use in schools too small to hire foreign language teaching staff or in larger schools for enrichment. The multi-media programs are based on a standard textbook and workbook, accompanied by a study guide prepared by the University. Students work with the materials in regularly-scheduled classes that meet with supervising teachers who do not necessarily have any background in the foreign language. The students use audio tapes individually or in small groups to practice dialogues and drills, view series of videotapes developed by the University, and take part in weekly "telelectures" presented through amplified telephone hook-ups by an instructor at the University. Examinations are given in written form and on audio tapes, which are sent to the language instructor for correction and grading. Evaluation of the program indicates that students reached levels of proficiency in all four skills equal to those reached by "matched" students in similar communities who received standard classroom instruction from regular foreign language teachers.

PROGRAM DEVELOPMENT AND PRESENT STATUS

The view from Pike's Peak of Colorado's "purple mountains' majesties" and "amber waves of grain" prompted Katherine Lee Bates to write "America the Beautiful" in 1893, and in many places the land is as inspiring now as then. But the geographic and, more particularly, the demographic patterns inspire nothing but problems for foreign language instruction in some of the small towns in the mountains and plains. The great distances between towns and the difficulty of travel in winter make busing students to regional schools infeasible, and students in many rural areas attend schools too small to offer a broad range of courses. To compensate for this situation, the Bureau of Independent Study at the University of Colorado offers high school students correspondence programs of independent study. For several years these included a mail-exchange program in foreign languages based on the grammar-translation approach. In the spring of 1968, however, the Bureau dropped this program because it was outdated and considered inappropriate to the students' primary language needs. In its stead, on the request and with the help of a school of 80 students located in Gateway, an isolated mining town, the Bureau of Independent Study cooperated with the Bureau of Audio-Visual Instruction at the University, the Colorado State Department of Education, and one of the state's outstanding Spanish teachers in developing a multi-media Spanish I program that made possible an audiolingual framework for correspondence study. In 1970, the materials for Spanish I were revised and a new program in Spanish II was developed; the following year a program in French I was initiated, and in 1972 a program in French

II was added to the Bureau's foreign language offerings. At present, over 75 students are enrolled in the program in seven schools, and the Bureau is considering expanding the foreign language options to include advanced courses in the two languages, as well as courses for Spanish speakers in both Spanish and English.

TARGET AUDIENCE

Students in small high schools in Colorado that do not offer French or Spanish, or students in other schools whose levels or schedules create the need for a special class.

STUDENT GROUPING AND SCHEDULING ARRANGEMENTS

Students meet as a group five times a week with the other students in their schools who are at the same level of language learning, under the guidance of a supervising teacher. Classes range between one and sixteen students.

ORIENTATION

At the beginning of each year, the Coordinator of Foreign Language Programs at the Bureau of Independent Study visits each of the schools in the program to establish personal contact and explain the program's procedures to the students and teachers. The first videotape in the series also contains an explanation of the program and the students are asked to fill out a questionnaire to demonstrate their comprehension of the program and its procedures. Supervising teachers are given detailed explanations of their role and responsibilities in the program and are given written directions and explanations they may refer to when necessary.

METHODOLOGY AND REPRESENTATIVE CONTENT

The program is one of modified correspondence study. Once a week, the language instructors at the Bureau use amplified telephones to give a 30-minute "telelecture" of individual and group drill and instruction, and answer questions from students and the supervising teachers about language-learning problems or procedural difficulties. In another period each week, the students view one videotape from the series created by the Bureau for each level of both languages. In the videotapes, native speakers act out the textbook dialogues in appropriate settings and then repeat the dialogues slowly, using backward buildup and other audiolingual techniques. For the remaining three periods each week, students work in pairs, alone, or in groups, as they and the supervising teacher decide, using a standard textbook and workbook as well as a study guide developed by the Bureau of Independent Study. Audio tapes developed by the Bureau and by commercial firms are used each day to practice dialogues and drills. Students also record the unit readings on tapes that are returned periodically to the language instructor for correction and evaluation. Faster students are encouraged to take on supplementary work, and slower students are directed by the study guide and the Bureau's instructors to exercises that will be of special value to them. The language instructor occasionally presents cultural information in the telelectures, but the teaching of culture stems primarily from the descriptions of French or Hispanic life included in the textbook. Short travelogues and other films are occasionally incorporated into the classes as well. Written examinations are administered at regular intervals by the supervising teacher and are corrected by graders and the language instructors at the University.

GRADING AND CREDIT

The supervising teacher and the language instructor cooperate in determining students' grades. The supervising teacher sends the language instructor comments on students' work in class, which the instructor considers along with his record of each student's performance in the telelecture quizzes, oral work, the written "homework," and tests to determine final grades. Credit is given as for any other course through the participating schools.

MATERIALS

The texts and workbooks (*Learning Spanish/French the Modern Way*, rev. ed. New York: McGraw-Hill), videotapes, audio tapes, and guide books prepared by the Bureau of Independent Study are supplied and distributed to the schools by the Bureau at the beginning of each year. Films and other supplementary materials are sent to the schools as needed. Each school must provide a half-inch format videotape recorder and monitor, at least two tape recorders, and a 16mm sound movie projector. These are rented or bought by the school from commercial distributors.

ROLE OF STUDENTS

Students enroll in the program voluntarily. They are expected to attend all classes and complete all the assigned work.

ROLES OF SUPERVISING TEACHERS AND LANGUAGE INSTRUCTORS

The supervising teachers do not teach the language: they coordinate the use of the audio-visual materials in the school; handle procedural problems; supervise examinations and classroom work; act as the liaison and contact person for the Bureau of Independent Study; send examinations, worksheets, and tapes to the language instructor for correction; cooperate in determining student grades; and attempt to keep "the students motivated, organized, and involved in their work." They may use their teachers' manuals to help students correct work. The French and Spanish language instructors, based at the Bureau of Independent Study, present the telelectures. They correct student worksheets, examinations, and audio tapes; assign grades in cooperation with the supervising teacher; and review materials to be used in the program.

ROLE OF COORDINATOR OF FOREIGN LANGUAGE PROGRAMS

The Coordinator is also the Spanish language instructor and is based at the University. She carries out the orientation program at the beginning of each year, describes the program at meetings of principals and teachers in Colorado, and cooperates with the State Department of Education in contacting schools that might need or want the program. She coordinates the preview and review of the materials, plans for the development of new courses, participates in the development of some materials, and arranges for the distribution and collection of all materials. The coordinator handles the bookkeeping operations of the program and hires and supervises the French language instructor.

ROLE OF ADMINISTRATORS

The Director of the Bureau of Independent Study at the University of Colorado develops the budget for the language programs each year, and approves the program's expenditures. He is responsible for hiring the Language Coordinator. The principals or district staff for each school make the arrangements for the program with the Bureau of Independent Study, appoint or hire the supervising teachers, rent or buy the necessary audio-visual equipment, publicize the program among students in their schools and determine which students will be allowed to enroll, arrange whatever extracurricular activities are possible, and schedule the classes.

ROLES OF SPECIAL STAFF AND CONSULTANTS

The Foreign Language Coordinator for the Colorado State Department of Education in 1968 helped determine the feasibility of the program and recommended Spanish teachers to assist in the development of the materials. Cameramen and technicians from the Bureau of Audio-Visual Instruction at the University of Colorado filmed and produced the videotapes. An extremely competent Spanish teacher was selected by the Bureau of Independent Study to help develop the materials for the program and teach in the Spanish videotapes. He, in turn, helped a French teacher develop the materials and videotapes for the French program. Native speakers of French and Spanish act and "teach" the dialogues in the videotapes.

TRAINING REQUIREMENTS

The language instructors must be able to teach effectively with the amplified telephone and audio and video tapes; this requires some familiarity with the media and an "aptitude for verbalizing contrastive analysis." The supervising teachers must understand and be able to implement the program's procedures and be able to operate the mechanical equipment. This training is provided in an afternoon.

FUNDING AND COSTS

The program has been funded, to date, through the user fees and through loans from the University of Colorado. Repayment of the loans has been put on a deferred-payment basis. The development costs for the two Spanish programs were approximately $7500 each and for the two French programs approximately $10,000. These costs include writing and typing the materials and scripts; the actors', teachers', and cameramen's wages; the costs of filming, developing, and printing the videotapes; the duplication of materials; telephone and postage charges; travel expenses; and publicity. The first school involved in the program, the Gateway School, contributed $500 toward the development of the first Spanish program, and a Research Grant from the University of Colorado financed the rest. The salary costs for the Director of the Bureau of Independent Study are not included in this figure; they were absorbed by the University of Colorado.

The fees charged to users fall into two categories: "fixed" and "per student." The maximum fixed costs for one full-year program of one level of either French or Spanish are $965, and include telephone charges, developmental costs, site visits by the Coordinator, instructor time, and audio and video tape rentals; for two full-year courses, either of one level of French and one of Spanish or two levels of one language, the maximum fixed costs are $1900. The cost per student is $50, and includes textbooks and other materials. Thus to enroll ten students in Spanish I would cost a school a maximum of $1465; to enroll ten students in Spanish I and ten in French I would cost a maximum of $2900. The time of the supervising teacher is not included in this figure. Lower fees are charged for second-level programs with only one to three students.

PROGRAM EVALUATION

In the second year of the program, an evaluator from the Bureau of Independent Study matched the experimental group of 53 students in the Bureau's foreign language programs in seven communities with a control group of 55 students who were completing regular foreign language programs with "in-school" teachers in seven similar communities. The students in the two groups were matched on the bases of language aptitude, general academic ability, and prior knowledge of Spanish, but differed in that the students in the experimental group were, on the average, at a slightly higher grade level than those in the control group, while the control group had a higher percentage of female students than the experimental. Degrees of teacher competency and its effect on student learning cannot be accurately quantified, and therefore could not be taken into consideration in the experiment. And random distribution of the students between the two types of instruction, which would have ensured a truer experimental design, could not be accomplished. Both groups were given the Pimsleur Spanish Proficiency Tests, Form A.

Based on an analysis of the two groups' scores, the researcher in the experiment concluded that "there is no significant difference in language achievement between students studying a foreign language by a supervised correspondence study method and those studying by the standard audiolingual method, with respect to: (a) listening comprehension, (b) speaking proficiency, (c) reading comprehension, (d) writing proficiency, and (e) total language proficiency."[1] The scores of the two groups fell around the fiftieth percentile in listening and reading comprehension, in the range of "Fair" (out of the three categories of Good, Fair, and Poor) in speaking proficiency, and around the twentieth percentile in writing proficiency.

The attrition rate in the control group was 9.8% (six students) over the year of the experiment; three left school and three dropped out of foreign language classes. The attrition rate in the experimental group was higher, 18.5% (12 students). Six of the students left school for reasons not related to the program, and six more dropped out of the program's foreign language classes. In the school whose scheduling pattern did not allow students to study as a group, the three students enrolled in the program dropped out, indicating that there is some value in the group study aspect. The program's attrition rate of 18.5% is considerably lower than that encountered in traditional correspondence study programs where the rate can be as high as 30–40%.

ADAPTABILITY OF CONCEPT TO OTHER PLACES

The format is extremely adaptable. A similar program could be developed and conducted by a state education department, a university, or a consortium of school districts. The logistics of initiating a similar program would involve establishing a coordinating agency; choosing a textbook/workbook series on which to base the program; developing video and audio tapes to present and supplement the content of the textbook/workbook series; organizing films, tapes, and other supplementary materials; developing a study guide and orientation program; recruiting language instructors, actors, and television technicians; contacting schools; developing an effective orientation program for supervising teachers; establishing procedures for the distribution of materials and other interactions among the coordinating agency and the schools; and arranging for funding of the developmental costs of the program.

The concept is of course not restricted to French and Spanish; conceivably any language could be offered through a program of this kind. Nor is it necessary that the supervising teacher be a certified teacher; a paraprofessional, whether a native speaker or not, could serve in this capacity. The University of Colorado materials, or rights of reproduction renewable every four years, are available at a fee to other users.

AVAILABLE DESCRIPTIONS

"Spanish and French High School Foreign Language Programs," a six-page pamphlet describing the program, is available from the contact person, who also has available for distribution a 16-minute slide and tape presentation showing the program's development, methodology, and evaluation.

PROGRAM INITIATORS

David F. Mercer and Lynn T. Sandstedt, formerly of the Bureau of Independent Study, University of Colorado, Boulder.

CONTACT PERSON

Mildred Murphy Drake, Coordinator of Foreign Language Programs, Bureau of Independent Study, 970 Aurora Avenue, Boulder, Colorado 80302 (303) 443-2211

NOTE

[1] David F. Mercer, *A Comparison of Standard Classroom and Correspondence Study Instruction in First Year High School Spanish* (Madison: University of Wisconsin, 1971).

TOTAL IMMERSION LANGUAGE PROGRAM (TIP)

ABSTRACT

Dissatisfied with the low level of fluency students were reaching in foreign language courses and with the small number of students continuing into advanced language study, Commack High School North in Commack, New York initiated the Total Immersion Language Program (TIP), which proposes to simulate as closely as possible the amount of daily contact with a foreign language that residence abroad might give a student. TIP consists of a three-year sequence of year-long full courses and quarter-long mini-courses, conducted almost entirely in French or Spanish, in advanced language, literature, and other subjects ranging from cooking to American history. Students work with appropriate French or Spanish texts and materials and use the foreign language as the "primary medium of communication" for three class periods five days a week throughout the three-year sequence—a total of approximately 1500 contact hours. The program is open to all interested students who have successfully completed the first two levels of language study. Both the growth of the program and students' test scores indicate TIP's success in helping students achieve outstanding competence and proficiency in all four language skills.[1]

PROGRAM DEVELOPMENT AND PRESENT STATUS

TIP began in September 1968 as a three-year experiment in Spanish designed to discover whether a program of conducting a sequence of non-foreign-language courses in a foreign language was practical and beneficial: whether, for instance, students could learn history as well in Spanish as they might in English and also improve their foreign language skills at the same time. A series of tests given throughout the three years in both history and Spanish indicated that "total immersion" was a viable approach, and the low rate of attrition pointed out the high degree of continued interest among students.

The success of the experimental phase encouraged the foreign language department to expand the Total Immersion Language Program in 1970 to include a sequence in French and over ten mini- and full courses in both French and Spanish. TIP is now a viable and growing part of the foreign language curriculum at Commack High School North. There are 1345 students in the school, of whom 422 are enrolled in French and Spanish courses; of these, 42 French and 58 Spanish students are enrolled in the TIP sequence at all three levels, and 53 other students are enrolled in single TIP courses. In the future, the TIP staff hopes to establish an entire school modeled on the "total immersion" concept that could serve as a district or regional center for students interested in perfecting their foreign language skills.

TARGET AUDIENCE

Students of French or Spanish, grades 10 through 12, levels III, IV, and V. Participation is voluntary. Non-TIP students in advanced language courses may enroll in individual TIP courses.

REPRESENTATIVE CONTENT

The TIP sequence, in both French and Spanish, consists in the first year of year-long courses in World History and level III of the language, and mini-courses in Conversation, Cooking, and Art Appreciation; year-long courses in Composition, Readings in Literature, and American History, as well as mini-courses in Cooking, Current Events, and Music Appreciation in the second year; and, in the third year, year-long courses in Civilization and Human Dynamics and Great Ideas, as well as mini-courses in Advanced Conversation, Cooking, and French or Spanish Life. Except in the American and world history courses, both teachers and students use only the target language in class and use foreign language texts and materials almost exclusively. The American and world history courses must, by law, be conducted at least partly in English; TIP students, therefore, use both English and foreign language texts and materials and speak both English and French or Spanish in these classes. In all courses, students are encouraged to use the target language, no matter what mistakes they make; corrections, if made at all, are informal and quick, except in the advanced language classes which deal specifically with language problems.

The Art and Music Appreciation courses are basically survey courses in which the work of artists from cultures related to the target language is discussed and illustrated by slides, art books, and recordings. The types of music studied in the Music Appreciation course cross a spectrum running from opera to folk songs and rock. An attempt is made to integrate artistic movements with historical trends. The Cooking courses center on the cuisine and culinary customs of the cultures of the target language; in class, TIP students may prepare *paella* or *soupe à l'oignon* with metric measurements and foreign recipes, talk about the French attitude toward wine, or sit down to an ethnic dinner after school with other TIP students and their parents. Foreign language newspapers and magazines are the springboard for discussion in the Current Events class, but topics in the Conversation classes may range from sex roles to the weather. Civilization is an all-inclusive study of the history of cultures in the target language area, especially those of Spain and France; the course in French or Spanish Life, however, generally concentrates on the present everyday life of Frenchmen or Spaniards, including their recreation activities, sports, educational system, dating customs, and other topics interesting to teen-agers. The course in Great Ideas deals with basic philosophical themes and their expression in the writings of French or Spanish philosophers or novelists; a class might center on a discussion of the questions posed by Camus in *L'Étranger* or could zero in on a discussion of the Spanish, and the students' own, concept of happiness. Human Dynamics is a course developed in English at Commack High School North and translated into the target language for use in TIP; it encourages the students to deal with their personal feelings, philosophies, and ideas through the use of games and discussions. Speaking only in the foreign language, students might work out a solution to an ethical or moral dilemma ("Of ten people of different capabilities, ages, and sex, which ones would you save if your fallout shelter had room for only six?"), or might take part (or not) in a discussion on the problems of being introverted. The advanced language courses and Composition deal more formally with the development of the four language skills. And in the course called Readings in Literature, students read poetry, plays, excerpts from essays and novels, and one or two short novels.

At each of the three levels, a double period was set aside each Friday for audio-visual activities, but budgetary problems this year have caused the time to be under-utilized. Videotapes and live dramatic readings, skits, and plays are regularly presented in the foreign language by the TIP students.

METHODOLOGY

The approach to language teaching is audiolingual. Apart from the use of the foreign language in teaching non-language courses and an informal "rap-session" format in the Human Dynamics and Conversation courses, the methodology in the program is traditional.

STUDENT GROUPING AND
SCHEDULING ARRANGEMENTS

Students are grouped according to language level, and meet with their level for three periods daily; all three levels of French or Spanish meet together for a double period of audio-visual activities each Friday. The school is on a non-rotating schedule of eight 45-minute periods a day (one period is lunch). Each of the three mini-courses in each level lasts for one-third of the year and is taught by a different teacher; these courses meet five times a week. The Composition and Literature courses in grade 11 and the Human Dynamics and Great Ideas courses in grade 12 are each scheduled to meet two days a week throughout the year. And the courses in American History, World History, and Civilization meet five times a week throughout the year.

CREDIT AND ARTICULATION

TIP courses are equal in credit to regular courses; credit in the mini-courses is given in French or Spanish and, in the year-long courses, in the appropriate subject area. The language courses are sequential (III, IV, etc.) and the non-language courses increase in difficulty throughout the sequence.

ROLES OF TEACHERS AND PARAPROFESSIONALS

Team teaching is practiced whenever possible, and TIP teachers regularly consult with teachers in other curriculum areas. Teachers work with the program director and each other in counselling students and designing the curriculum; and they conduct and lead some extracurricular activities, including a weekly "HELP" language class and field trips. Native speakers visit the program occasionally to talk about their countries.

ROLES OF PROGRAM DIRECTOR AND
SPECIAL CONSULTANTS

The chairman of the foreign language department serves as a part-time director of TIP and is responsible for conducting program evaluations, organizing meetings with teachers and an annual meeting with parents, and for supervising the program organization and scheduling in cooperation with the school administration. Consultants from Experimental and Innovative Programs of the New York State Department of Education conducted an interim evaluation of the program in 1968, and aided the director in the preparation of a technical report on the final results of the experimental phase in 1969.

ROLE OF PARENTS

Parents of qualified sophomore students are invited to the school each year for a meeting on TIP, which is conducted in part by parents already involved in the program. Parents attend frequent foreign dinners at the school as well as plays and skits presented by the students.

TRAINING REQUIREMENTS

There is no special training program for the total-immersion language teachers, but it is self-evident that they must be qualified in another subject area, and the director notes that the TIP teachers as a group possess "goodly amounts of patience, enthusiasm, and understanding" that undoubtedly contribute to the success of the program.

FUNDING AND COSTS

The cost of all aspects of development and operation in the experimental phase of TIP, approximately $64,000, was met jointly by the New York State Department of Education and Commack Public Schools. At present TIP is funded through regular district allocations. The annual expenditure per pupil in the district is $1600.

The $64,000 developmental costs included the teachers' salaries over the three years, released time for meetings on curriculum development, resource materials and books for a small library, textbooks, and audio-visual equipment. In the first year, TIP teachers and the director were each provided with one extra released period per day. There are now no special or additional operational costs for TIP.

PROGRAM EVALUATION

In the first year of the experimental phase, the TIP students were matched with a control group of Spanish III students, who were also enrolled in a regular World History course, on the bases of sex, I.Q. as measured by the Lorge-Thorndike Intelligence Tests, scores on both the Iowa Test of Educational Development (ITED) and the Verbal Reasoning Section of the Differential Aptitude Test (DAT), and final grades in the grade 9 social studies course. A difference in favor of the TIP students in their Spanish II final grades was compensated for in evaluating the test results. The TIP group and all but four of the students in the control group had the same teacher for Spanish III, but the TIP students were all in the same class.

An extensive testing program utilizing *A-LM* Spanish III Unit Tests (1962 edition), the New York State Regents' Examinations in Spanish III and World History, and tests prepared by the high school staff was conducted with the TIP and control groups in the first year. In the second year, the TIP group and a (non-control) group of Spanish IV students were administered the MLA Cooperative Foreign Language Test in Spanish (Form MA), which has national norms. And, during the third year of the experiment, the TIP group was given the College Entrance Examination Board's Spanish Listening Comprehension, Achievement, and Advanced Placement examinations, and took the MB form of the MLA Cooperative Foreign Language Test in Spanish at the end of the year.

The TIP students scored slightly higher in the Regents' Examination in World History in the first year, indicating that they were learning as much in a TIP non-language course as the control group in a regular world history course. And the mean score of the TIP students was 17% higher than the control group on the Spanish III Regents' Examination, even when their scores were adjusted to compensate for their generally higher grades in Spanish II. Thus the results of the first-year testing program indicated that TIP was both beneficial and practical.

By the end of the third year, the mean scores of the TIP students on the College Entrance Examination Board Spanish tests in Listening Comprehension and Achievement were higher than those of 90 percent of the students in the national norm group. And in the MLA (Form MB) test, the mean scores of the TIP students placed the group at the 99.9 midpercentile rank in speaking, 99.4 in writing, 99 in listening, and 93 in reading in the fourth-year high school norm group.

The director of TIP places several limitations on the interpretation of these data in recognizing that there was an initial difference between the students in the TIP group and those in the control group "in terms of motivation, interest, and willingness to submit oneself to a different and probably more demanding experience." This difference was controlled to some extent, but the director notes that "adherence to a strict experimental design would have required random assignment of volunteering students to the experimental and control groups as well as the inclusion of non-volunteers in the program." However, the test results of the TIP students do seem to indicate the value of the program in helping students attain high levels of competence and proficiency in a foreign language.

ADAPTABILITY OF CONCEPT TO OTHER PLACES

The three primary considerations in adapting the total immersion concept to other schools are student interest, the capabilities and qualifications of the teachers, and the availability of funds for purchasing materials and texts and time for curriculum writing. Some of the TIP courses, such as those in cooking or composition, could be adapted fairly easily; others, such as Human Dynamics, would require a great deal more time and imagination to develop or adapt to different situations. But there is no need to adapt "whole cloth." The teachers involved in the experimental phase at Commack felt that two classes a day would have been sufficient to meet the program's goals, and indicated that many variations in the content and type of courses and activities are possible; in the experimental phase, for instance, the students met every lunch hour for 30 minutes of conversation, slide shows, and other activities related to Spanish and the Hispanic cultures, and some of the courses were quite different from those now included in the sequence.

Other considerations in adapting the total immersion concept include the possible impact of the program on other curriculum areas and any state or local requirements that might apply. Some features of the Commack program itself, such as the weekly double period of audio-visual activities, depend on the school's scheduling patterns and the cooperation of the school administration. At least one high school, Xaverian High School in Brooklyn, New York, has used the Commack experience in developing its own very successful program. And in 1968 evaluators from the New York State Department of Education wrote that TIP "deserves emulation in some schools throughout the state."

AVAILABLE DESCRIPTIONS

A program guide is available from the Bureau of School and Cultural Research, State Education Department, Albany, New York 12224. A technical report (BSCR-002-71), centering on a description of the evaluation procedures and results of the experimental phase of the program, is also available from the Bureau of School and Cultural Research, or from ERIC (ERIC ED 053 586). TIP was described briefly in Barbara Ort and Dwight R.

Smith, "The Language Teacher Tours the Curriculum," *Foreign Language Annals*, 3 (1969), 55–57.

CONTACT PERSON

Stefano Morel, Chairman, Foreign Language Department, Commack High School North, Commack, New York 11725 (516) 449-5800

NOTE

[1] Quotations throughout are from the *Technical Report on the Total Immersion Language Program* (BSCR-002-71) prepared by Stefano Morel and distributed through the New York State Department of Education.

SECTION II

ABERDEEN-L'UNION JUMELAGE

Pen pals have been around a long time, but intercontinental exchanges between entire classes as a basic part of foreign language study are relatively recent. The Aberdeen-l'Union Jumelage began in the fall of 1970 with a twinning of 38 level II French students at Aberdeen High School in Aberdeen, Maryland with an equal number of students at a comparable level of English study at the Collège d'Enseignement Secondaire in l'Union, France. Students exchanged personal letters, photos, records, and small gifts with their French pen pals, and made class exchanges of tapes and slides. In March of the second year of the twinning, 30 French pupils and their teacher visited Aberdeen for two weeks, and, the following June, 35 American students spent two weeks in l'Union. In the third year, correspondence between the two original groups continued, and a new exchange was begun between level II students in Aberdeen and their counterparts in l'Union, with an exchange of visits planned for 1974.

The program director originally made contact with the French students through a French friend in l'Union whose son's English teacher agreed to the twinning and later made arrangements for the homestays in France. Although only 38 of the Aberdeen students had pen pals the first year, the entire level III group of more than 60 students was involved in some aspect of the exchange the second year. Those who had no pen pals suggested and prepared materials for class exchanges, worked on publicity, wrote letters of thanks, participated in almost all the planning and activities for the French students' visit, and helped plan their classmates' trip in June. Meanwhile, for two years much of the cultural focus in French class was on l'Union and the Toulouse area; students studied the contrasts between the two countries, prepared class exchanges, and shared their letters from France.

When the French students came to Aberdeen, living in most cases with their pen pals' families, they spent one week in school going to classes and speaking to students studying French and one week during Easter vacation in out-of-school activities. The project had begun with a relatively small group of parents, students, and teachers, but soon spilled over into the entire school, town, and county. The visiting students met the town mayor and a state senator, were received by numerous community and fraternal groups, met with an unexpectedly large number of visiting students from other schools, and were invited to visit the U.S. Army Ordnance Center in Aberdeen as well as the behind-the-counter operations of the local McDonalds. They also visited the White House and monuments in Washington, D.C., took a trip to New York City, Atlantic City, and Amish country, and visited a nearby Coca-Cola plant.

When the Aberdeen group returned the visit, accompanied by the director and another French-speaking teacher, they flew Air France to Paris and then immediately boarded a train for l'Union. At the train station in Toulouse, they were greeted by television cameras and 40 majorettes. They attended the last week of school with their pen pals, spoke to many English classes, were received at the town hall by the mayor and city council, attended parties in private homes, were given a tour of Toulouse by the assistant mayor, and visited such places as the building grounds for the supersonic Concorde, the offices of the daily paper, a wine and fruit cooperative, and the historical sites of Carcassonne and Rocamadour. Individual families took their guests to such places as Albi, Lourdes, and Andorra. Following the homestay, the group toured Paris for three days.

There is no doubt in the minds of the students, teachers, and parents involved that the twinning program has been a success. Close friendships and understandings and continued exchanges are just some of the results. Enthusiasm and generosity on the part of parents and community groups in both countries overwhelmed the participants; an overflow of parents volunteered to house students in Aberdeen, while in l'Union arrangements for the homestay brought many French parents and the teacher together for the first time. The visits were widely publicized in local newspapers in both countries, and the American mayor and governor continue to send Christmas greetings to l'Union. All those involved agree that the Jumelage not only gave the students a concrete reason to study French, but also gave them the opportunity to use the language in a personal, meaningful, and instructive way.

TARGET AUDIENCE

Students of all abilities, levels II through IV of French.

COSTS

All travel arrangements were made by the director with the assistance of a local travel agency. Each student paid $330 to cover all train, plane, and bus transportation as well as hotel and food costs in Paris. Students were responsible for securing their own money. A "travelship" for two students was contributed by various fraternal organizations in Aberdeen. Host families donated room and board. Incidental costs for postage and film processing during the exchange were paid primarily by students.

CONTACT PERSON

Ethel Sellman, Chairman, Department of Foreign Languages, Aberdeen Senior High School, Paradise Road, Aberdeen, Maryland 21001 (301) 272-3663

ADVANCED
FRENCH
CONVERSATION

Cassette recorders are the key to personalized language instruction in an advanced French conversation course at the Wheatley School in Old Westbury, New York. Each semester 15 seniors who have completed their foreign language requirements participate in a one-semester elective course designed to enable them to speak with fluency on a wide range of topics.

With texts providing an initial vocabulary base, students examine in class each week one aspect of French or American life, using French newspapers and magazines, recorded French radio broadcasts, films, and tapes as the basis for informal, round-table discussions. Classes are one period long and meet five days a week. Homework assignments involve the use of each student's cassette tape recorder and are given in two forms that alternate each week. At the end of one week's discussion, each student prepares a 10- to 15-minute cassette recording in which he discusses any aspect of the subject covered in class; reads a poem, article, or story for pronunciation practice; and talks freely on any topic he chooses—from music or sports to current events or personal problems. The teacher answers each student personally on tape, makes corrections, gives drills on weak points, and comments on classroom work. The following week students work with a 30-minute teacher-prepared cassette recording and mimeographed sheets that provide questions, vocabulary, and directions. These tapes may include short-wave radio broadcasts and related questions that students answer orally or in writing, popular French songs for dictation and word identification, and grammar drills that use song excerpts, skits, vocabulary games, or jokes. Each student prepares a total of five tapes and completes five teacher-prepared tapes during the semester. Credit is given on a pass-fail basis.

Students have responded positively to the cassette exercises: they have consistently prepared longer recordings than required, have asked that the course be extended to one full year, and in end-of-semester evaluations agreed that the course was enjoyable and beneficial. Michael Agatstein, the teacher and initiator of the course, notes that they have approached the taped free discussions with imagination: "One student played the music of 'Peter and the Wolf' and told the entire story in French along with the music. Another played a background recording of the sounds at a Cape Kennedy moon shot with appropriate comments. One student dared to give me a 15-minute discussion on the theories of Pascal, and when I responded with some opposite points of view, carried on the discussion in his next cassette." Agatstein has found that students who are shy in class open up on cassettes, that students can prepare their tapes and respond to his at their own rate, that he can make corrections without embarrassing the student, and that the mutual feedback has indeed made French a personalized experience. Over 50 observers from high schools and colleges have reacted favorably to the course format and results.

TARGET AUDIENCE

Students in grade 12 who have completed foreign language requirements in French.

MATERIALS

Cassette recorders for each student; a basic text, *L'Art de la conversation* (Harper and Row); newspapers and magazines from France; films; and teacher-prepared recordings of radio broadcasts in French.

COSTS

Students purchase their own cassette recorders, approximately $40 each, and their own cassettes. Texts and other materials are financed through the regular school budget.

AVAILABLE DESCRIPTION

A speech delivered by Agatstein at the AECD/NALLD Seventh Annual Business Meeting, March 1971, "Individualization of Language Learning through the Cassette Recorder," appears in the *Journal of the National Association of Language Laboratory Directors*, December 1971.

CONTACT PERSON

Michael Agatstein, Wheatley School, Bacon Road, Old Westbury, New York 11568 (516) 334-8020

AUGUST MARTIN
HIGH SCHOOL
FOREIGN
LANGUAGE
PROGRAM

"Fasten your seat belts" and "clear the runway" may not be typical dialogue sentences in most foreign language courses, but they show up frequently at August Martin High School in Jamaica, New York, where most courses have an aviation "slant." In 1971 the school, located just one mile from Kennedy International Airport, was converted into a comprehensive high school that offers courses related to aviation and the air transport industry in addition to a full academic curriculum. Students can elect programs leading to higher education, employment in business and industry, or specialized work in aviation-related fields. Among the school's requirements for all students are one year of typing, one year of practical arts, and two years of foreign language study. Each year 600 volunteer freshman students are accepted at the school; in 1972–73 there are 1200 students in grades 9 and 10, and by 1974–75 the school will be filled to its capacity of 2400 students in grades 9 through 12.

Language courses are offered in French and Spanish; they develop all four skills and use standard audiolingual texts and methods. However, at all levels the vocabulary of aviation is integrated into the regular lessons whenever appropriate. For example, in a unit on food, students might simulate a dialogue between an air hostess and passengers having a meal on board. In a unit on travel, "take-off" and "landing" would naturally be worked into a dialogue between a tourist and a ticket agent. Spanish IV currently involves the study of literature balanced with activities related to the topic "Hotels and Motels," and career electives are planned in both languages as more students move into advanced levels in grades 11 and 12. Language students have visited Air France and Iberia Airline terminals at Kennedy Airport, and some students observed a class at a stewardess training center. Throughout the first year, five airline hostesses who spoke French and Spanish volunteered to work with students in the resource center as their flight schedules permitted.

The school year at August Martin is divided into four ten-week cycles and the day into 18-minute modules. The schedule provides for at least two modules of independent study each day for each student and the integration of "extracurricular" activities into the school day. In foreign languages, class meetings are held four times a week for a total of ten modules, and students may use the free modules on the fifth day to go to the language resource center for assistance from a teacher or paraprofessional or for practice with taped drills in a laboratory donated by Pan American World Airways. A system of flexible grouping allows students to be transferred from one ability group to another, and the four-cycle year permits students to repeat one phase of work for ten weeks, rather than be "kept back" for a whole semester. There are special courses that let students complete one year's work in two years or three year's work in two and courses with an emphasis on conversational skills for students with low English-reading scores. Some students choose to study a second foreign language independently during their free modules with the aid of a teacher in the resource center. And special assistance is available at foreign language tutorial sessions before the school day begins.

Airport facilities are often used for "off-campus" instruction in a variety of subjects, and a flight simulator is being built within the school itself. Airlines have treated students to flights for aerial geography lessons and talks with pilots, technicians, and airport personnel. Students meet at least twice per cycle with guidance counselors to determine their course of study or any grouping readjustments that might be needed, and other "orientation" is provided through collections of career-related literature available in the Occupational Resource Center and foreign language travel posters liberally scattered throughout the school building. An Advisory Committee for the school appointed by the Board of Education is headed by an employee of one major airline; and representatives from other aviation industries, labor unions, parent groups, and area colleges have cooperated in planning for maximum use of local facilities to expose students to an industry that may one day employ them.

TARGET AUDIENCE

Students apply voluntarily to August Martin and are accepted on the basis of reading scores and attendance records in junior high school. To recruit students, brochures are sent to feeder schools, and administrators from August Martin present assembly programs in the junior highs explaining the program. Students who apply to the school are aware that they will be required to take two years of foreign language.

CONTACT PERSON

Samuel J. Larocca, Chairman, Department of Foreign Languages, August Martin High School, 156-10 Baisley Boulevard, Jamaica, New York 11434 (212) 528-2920

COMPUTER-
ASSISTED
INDEPENDENT
LATIN
STUDY

Ten students at University High School in Urbana, Illinois are doing two years of independent Latin study in one with the help of a computer system named PLATO III (Programmed Logic for Automatic Teaching Operations). The system consists of a CDC 1604 computer connected with student stations at the University of Illinois's Computer-Based Education Research Laboratory, across the street from the high school. Each student station has a television monitor, which can show photographic slides and student- and computer-generated words and diagrams, and an electronic keyboard, like a typewriter's, with alphabetic and numeric symbols and several "functional" keys. The functional keys give a student control over the computer program; for instance, he presses -NEXT- to have an answer evaluated and move on, -ERASE- to erase a mistake, and -HELP-, -DATA-, or -LAB- to use audio-visual or other materials not included in the lesson's main program sequence. The programs were written by Richard

T. Scanlan, a professor at the University of Illinois, using a computer "language" called TUTOR that was especially designed for people with little experience in programming.

Once a week, at a scheduled time, the students meet voluntarily with the Latin teacher for any help they may need; they also meet with the teacher at other scheduled times during the week for individual tests on the week's work. The rest of the time, generally about four to seven hours a week, the students work with their textbooks and with the computer. On beginning a computer lesson program, the student first sees a "choice table" that tells him what the various parts of the lesson are and lets him choose the order in which he will do them. At this point, he may use the lesson's final test as a pretest to see if he needs to complete all the lesson's components. The student then begins the lesson.

The lesson programs contain translation exercises, vocabulary, grammar explanations, dialogues, drills, and series of questions, called "problems," that the student solves using previously learned or given information. Given a problem, the student types his answer, presses -NEXT-, and if the computer checks his answer as correct, moves on. If the answer is not correct, however, the computer may "branch" him into progressively easier problems or series of problems based on the same concept until he deduces a correct response. A student may also elect to do the alternative problems if he wants more practice. Where appropriate, the computer has been programmed to accept more than one correct answer as well as to address students by name and to type out "Bravo" and other encouraging words when the student solves certain problems. It has also been programmed to judge sentences; it crosses out incorrect words in a student's translation, underlines misspelled words, and indicates with arrows the proper placement of words that are out of order. The computer also stores, for a limited time, both the correct and incorrect responses individual students make; the teacher occasionally inspects the answers so as to be better able to identify students' learning problems. Working with the computer, students tend to progress about twice as fast as they do in a regular class; this enables them to complete two years' work in one.

PLATO III is also used by several students in Urbana High

School to learn reading and writing in Russian, and by University of Illinois students to learn French, Russian, Latin, Chinese, Japanese, and Spanish. The University of Illinois is currently installing a more sophisticated computer system, called PLATO IV, that will have a new plasma panel display unit (replacing the television monitor) and slide projector, a larger computer, and an audio component that will enable students to record and respond to verbal messages. PLATO IV will be able to handle as many as 4000 student stations throughout the state and nation on a time-sharing basis. No doubt the number of schools using computers in teaching foreign language will expand once PLATO IV is installed. The estimated rental costs for PLATO IV are $0.50 per student per terminal hour; this covers all operating costs.

CONTACT PERSON

Richard T. Scanlan, Associate Professor of Classics, 4072 Foreign Language Building, University of Illinois, Urbana, Illinois 61801 (217) 333-1008

CONCORDIA
LANGUAGE
VILLAGES

"The next best thing to being there" is the slogan of the Concordia Language Villages, a foreign language summer camp program sponsored by Concordia College in Moorhead, Minnesota, where campers in the village of Bretagne can play *boules* or use francs to shop at their local *confiserie*, and where those in the *Skogfjorden* snack on sardines before rehearsing a scene from *Peer Gynt*. Along the wooded lakefronts of Minnesota are separate camps for five different languages—French, Norwegian, German, Russian, and Spanish—each simulating the ambiance of the countries where the language is spoken. Beginning, Intermediate, and Advanced campers, ranging in age from 9 to 18, work and live with a staff of teachers and counselors from the U.S. and abroad for two-week sessions. They learn and use their chosen language around the campfire, on the beaches and trails, as well as in more formalized open-air classes conducted with special camp-oriented curriculum guides. The program includes an intensive "credit course" for students who stay for four weeks and wish to have their progress at camp recommended for credit at their home schools. There are also German, French, and Norwegian camps in the mountains of Montana, where hiking and climbing take precedence over sea-level sports, and a new program begun in 1972 enables some campers to actually go "there" to camp along the trails of Europe and Mexico.

Emphasis is on the informal use of the target language in all camp activities: meals, shopping at the kiosk, swimming, canoeing, arts and crafts, skits, folk dancing and singing, horseback riding, hiking, fencing, soccer, and sports and arts related to specific foreign countries. Eating the *norsk koldtbord* Viking breakfast in the Norwegian camp, dining on *borsch* in the Russian villages, or being served *tacos* and *paella* in the Spanish camp help acquaint campers with the foreign cultures. The French students celebrate Mardi Gras—a bit off season—and have their own orchestra and chorale, while the German campers publish a newspaper, put on a *Maskenball*, and stage *Wilhelm Tell*.

In the more formal large- and small-group instruction, English is used as little as possible; hand signals, pictures, realia (kitchen utensils, sports equipment), flash cards, and posters are used to aid in comprehension. Short dialogues, word games, and a variety of drills are used in an oral-aural approach to instruction at the first two levels. Teachers try to build student confidence and feelings that the language is fun, and to prevent stumbling, boredom, meaningless parroting, and feelings of failure. Games like Buzz, providing number practice, or Simon Says are played in each small-group session, and, rather than talk about volleyball, students play it during instruction time, learning the vocabulary as the game proceeds. All dialogues in the student manual relate to the camp experience, focusing on topics like sports, outdoor clothing, the weather, and typical cabin talk. At the Advanced level, dialogues are replaced by a printed narrative, conversation, article, or song that serves as a springboard to directed conversation. Subjects range from pop singers in the foreign country to nature, "franglais," and ghost stories.

Deans for each language camp are qualified language teachers who etsablish the program's content, scheduling, and staffing, and meet monthly during the year for planning and evaluation. The counselors are American and foreign teachers and college students who assume a variety of roles. "One time a counselor may be teaching a folk song; at another time, selling the camper [a coke] . . . all in the language. The relationship between teachers and students is a very informal one, but it's also one that is nurtured over a 24-hour-a-day period." The staff also includes counselors-in-training, registered nurses, lifeguards, and food service personnel. Staff members meet with the director and coordinator (both from Concordia College) for three weekend symposiums in the spring and for two days before camp begins for an introduction to the general camp philosophy and training in the use of the curriculum guide and audiolingual techniques.

TARGET AUDIENCE

Students of all abilities, ages 9 to 18, with or without previous language study. For the four-week credit program, it is recommended that candidates be ready to enter at least the ninth grade, "be highly motivated, and reflect an enthusiastic interest in foreign languages."

MATERIALS

Teachers' guides and student manuals were prepared for each level in each language under a grant from the Louis W. and Maud Hill Family Foundation. The manuals contain dialogues and pictorial materials. The teachers' guides give directions for methods of presentation and provide many games and songs, translations, and vocabulary.

COSTS TO STUDENTS

Costs to students range from $165 for the two-week sessions at any of the Minnesota camps to $275 at one of the Montana camps; the programs abroad range from $595 for three weeks in Mexico to $1195 for five weeks in Russia.

CONTACT PEOPLE

Odell M. Bjerkness, Director, Language Village Program, Professor of Modern Languages, or Alvin P. Traaseth, Coordinator for International Programs, Concordia College, Moorhead, Minnesota 56560 (218) 299-4544

NOTE

[1] Quotations are from the survey questionnaire.

COORDINATION
OF
SKILLS IN
AN
INDIVIDUALIZED
PROGRAM

Four different kinds of activity groupings, made possible by modular scheduling, are the backbone of individualized instruction in French at Norman High School in Norman, Oklahoma. The school day is divided into 15-minute modules, several of which are unscheduled and used as "Independent Study Time" by all students in the school. For the French program, which involves 150 students at four levels, two teachers developed behavioral objectives and learning packets, based on text units, that cover individual grammatical concepts and cultural materials. Students work on these units during Independent Study Time, while three different kinds of classroom sessions are used at each level to develop speaking and listening skills through an audiolingual approach. The purpose of individualization in this program is not so much to allow for complete self-pacing as to enable students to do out of class the reading and grammar work they can do without direct supervision and to use class time and its "socializing atmosphere" for intensive oral practice.

272

Students meet in "Large Groups" (for example, all 50 students in French I) for one two-module block each week; an initial presentation of the unit is made, and students are given unit information sheets that direct them to explanations in the texts and exercises in the workbooks. During their Independent Study Time, they work with these sheets on their own and complete written and taped exercises, reading assignments, and vocabulary-building work. They then check their results with a key and report to the teacher in the lab for individual help, testing, and, if necessary, retesting. The amount of time spent in the lab for these activities varies from two to ten modules per week, depending on individual students' needs.

Students also meet with their teacher in "Small Groups" of 10 to 15 for one three-module block a week. These sessions focus on conversation and directed dialogues, which reinforce orally those items dealt with in the unit exercises. Finally, "Lab Group" sessions with about 25 students are held twice weekly for two-module blocks for quick-change drills on tape and oral practice of the exercises in the text; these activities are conducted by the teacher in lockstep fashion.

Broad deadlines are established for the completion of each unit. Students work as much as possible at their own rates within these deadlines, spend more time when necessary on individual problems, and take written and oral tests individually. They may retake tests until achieving a minimum of 75 percent mastery, as long as they do so within the specified time limit. Faster students may move to more advanced units if they complete the unit exercises and pass the unit tests before the deadline, but it is preferred that they work on enrichment or special-interest units rather than move too far ahead of the class. These supplementary units focus on comprehension and speaking skills, practical or specialized vocabulary, and French culture and history.

Considerable time and flexibility are demanded of teachers. However, the program director believes that students learn more easily when they do not feel pressured to move ahead before mastering a given topic and know they can be retested without penalty. This, she believes, justifies the increased demands on teachers. The director also states that the same approach could be used in a traditional scheduling system by setting aside certain days of the week for independent study.

TARGET AUDIENCE

Students of all abilities, grades 9–12, French levels I–IV.

PHYSICAL FACILITIES

Language laboratory with teacher console and audio-active units for 30 students.

FUNDING

The program and language laboratory are funded through the annual school budget expenditure of $562 per pupil.

CONTACT PERSON

Virginia Bell, Norman High School, 900 West Main Street, Norman, Oklahoma 73069 (405) 321-7410

DELAWARE-PANAMA
EXCHANGE
PROGRAM

Under the Alliance for Progress, the state of Delaware and the Republic of Panama are paired as "Partners of the Americas." This partnership was used to the benefit of many schools and students by the creation of the Delaware-Panama Exchange Program. The Delaware Supervisor of Foreign Language Education, with local members of the Partners of the Americas and the Delaware branch of the American Association of Teachers of Spanish and Portuguese, piloted an exchange program in the summer of 1966 involving four students of Spanish from two high schools in the Dover area. For six weeks they lived as guests in the homes of young people their own age in the City of Panama and attended classes at the Instituto Pan-Americano, a bilingual high school. The following March, six students and two teachers from the Instituto came to Dover for a six-week stay. By 1971, the program had grown to include 30 schools in Delaware, which hosted 93 students and teachers from Panama City and the Chiriqui

Province, and sent more than 40 Delaware students to Panama. Except for one year's interlude at the time of a junta takeover in Panama, the program has been running smoothly for seven years.

In Panama the Delaware students attend classes in Spanish and serve as native-speaker aides in English classes at their Panamanian schools. The Panamanian students in Delaware go to the schools in the area of their host families, attending classes in English and acting as Spanish-speaking aides. In addition, there is an exchange of teachers, who may provide instruction in their native language or use the language of their host country to teach mathematics, arts and crafts, home economics, or history, or talk about their country to a variety of classes. In Panama, the Delaware students have met the President of the Republic and the American Ambassador, and have visited places of interest in Panama City, the beaches of San Carlos and Coronado, the Island of Taboga, and the Canal Zone. They have been treated to many special fiestas, and, most importantly, have lived the way of life of their host families, speaking Spanish as their major language. The Panamanian visitors to Delaware have met city and state officials, spent weekends visiting New York City, Washington, D.C., and Williamsburg, and made field trips to local museums and other cultural spots. They frequently give musical programs and poetry recitations to their host schools or local civic groups, and have started a "fiesta circuit" right in Delaware.

A member of the Partners of the Americas who was also a teacher at the Instituto and teachers from David, Panama have served as coordinators of the Panama phase. The Delaware State Supervisor of Foreign Language Education coordinated the Delaware phase until her departure from the state in 1971, when the responsibility was assumed by the Delaware branch of the AATSP. The coordinators set up the procedures for selection of participants in their respective countries and arrange for living accommodations, travel, and reception of visiting students. They also provide special study sessions for the participants before departure involving individual readings and informal talks about life in the host country. The warmth and generosity offered by host families in both countries, the interest shown by various civic groups, and the very positive reactions of the participants in their evaluations of the program indicate that the exchange has indeed achieved its objective of cross-cultural understanding. Some students felt that they became more proficient in the foreign language during the six-week trip than in their previous years of language study, and the presence of native-speaker aides in so many classrooms has been a culturally-enriching and motivating experience. The exchange-related activities of the Partners of the Americas have also spilled over into several college-level activities—an exchange of agricultural students and resources, for example.

TARGET AUDIENCE

The program is open to selected students from Delaware who have completed at least two levels of high school Spanish, who "will represent well [their] families, schools, and the State of Delaware," who are recommended by their Spanish teacher, who have a doctor's certificate of good health, and who are willing to live according to the customs and rules of the homes and the society in the host country, to serve as aides in English classes, and to attend other classes taught in Spanish.[1]

MAJOR GOALS

(1) "To use the bond of common interest in language study found among young people of Delaware and young people of the Republic of Panama to further their knowledge of each other's country and hopefully their mutual understanding and respect"; (2) to help promote the study of Spanish and English in each country by providing a "greater sense of reality" to foreign language study.

FUNDING AND COSTS

Participants pay for their own trips. Estimate of total costs, including round-trip air fare, travel in Panama, travel and health insurance, passports, and spending money, is $400. Host families provide room and board free of charge. Administrative costs are borne by "interested persons," civic groups, and contributions from the Partners of the Americas.

PROGRAM INITIATOR

Genelle Caldwell, former Supervisor of Foreign Language Education for the Delaware State Department of Public Instruction, now Coordinator of Foreign Language Education, Henrico County Public Schools, Box 40, Highland Springs, Virginia 23075

CONTACT PEOPLE

Sharon Chaffinch, 302 Cedar Street, Bridgeville, Delaware 19933; William H. Bohning, Coordinator of Foreign Languages, Newark School District, Newark, Delaware 19711; Joan Abraham, 216 Pennsylvania Avenue, Dover, Delaware 19901

NOTE

[1] Quotations are from "Criteria for Selection of Students, Chaperones, and Programs of Foreign Study and Travel Abroad," *A Guide to Curriculum Development* (State of Delaware: Department of Public Instruction, 1968).

EDMONDS
GERMAN
LANGUAGE
SCHOOL

Some teachers may feel they stand on their heads to get their students to learn, but in the Edmonds German Language School in Edmonds, Washington it's students who stand on theirs, and they appear to be learning German quite well. Every Saturday morning about 45 self-enrolled students, ranging in age from 4 to 65, meet for three hours in the classrooms of a local parochial school to learn or practice German in a variety of ways. Some stand on their heads and do rolls and flips in gymnastics classes conducted in German; others learn German folk dances and songs; others learn recorder pieces by Bach and Telemann, or practice in the school's string quartet. In slightly more formal language classes, audiolingual drills are used and are often varied with other types of exercises. A couple of advanced or intermediate students might get together for a conversation session with a teacher, while around them four-year-olds learn vocabulary words by pasting magazine pictures in a scrapbook. Two seven-year-olds and some onlookers may be in the corner learning how to count while playing checkers, and some younger ones might be playing ring-around-the-rosy in German. Bingo, Hangman, and other word and number games are very popular, and all classes are treated to frequent slide shows and films to gain a good picture of Germany and German life. Special individualized tutoring is available after class, but most of the classes are so small they amount to the same thing. For fun, some native German speakers, friends of the teachers, volunteer to help students learn grammar, lead folk dances, give lectures, or just talk with individual students. There are no tests, no grades, and, for credit, only the satisfaction students feel themselves.

The fall quarter is highlighted by a Christmas pageant, complete with carols, ensemble music, and *Krippenspiel*. At the end of the spring and summer quarters, the school holds a *Maifest* and a *Sommerfest* in which each class displays its talents and achievements in plays, puppet shows, folk dancing, music, and gymnastics. The school makes frequent field trips to a lodge in the Cascade Mountains, owned by a German social and travel club, for picnics and contact with Germans. And the students go to German restaurants for parties and to German food or import shops to talk and shop.

The Edmonds German Language School was founded in the spring of 1971 by a group of parents, German teachers, and a professor at the University of Washington. The school is incorporated as a nonprofit organization, with a board of directors elected at an annual meeting of the adult students, parents, and teachers. The board appoints a treasurer, contracts with the parish to use the school, approves financial transactions, and appoints a principal. The principal, who is usually also a teacher, chooses the teachers. Most of the five teachers are native speakers, some are teachers in local colleges or schools, all have been to Germany, and most importantly, for the students and the school, all are committed to the school's motto—"Learning can be fun!" Some have special talents—in music, for instance—that they put to use in the school's programs. In past years, the Edmonds German Language School has served as an inservice training ground for prospective German FLES teachers. One summer it was the site of a week-long demonstration workshop for German teachers interested in unusual approaches to language teaching. At times there have been up to 70 students enrolled in the school. There are about 15 similar schools throughout the state, some of which provide instruction in as many as four languages.

FUNDING AND COSTS

The school year is divided into four quarters, with vacations that coincide with those of the public schools. Students may register for as many quarters as they like. Tuition is $24 a quarter or $64 a year. Students are also required to pay an annual registration fee of $3 per family and an annual insurance premium of $1.50 per student. From these fees, the school rents the classrooms, pays the teachers, and covers developmental, office, and materials costs. Teachers are paid $5 an hour. Board members serve without pay. The local German Consulate occasionally provides books, travel and other films, publicity, and contact with native speakers. The school also acquired some textbooks when a local school district replaced its textbook series with another.

AVAILABLE DESCRIPTIONS

Willi W. Fischer, F. William D. Love, and Victor E. Hanzeli, "Community-Based Foreign Language Teaching in Washington," *Modern Language Journal,* 40 (1971), 514–18.

PROGRAM INITIATOR

Willi W. Fischer, Department of German, Denny Hall, University of Washington, Seattle, Washington 98105

CONTACT PERSON

Virginia Low, Principal, Edmonds German Language School, P.O. Box 268, Edmonds, Washington 98020

FLEXIBLE FOREIGN LANGUAGE CLASSROOM

The Flexible Foreign Language Classroom, now in its second year at the Walden School in New York, New York, is a modified open-classroom program of individualized instruction in French or Spanish. The director recommends the format for "teachers who have to work alone, with little financial or material help, who would like to individualize their classrooms [and] provide for greater oral practice on the part of their students." All 175 students in the high school are required to take three years of one language; there are approximately 18 students in each foreign language class. The program was started in French II and III (the classes taught by the program director) and now also includes two levels of Spanish.

Half of each class period is conducted in a traditional manner; students meet as a group with the teacher for conversation practice, presentation of cultural material, written tests, and explanations of grammar. In the remainder of the period, students may work alone, completing written exercises at their desks or tables in the back of the room or using the tapes in a special area at the side of the room. They may work with partners, drilling each other orally with teacher-prepared worksheets complete with answers, or meet in small groups for conversation and practice with dialogues. Foreign language games, puzzles, and comic books are available for those who want to take a break. Faster students frequently help slower ones, and twelfth-grade French students work as assistants in lower-level classes in the program, receiving advanced credit. The teacher circulates among the students helping with individual problems.

In their individual work students progress as much as possible at their own rates, but are required to meet specified (but generous) deadlines for each unit; following a guide prepared by the teacher, they complete a sequence of both written and recorded exercises and take individual oral quizzes based on these exercises at any time they choose within the specified period. Faster students who have completed the exercises and passed all the oral quizzes before the deadlines may work with supplementary tapes, written exercises, and readings selected with teacher guidance from the open bookcase at the side of the room. Slower students work with teacher-prepared remedial worksheets and may receive more individual assistance from the teacher or teaching assistants during the time allotted for individual work. Written unit quizzes are given to the class as a whole at dates announced well in advance. Students who fail are given remedial work and help and can retake the test if they choose.

The program demands a lot of time from the teacher for preparation of guides and worksheets. It does not require a great deal of hardware. For each classroom, there are two reel-to-reel tape recorders, ten headsets and two jackboxes, two microphones, sets of commercially prepared tapes and teacher-prepared tapes, a bookshelf, and file cabinets for students' individual worksheets and records. The director stresses that the basic format of the Flexible Classroom can be adjusted to suit different needs or resources in other schools; emphasis could be placed, for instance, on independent study, small-group conversation, reading, writing, listening, or speaking.

FUNDING AND COSTS

The program is funded through the regular school budget. Equipment costs are $200 per classroom (in addition to material already in the school but previously underutilized); the cost of tapes averaged $100 per level per language. Two teachers in the program received $200 each for preparing materials during the summer of 1972.

CONTACT PERSON

Joan S. Freilich, Walden School, 1 West 88th Street, New York, New York 10024 (212) 787-5315

FRENCH DRAMA

Advanced French students at Walt Whitman High School in Bethesda, Maryland have Broadway beat. Not only are they the directors, actors, editors, prop managers, designers, technicians, carpenters, and tailors in a one-semester French Drama course offered each year, but they are also their own critics and some of the most appreciative members of their own audiences. From a list of plays drawn up by the program director, the students in French V, VI, and VII select one long play that all three levels stage together and several scenes or shorter plays that each level presents separately. The students elect a director, cast the roles so that everyone gets a chance to act, and choose or are assigned to committees responsible for editing the major play to a length of two hours and designing and making the scenery, props, and costumes. The class meets as a single group each day for two hours, and occasionally in the weeks preceding the presentation of the long play meets after school for a couple of hours. In class the actors go over their lines with the program director and practice pronunciation and intonation, while others work with the student director in practicing their moves and interaction. The committees scrounge and make props, scenery, and costumes from any place and any thing they can. They assembled the old auto for *Knock*, for instance, from painted food cartons; they borrowed costumes from the theater department of George Washington University for a production of *Cyrano de Bergerac*; and they used poster paint and paper for backdrops and choir robes from the school's music department for their sixteenth-century finery. The excitement of the production and the special feeling that grows in theater troupes keep the students' imaginations and interest high, and obstacles seem to be overcome easily.

French Drama is as much an intensive academic study of French drama as it is a theater production course. In class the students read and discuss from 15 to 25 plays, depending on their level, which are representative of movements in French drama from the sixteenth century to the present. They also talk about traditions of the theater, the influence of existentialism on playwrights, French drama in comparison to Shakespeare, or the popularity of Anouilh. Virtually all the class discussion is in French, although English has been found to be more practical during rehearsals and other aspects of production. Students also present oral reports in French on independent projects like "The Development of the Farce," "Jansenism," or "A Comparative Study of Racine and Corneille." Generally research is done during class time, on days when the students are not rehearsing or working with a committee. Students are graded on the quality of their reports to the class, their diligence in rehearsals, and their participation in class.

The troupe puts on performances of the short plays for French classes in the district's junior and senior high schools, and stages the full-length play in the school auditorium for all French classes at the end of the year. Reaction to French Drama has been very positive; students in the course like it so much they do not object to memorizing the lines and in feedback sessions have been unanimous in their approval. And, especially at the high school level, the audiences have enjoyed the performances very much; in

FRENCH DRAMA – 287

fact another high school in the district just instituted a course similar to French Drama on the request of students who saw last year's production of *Cyrano*.

PROGRAM GOALS

(1) To encourage and continue the development of the four basic language skills; (2) to make the learning of French language, literature, and culture stimulating and fun; (3) to develop a broader interest and understanding of French literature and literary movements.

TARGET AUDIENCE

Students in French V, VI, and VII. In 1972–73 there were 14 students in the course.

COSTS

The program director receives a very small amount of money for the program from the school each year and sometimes is given materials from the art department. Costs vary from play to play, but are minimal in all cases; for some plays, such as *En attendant Godot*, the costs can be lower than $10.

CONTACT PERSON

Estelle Stone, Walt Whitman High School, 7100 Whittier Boulevard, Bethesda, Maryland 20034 (301) 320-5900

FRENCH INSTRUCTION IN THE PRIMARY GRADES

More than one million people in Louisiana still speak French, yet for years the use of French was discouraged—and even punished —in the state's public schools. To reverse this trend and to revive and preserve French language and culture in the state, the Louisiana Legislature passed an act in 1968 requiring French instruction in the elementary grades. There were, however, two major obstacles to establishing an ongoing program: the lack of certified French teachers at the elementary level and the lack of funds. These problems were finally resolved in a cooperative effort involving the State Legislature and the State Department of Education, which supplied a grant for teachers' salaries; the Council for the Development of French in Louisiana, which carried out a search for teachers by going straight to the Elysée Palace in Paris; and finally the President and government of France, who agreed to expand their cultural affairs program by sending to Louisiana 100 qualified, experienced teachers who have chosen to teach outside their own country in lieu of military service, as well as seven consultants. The teachers have the title of "French Teaching Assistants"; they are supplementary staff and do not displace any Louisiana teachers.

The state-wide pilot program began in September 1972 with 16,500 pupils in grades 1–3 from 88 schools in 20 of Louisiana's parishes (counties). Fourteen of these are "Acadiana Parishes," where there are sizable numbers of French-speaking families. The Foreign Language Section of the State Department of Education worked with the consultants from France and a Project Evaluator to develop the goals and procedures for a two-year pilot program in French, incorporating curriculum guides prepared by Title VII bilingual programs in the state. It was hoped that students from French-speaking homes would, by developing skills and pride in their native language, get back into the "mainstream" of the state's education system and that English-speaking students would develop skills in the second language.

Each of the 100 teachers has a maximum of six class sections per day; for each section, there is half an hour of instruction in French language arts, and half an hour in such areas as physical education, art, music, or math conducted in French. The teachers move from class to class or from school to school with their own equipment and materials. They are the actual teachers of the French language component and work on aural-oral skills in large and small-group sessions, using a variety of visual aids as well as tapes and records. In the other subjects, the teachers from France may assist or supplement the regular classroom teacher's presentation: for example, in math, they usually reinforce material previously learned in English. Or they may take turns with the regular classroom teacher in presenting lessons in art, music, or physical education. The classroom teacher, who works closely with the French teacher to keep presentations consistent and well integrated, keeps a skills chart for each class showing individual students' progress in French; although there are no grades, each child is aware of his progress in relation to the rest of the class. Each school or group of parish schools plans its own special or extra-curricular activities in French, for example, festivals and dramatic presentations, or open house and demonstration classes for the benefit of the parents.

Before being assigned to schools by the Foreign Language Section, the French teachers have a full-week training session. Continuous inservice training is provided by the consultants from France, who visit each teacher in their assigned region every two weeks. There are also group meetings within each parish every three months, attended by the teachers, the local supervising staff, consultants, and the project evaluator. In May, there is a three-day workshop for all 100 teachers, to "compare notes" and make plans for the coming year. In addition, an extensive evaluation program is planned, using proficiency tests and attitude surveys. It is hoped the results will demonstrate that both English-speaking and French-speaking students "exhibit noticeable linguistic gains in the areas of listening comprehension and global understanding of French," as well as "minimal oral proficiency and mastery of both structure and lexical items in French," and that significant gains in overall achievement can take place in bilingual education.

TARGET AUDIENCE

In the two-year pilot program, all students in grades 1–3 in all participating schools are enrolled in the program. More grade levels will be included each year.

FUNDING AND COSTS

The first year, a $250,000 grant from the Louisiana state government and $250,000 from the State Department of Education covered the total cost of the program. Teachers receive $3900 a year, plus a mileage allowance for those required to work in two different schools. Teachers pay for their own housing, but the French Education Consultants, the Council for the Development of French in Louisiana, and the Local Educational Authorities (LEA) cooperate in locating suitable living accommodations.

CONTACT PERSON

H. B. Dyess, Foreign Language Supervisor and Coordinator of Bilingual-Bicultural Education, State Department of Education, P.O. Box 44064, Baton Rouge, Louisiana 70804 (504) 389-6486

HIGH SCHOOL
CADET
TEACHING
PROGRAM

For the last four years, high school students in French and Spanish in the public schools of Danville, Illinois have been serving as "cadet teachers" in their own informal FLES program. At present, 28 cadet teachers offer language instruction to a total of over 1300 students in kindergarten through the sixth grade, using a curriculum guide they helped prepare in their high school language classes. The program is designed to stimulate interest in foreign languages and foster cross-cultural understanding in the elementary grades and to encourage upper-level students to continue language study by giving them a concrete way to use their foreign language skills.[1]

The program began in 1969 when several teachers in two elementary schools expressed concern for Mexican-American children in their classes who were having learning difficulties because of the "language barrier." Eleven high school students in their fifth year of Spanish volunteered to work as bilingual tutors for individual students in these two schools. Because of the success of this program and the widespread interest it aroused, the role of the cadets the following year was expanded: they were to provide exposure to a foreign language to English speakers as well as Spanish speakers and to develop a "bicultural attitude" among all students involved. High school students in their third and fourth year of Spanish also became eligible for cadet teaching, and 15 cadets gave Spanish instruction to full-class groups in several schools. The foreign language coordinator and primary teachers developed a curriculum outline that could be used and expanded by the cadets at all primary levels. In the third year, an elementary school principal of Belgian-French descent asked to have French instruction in his school, and in 1972–73 eight cadet teachers were involved in French and 20 in Spanish in 12 elementary schools.

Each cadet gives 20 minutes of instruction three to five times a week; many cadets teach two or three different classes. During a portion of the children's language arts time, the cadet teacher presents a "bilingual, bicultural program, involving simple conversation, games, music, and customs." Both English and the foreign language are spoken, and the cadet works closely with the classroom teacher to coordinate language instruction with the regular classroom activities. In kindergarten Spanish, for example, one of the first objectives is for the pupil to count as far in Spanish as he can in English. Students repeat numbers from one to ten, count and name fingers, toes, and classroom objects, color pictures of numbers, discuss their age, and sing number songs in Spanish. By the time students reach the sixth grade, they have celebrated most Spanish and American holidays in Spanish, have learned to name parts of the body, clothes, food, days, months, seasons, and directions, have planned a fiesta, and can go on to tell time, use basic classroom commands, write short conversations, and speak in complete sentences in Spanish.

Meanwhile, the classroom teacher provides cultural activities in conjunction with the cadet's program and lays the groundwork for the cadet's presentations. The cadets meet daily with the coordinator of foreign languages, and, as part of their high school foreign language course, they design the curriculum and objectives and create materials to be used in the elementary classes. This year the fifth-year Spanish class is also preparing a complete guide for the elementary school language curriculum that will be incorporated into the general district-wide curriculum guide.

Elementary principals and teachers find that, because it stimulates interest in language and sets goals for elementary students, the program is "an excellent means of establishing articulation between the elementary and secondary levels." On the other end of the scale, at the advanced levels, the opportunity to use what they have learned in language instruction has generated much interest among the high school students. The cadets have been pleased at the chance to practice teaching, the enthusiastic response from their pupils, and the chance to create, implement, and revise a curriculum. Parents of both the primary and secondary students have expressed "sincere appreciation" for the opportunities provided through the program. Finally, the district has developed a formal, state-subsidized bilingual program, in which the cadets continue to participate as teaching aides.

TARGET AUDIENCE

Cadets are volunteers from third-, fourth-, and fifth-year high school foreign language classes. Their pupils are in kindergarten through the sixth grade, in classes selected by cooperating elementary school principals.

MATERIALS

Many materials used in the program are prepared by the cadets as part of their high school course in foreign language: dittoed worksheets, pictures, flash cards, and tape recordings. Basal readers in French and Spanish, Mother Goose and math books in both languages, rented films, movie and overhead projectors, tape recorders, and record players are also used.

FUNDING

Books, ditto masters, paper, film rentals, tapes, and hardware equipment are provided by the individual elementary schools. The cadets provide their own transportation to the elementary schools.

CONTACT PERSON

Dorothy Sturm, Foreign Language Coordinator, Danville Public School District 118, 516 North Jackson Street, Danville, Illinois 61832 (217) 443-2900

NOTE
[1] Material is taken from the survey questionnaire and from a speech presented by Marian Hall, Primary Supervisor, and Dorothy Sturm, Foreign Language Coordinator, at the 1972 Central States Foreign Language Conference.

INDIVIDUALIZED
FOREIGN
LANGUAGE
ISLANDS

Mountain View High School in Mountain View, California has used modular scheduling to good advantage in its program of individualized instruction in German and Spanish. One large room has been set aside for each language as a "language island," and German or Spanish students are scheduled into the rooms, regardless of their level, for a total of 40 minutes a day at whatever times are most convenient for them. During any one module, therefore, students in levels I–V may be using the same room. Classroom organization and individualized instruction are crucial in keeping the program running smoothly.

The island is divided into five specific areas, each with a different function. Against one wall are stations for tape recorders and phonographs, study carrels, and a bookcase containing tapes, records, and other materials. On another side is a library and reading area, complete with couch, where students can look at foreign language books and periodicals. In the center of the room are four circular tables, where students work by themselves or in groups of two or three using materials that they choose from several available texts and Learning Activity Packets prepared by the teachers. Off to one side is a large table used by the teacher for conversation sessions with groups of five or six students at approximately the same level of proficiency. Against another wall is the teacher's desk, bookcases, and file cabinets for storing tests, test tapes, student files, and records.

On beginning a new unit, the student receives a Learning Activity Packet with a checklist of all the activities he must complete to receive credit for the unit. These include dictations, written exercises, written reports, readings in a variety of texts, translations, and the use of tapes and records. Each activity is accompanied by a test, evaluated by the teacher or a teacher aide, on which students must score at least 80 percent correct before going on to the next activity. "Grades are given only at the end of each quarter and are based upon units completed, upon progress in relation to ability, upon effort, and upon will to learn the language."[1] Credit, therefore, is based directly on the amount of work a student completes and the teacher's perception of his diligence.

Students are encouraged to work together, giving or taking dictations, running through drills, exercises, and tests, practicing with vocabulary cards, or speaking with each other in the target language. In addition, all students take part in at least one small-group conversation session each week. In these sessions, the teacher leads the students through dialogue repetition and encourages them to engage in free conversation. Teacher aides, who are advanced students, and native speakers who live in Mountain View also work with the students in conversation practice and provide assistance with the drills, translations, and other activities. Occasional foreign language films, lectures on a country's history or culture, slide shows, and visits from people knowledgeable about foreign cultures spice up the program's fare.

TARGET AUDIENCE

Students in grades 9–12, enrolled in levels I–V of Spanish or German.

PRESENT STATUS

There are 180 students in the Spanish program and 80 in the German. The Spanish teacher is a full-time language teacher; the German teacher teaches language part-time.

AVAILABLE DESCRIPTIONS

"Individualized Foreign Language Islands: Sample Materials," a booklet, is available on request from the contact people. And the program is described in the December 1970 issue of *Individualization of Foreign Language Learning in America* (ERIC ED 051 684).

CONTACT PEOPLE

Sheila Vidal (Spanish), Coordinator of Individualized Program, and Robert McLennan (German), Vice Principal in Charge of Curriculum, Mountain View High School, P.O. Box 640, Mountain View, California 94040 (415) 967-5543

NOTE
[1] Collie J. Kidwell, Robert McLennan, and Sheila Vidal, "Individualized Foreign Language Islands: Sample Materials" (Mountain View, Calif.: Mountain View High School, 1972).

INDIVIDUALIZED
INSTRUCTION

The move to individualization was slow and smooth for Lynn-brook High School in Sunnyvale, California. Wanting to create a situation in which students could learn languages at different rates, the foreign language department chairman in 1969 began individualization in one of her French III classes. Using the experience to good advantage, the next year each of the school's six foreign language teachers experimented with individualization in at least one class and the following year individualized all classes in levels I–V of French, German, and Spanish. During spring and summer workshops, the teachers prepared Learning Activity Packets and accompanying tapes, with dialogues, drills, and grammar explanations structured around behaviorally stated enabling and final objectives. Following an orientation session, students meet five periods a week to work with these materials on their own or in small groups, as they choose. They work at a rate that they find comfortable, although progress must be made each day in order to receive credit. When a student has finished the enabling objectives in a unit or subunit, he is evaluated by the teacher or a teacher aide—a language student who is at least one unit ahead of the other. For their work, teacher aides receive graduation, but not language, credit. If a student has trouble with a specific exercise, he may go to a teacher aide or to the teacher for drills or explanations. If he feels he can complete the final objectives in the unit he goes to the teacher for testing. Unit grades are A, B, C, or No Credit, and final grades are determined on a "balance between quality and quantity." Most of the teachers hold frequent group meetings to explain general points of grammar, conduct special activities, and help maintain an "esprit de corps."

Some of the units require extracurricular food or craft projects to be done by students on special occasions like Christmas. From time to time, lunch-hour conversation groups are formed, and occasionally groups of advanced students go to foreign language movies in the area. Some French students meet Saturday mornings in a mini-course on French cuisine. Each language group presents a foreign language songfest at the department's Christmas program. And the French, German, and Spanish students are active in the school's annual Foreign Language Week.

Since the program began there has been a slight decrease in attrition. The Lynnbrook High program was one of the five programs included in the generally favorable report of student attitudes toward individualized instruction written by Robert Morrey for the Stanford Conference on Individualizing Foreign Language Instruction in 1971. And local evaluation indicates that both students and teachers are in favor of the approach.

TARGET AUDIENCE

Students in grades 9–12, levels I–V of French, German, or Spanish. In 1972–73, there were 2200 students in the school; 250 were enrolled in French, 165 in German, and 400 in Spanish.

FACILITIES

Each classroom is divided into specific functional areas. At one side is a listening area with a reel-to-reel tape recorder, multiple jackbox, and several headsets. On another side is a study area, and one other is used for testing and tutoring. The school has a 36-station language laboratory, which adjoins a Resource Center with a foreign language library, a viewing area for films, filmstrips, and slides, and a listening area where students can use the center's 23 cassette recorders. Most teachers require students to spend a certain amount of time in the Resource Center each week.

FUNDING AND COSTS

Each teacher has assumed an increased classload to free funds for hiring a paraprofessional to direct the Resource Center. The annual expenditure per pupil in the district is $1300.

CONTACT PERSON

Elna Carroll, Chairman, Department of Foreign Languages, Lynnbrook High School, P.O. Box F, Sunnyvale, California 94087 (408) 257-1400

LATIN,
HORSESHOE
STYLE

At Bishop Scully High School in Amsterdam, New York, all 130 students who elect to take Latin continue through level IV, and, from reports by the teacher, principal, consultants, and parents, they all like it. Sister Anna Roberta Benson teaches all sections of Latin, levels I–IV, on a system of modular scheduling, and her "trick" is the harnessing of audio-visual aids of all kinds to the humanistic, value-oriented approach she feels the study of classical language requires. The program's main goal—to encourage creative student involvement in the study of Roman civilization and language and its Greek background—is achieved by allowing students to conduct all classes.

The key is the overhead projector. At the beginning of the year, students receive their own transparencies and grease pencils. Homework assignments are put on transparencies and projected

by students in color. The class sits at desks in horseshoe forma-
tion; only the elected class leader faces the teacher, who sits back
and watches. Following a Procedure Sheet, a flexible outline of
things that can be done in class, students discuss the concepts and
problems raised by the homework presentation. They do not have
to raise their hands to talk, but surprisingly, there are "no colli-
sions verbally."[1] "They explain to each other and argue with each
other, until light dawns for all." Conversation can be lively, cas-
ual, or heated, but the teacher enters only when no one in the
group can solve a problem—"almost never." Some modules are
set aside for small groups receiving individual assistance from the
teacher and others for large-group sessions combining several sections for lectures or cultural presentations using the overhead projector, sometimes with an extra-large screen for a "total" effect.

Mythology and Roman history as presented in literary selections, songs, tapes, films, and the omnipresent color transparencies
are the main cultural focuses of the program at all levels. Development of the four skills is equally important, and the horseshoe
discussions provide the opportunity for practice and clarification.
Latin structures are frequently compared to those in English, and
students list in a Phonology Book the linguistic violations, chiefly
of levels of pitch and juncture, which they note on radio, on
television, and in conversations. In every class meeting there is a
"News Report" in which students take turns telling stories that
relate information received in class to classical references in the
media. Each student has a Record Book in which he enters each
day's accomplishments following the Julian calendar. At all levels
students often "bug" French, English, or science classes with a
microphone to listen in on relevant discussions in other classrooms through the FM radio in the Latin Resource Center. As one
beginning-level activity, students make birthday cards illustrating
in designs and words the good qualities of the mythological characters in the story of the constellation of their astrological signs.
At level IV students learn the Greek, Russian, and Hebrew alpha-
bets and the pronunciation of some words, study their interrela-
tionships, and compare them with Latin and French words they
already know. Finally, each spring vacation the teacher takes a
group of her advanced students to Italy, where for ten days they

see the art work and landmarks of Roman history that are the focal point of four years of study.

The students' enthusiasm has been shown not only through the care they give to their homework assignments, by their mutual generosity in class, and by their very active participation in the Latin Club, but also by their reports to parents, who have asked for and received their own monthly evening Latin classes conducted by Sister Anna Roberta. The school principal observes that "it is amazing, the numbers attending and the appreciation they have for her presentations." He also notes that the students' language program "is truly excellent and a great example of a humanizing, liberal course on the high school level." Morton Spillenger, Associate in Foreign Languages Education for the New York State Education Department, says that the students he observed, "without any intervention from the teacher, performed exceptionally well, each one making his contribution to the class on the basis of his particular interest and motivation."

TARGET AUDIENCE

Students in grades 9–12, levels I–IV of Latin.

EQUIPMENT AND MATERIALS

The basic hardware equipment consists of one overhead projector, a Day-lite screen, an electric pointer, several reel-to-reel and cassette tape recorders with amplifiers, an FM wireless microphone and radio (for listening in on lectures in other classrooms), a filmstrip projector, a carousel slide projector, a Viewlex filmstrip machine (with an 8-inch screen, for "make-up" work), a record player, a Unidyn Dynamic microphone ("to show the power of the human voice to communicate on all five levels of pitch, tone variation, and melody"). A variety of texts, readers, workbooks, records, filmstrips, and commercially- and teacher-prepared tapes and transparencies are also used.

FUNDING AND COST

All aspects of the program are funded through the annual school expenditure of $480 per pupil. The trip to Italy, however, is paid for by the students themselves. The total cost of the basic hardware materials was about $650.

CONTACT PERSON

Sister Anna Roberta Benson, Bishop Scully High School, Amsterdam, New York 12010 (518) 842-4100

NOTE
  [1] All quotations are from personal communications to the survey staff.

MIDDLE SCHOOL FOREIGN LANGUAGE: A MEDIA APPROACH

What does a teacher do when he has 60 students in every class and, at most, only part-time help from a student teacher? In the two middle schools of North Syracuse, New York, six foreign language teachers were faced with this dilemma when severe budget cuts in the district prevented the hiring of additional staff at a time when student enrollment was rapidly increasing. Their solution was the development of a "media approach" that, in essence, bombards students with recordings, transparencies, slides, filmstrips, and, most importantly, videotapes. Working after school and during the summer, the staff previewed several commercial videotape series before choosing the ones they felt were most appropriate for level I Spanish, French, and German. From these they selected segments for classroom use, and, with much editing and reassembling, the film segments were correlated with other media and put into a sequence of instruction built around the course objectives the teachers wrote. Not a single textbook is used; written exercises, instruction sheets, and tape recordings are prepared by the teachers and duplicated at the schools. Over 500 students in grade 7 are enrolled in the media program in three languages. The teachers are currently developing a media curriculum for the eighth grade. There is one teacher in each language in each school, and each teacher has, in addition to two seventh-grade media classes, two or three eighth-grade classes. A student teacher for each language works at each school whenever possible, and students are recruited on a day-to-day basis to serve as group leaders.

Each class meets daily for 40 minutes; once or twice a week a class views a videotape, the basis of several days' work. First, the teacher tells the students what they should watch for in the tape and explains the objectives of the lesson. Then they view the show, usually a segment of a continuing mystery or a short skit. At the end of the tape, the teacher leads a follow-up session with the whole class; this involves repetition of sentences from the videotape or simple questions that help the students become familiar with the material. Then the class divides into groups of about ten. Each group is told precisely what it is expected to do: the mechanical aids to use, the worksheets to follow, and the exercises to begin. The small-group work is used to reinforce the vocabulary and structures introduced in the film. Different groups might work with taped pattern drills based on the film dialogue, do written exercises on a worksheet, see slides related to the videotape, or be drilled by the teacher. The six groups may be doing six different things; while the teacher works with a group, the student teacher (or aide) supervises the rest of the class, or vice versa.

Students stay in the same groups for a few days and take turns working on the various activities. The teacher also introduces each group to some new material as a prelude to the next videotape. Activities are meant to be as lively and varied as possible. "Every activity is a form of self-test, since it is based on precisely stated objectives." For example, students are expected, "given a visual stimulus, to write a letter of at least five sentences, using vocabulary items from the first four units . . . [or] given the flash cards of buildings and the maps of Cadolzburg, to locate selected buildings by writing the German name of the building and its definite article on a local road map." The teacher might also have members of a group take turns doing "reflex drills" in which the student says as many sentences as he can in one minute. Another frequent activity involves asking students to complete an exercise (such as "describe your best friend") in three to five minutes, and then to begin a new exercise immediately thereafter. A high noise level is always preferred to restlessness or boredom.

Although no texts are used, students see the written language on worksheets, transparencies, and flash cards. The videotapes stress conversational skills through dramatizations, but most also include sections that teach vocabulary and grammar more directly. One sentence in a videotape, "It is five o'clock," might set off intensive drilling in numbers and telling time in the small-group follow-up session. One teacher has videotaped herself teaching grammar so that part of the class may watch the lesson while she works with a small group. Finally, cultural concepts are often introduced in the videotapes. A story in Spanish that takes place on a beach in Spain will demonstrate details like signs for drinking water, cabañas for changing clothes, food vendors (and their cries), and a list of flavors at an ice cream stand. Cultural information is also included in the filmstrips, slides, and records.

One period a day is set aside in both schools for Special Activities Classes, when students can come to the foreign language classroom to ask questions, review tapes, or catch up on a missed videotape. Student opinions and suggestions are constantly solicited, and the staff members meet weekly to share and develop ideas and materials. Since the teachers cooperatively prepare their own instructional sequence, a good degree of articulation is achieved within the middle school program. Monthly progress reports indicate which units of work each class has completed, and the two teachers of a language try to cover the same material, since their students are required by the district to take a common final exam. Articulation with the high schools poses more of a problem, since the middle school students continue into programs that are more traditional and textbook-oriented. The staff is, however, trying to expose high school language teachers to the media approach: all are invited to visit the middle school program and evaluate it. Next year the district will require the high school language teachers to visit the middle school classes for one day each semester, and every ninth-grade teacher will prepare a multi-media unit with an eighth-grade teacher. The program has aroused much skepticism on the part of administrators, other teachers, and even incoming student teachers and their college supervisors. But once people have been persuaded to visit the program in action, the skepticism has in almost all cases dissolved into surprise and approval. Members of the middle school language staff were asked to describe the program at the 1972 Conference of the New York State Federation of Foreign Language Teachers.

TARGET AUDIENCE

Students in grade 7 and in 1973–74, grade 8, who are not more than one year below reading level. (Otherwise they must take reading instead.)

MATERIALS AND EQUIPMENT

The "core" materials are the videotape series *Parlons Fran-çais* and *Una advéntura español* (D.C. Heath), the filmstrip series *So Sind die Deutschen* (Center for Curriculum Development) and *Vorwörts* (flash cards from the Nuffield materials). Portions of *La Familia Fernandez* and *Je parle Français* filmstrip series (Encyclopaedia Britannica Educational Corp.) and *Vamos a ver* (Time-Life Films) are sometimes used. Other materials include: flash cards in three languages; commercial and teacher-prepared slides; teacher-recorded tapes (copies of these are made for home use by students); cassette recorders, reel-to-reel tape recorders, overhead projectors, and television. Recently trapezoidal tables were acquired to enable freer movement and grouping in the foreign language classrooms.

FUNDING AND COSTS

Specific costs are approximately $7500 for videotapes, filmstrips, and other instructional materials; $10,000 for curriculum development over two years (including $800 per teacher for 200 hours of summer work and overtime work during the year on the seventh- and eighth-grade programs); $400 for file cabinets; $1000 for tables, and $250 for consultants. During the organizational phase, teachers were also awarded two inservice credits for curriculum writing. All expenses are financed by the district budget. The average annual expenditure per pupil in the district is $1100.

CONTACT PERSON

Elizabeth S. Hemkes, Coordinator of Foreign Language (and teacher of German), 200 Lawrence Road E., North Syracuse, New York 13212 (315) 454-9238

PAN-AMERICAN COMMUNITY THEATER ORGANIZATION (PACTO)

The Pan-American Community Theater Organization is many things at once: an interdisciplinary Spanish course at North Salinas High School in Salinas, California; a bilingual performing group for the Salinas community; and a troupe that tours California and sponsors joint productions with a student theater group from Mexico. But most importantly, it is a source of pride for a Spanish-speaking community that has been unsure of its place on the Salinas scene and a source of cultural understanding—and practice in Spanish—for English-speaking students.

North Salinas High School is on the outskirts of the city, on a line where housing developments increasingly encroach on open fields. Its students come from urban and agricultural areas, from middle-class city families, and from families of migrant farm-workers. When PACTO began in 1967, neither the Anglo nor the Mexican-American residents knew much about Mexican culture;

311

Spanish speakers had little pride in their heritage and did not even have a movie house to call their own. Hoping to relieve the social and economic isolation of Mexican Americans in both the school and the community at large, teachers from North Salinas High applied for, and received, federal funding for a project that would build the self-esteem of Spanish-speaking students and adults, develop awareness and appreciation of Hispanic cultures among Anglos, and "attack what is both an emotional and cultural problem through an emotional and cultural framework"—the theater. The director notes that "Chicano militancy has [since] come to Salinas" and that the techniques and goals of PACTO have been readjusted to meet changing—and challenging—community needs.

Three full-time teachers and three intern teachers with backgrounds in drama, Spanish literature, music, and dance work with classes composed of both Spanish- and English-speaking students who are studying Spanish and Latin American (essentially Mexican) culture. In class, plays are read, discussed, and produced in both Spanish and English. Students see Spanish-language film classics, listen to music, study filmstrips, books, and periodicals about Spanish and Latin American drama, watch performing groups or talk with guest lecturers from a nearby university, and work with tape recordings to improve their accent, diction, and auditory discrimination. Mexican-American students whose English is poor can participate—and feel successful—in a Spanish play, while those whose English is better participate in the English productions. The Anglo students, too, can perform in Spanish- or English-language productions. Rehearsals are conducted both in class and after school, and the students often videotape their rehearsals in order to improve their performances. They make their own props with whatever is available, keeping them simple so that sets can be moved around easily. Then they take their plays and their sets to the community—in daytime and evening performances in the school auditorium—and around the state. Travel is an important element in PACTO, whether to a nearby presentation of the "Teatro Campesino" in San Juan Bautista, or to Mexico for ten days, an annual trip in which as many as 80 students participate.

The PACTO actors and actresses have presented such plays as Sastre's *La cornada*, Lorca's *Bodas de sangre* and *La casa de Bernarda Alba*, all in Spanish; *Los intereses creados* by Benavente in Spanish and English, alternately; and Sophocles' *Antigone* in English. In 1972 they premiered an English translation of a play by Rodolfo Usigli, *The Gesticulator*, presenting it first for the Salinas community. Then they went on tour—to the Northwest Drama Conference in San Jose and to the Ethnic Studies Department of San Joaquin Delta College in Stockton. Finally, El Grupo de Teatro de la Universidad de Guadalajara visited the school and performed the same play in Spanish, then took the props produced by PACTO and went on their own 1972 California tour. This cooperative venture was so successful that plans were made to sponsor a similar tour in 1973, but lack of funds for underwriting the tour in advance prevented fulfillment of this proposal. Funding for 1974 is being sought, however, in order to continue this international project.

In the fall of 1972, a PACTO tour group presented an English-language version of S. N. Berman's play *Biography* in Sonora at the first northern California high school theater festival; half of the 40 students in the group were Mexican Americans. In 1973, a student television production crew flew to San Diego where they videotaped a one-act play for the Media Education Conference of California to demonstrate the capability and competence of the PACTO troupe and film crew. Another presentation of the same production was later given in Sacramento.

PACTO has brought Mexican-American and Anglo students together in a common pursuit, in most cases for the first time, and it has brought the Spanish-speaking residents of Salinas closer to the school and to their own cultural roots. Both the local Spanish- and English-language newspapers have given the program extensive coverage. Finally, largely because of the "persistence" and outcomes of PACTO, an ESEA Title III program called "Cycle VII" was begun in 1972–73 in several Salinas schools to reduce the dropout rate among students of Mexican descent. At North Salinas High, Cycle VII involves five teachers and 150 Mexican-American and other students who take classes together in Spanish in both academic and vocational areas. Three classes of Chicano

Theater, conducted bilingually, indicate continued interest in *teatro.*

TARGET AUDIENCE

One hundred fifty students in grades 9–12 who are either native speakers of Spanish or who are interested in Spanish-language drama and Hispanic cultures are enrolled in PACTO classes (Chicano Theater) and receive regular grades and credit for the course. An additional 100 students participate in PACTO's presentations but are not enrolled in the course.

FUNDING AND COSTS

The first year, 1967–68, PACTO was funded by a $4500 grant from the U.S. Office of Education. Since then, money has come from regular school budget provisions for drama and fine arts. Students conduct money-raising projects to finance their trips to Mexico and most tours in California; the San Diego Media Education Conference, however, awarded them a $890 grant for travel expenses to San Diego in 1972. The Cycle VII aspect has received a two-year ESEA Title III grant (1972–74) of approximately $200,000. The average annual expenditure in the district is $1000 per pupil.

AVAILABLE DESCRIPTION

The proposal for PACTO submitted to the U.S. Office of Education is available from ERIC (ERIC ED 001 989).

CONTACT PERSON

Lewis W. Heniford, Director, PACTO, North Salinas High School, 55 Kip Drive, Salinas, California 93901 (408) 449-1551

PETIT
LYCÉE
AND
COLEGIO
ESPAÑOL

During the summer in Beverly Hills, California, FLES students can spend six weeks in the Petit Lycée or the Colegio Español, French and Hispanic "cultural islands" conducted by some of the district's FLES teachers within the setting of a local school. These enrichment programs, often called "summer schools abroad at home," were begun in 1966 in order to make students strongly aware of the cultural and historic backgrounds of the people whose languages they study in the regular FLES sequence, as well as improve their language skills. During the first four years, the Colegio and Lycée were held simultaneously each summer, but after 1969, because of the cost, they began to be held in alternate years. Each summer an average of 65 students in grades 4–7 attend either the Colegio or the Lycée for four hours daily, signing a pledge to speak only in the target language.

The day begins with a short session bringing all students

together for "warm-up" exercises, announcements, and orientation in the day's activities. In the Colegio, this is followed by singing and instruction in the piano, guitar, drums, maracas, or guiras. Students then break up into three classrooms, where two periods are devoted to audiolingual language instruction and drama, and one to history, culture, and folklore. The remainder of the day is spent in sports, arts and crafts, music and dancing, discussions with guest speakers, or field trips. There are three teachers in each language who often work in teams and meet daily for evaluation and planning. In the Colegio, there is also one exchange teacher from Mexico, when possible, and 10 to 15 students of Mexican descent are recruited from Los Angeles schools to attend classes and give participants a chance to talk with peers who are native speakers. On occasion, students from Beverly Hills' sister city, Acapulco, visit the Colegio. And select groups from the Colegio have gone on field trips to Mexico with the help of the Beverly Hills Sister City Committee.

The cultural focus of classes in the Colegio Español is Mexico, but Latin America and Spain are also studied. A typical day in the Colegio includes two periods of skills instruction in small and large groups. Then each *Casa*, or large group, might rehearse the play it will present at the *Fiesta Folklórica* at the end of the summer. During another period, a teacher might discuss history and geography with half the class, while the other half watches a cultural film. Castanets, baskets, serapes, pottery, bull-fighters' capes, and other realia are used in cultural discussions, and students might examine the designs of Indian costumes in a session on handicrafts. Professional Spanish dancers often conduct folk dancing lessons, introducing the students to castanet exercises and footwork techniques. Some students attend a weekly cooking class, while others play soccer with a Latin-American college student. Special activities have included a visit to the Mission San Gabriel to see examples of Spanish architecture, furniture, and religious articles, a film at the Spanish "Café Colón" featuring Mexican film stars, and a visit to the Exposición Nacional de Mexico.

In the *Châteaux* of the Petit Lycée, instruction in skills, drama, history, and geography is supplemented with work in literature and creative writing in French. The major cultural focus is France, but French-speaking Canada and North Africa are also studied. There are often special joint meetings for films and guest lectures, and time for independent activities in "La Bibliothèque," which contains French educational games, several shelves of books, and realia from different French-speaking countries. Sports include *le football, le ballon-prisonnier,* and dancing, often under the direction of a professional dance instructor. One summer a boy from the Basque region of France visited the classes for two days. Other guests have included a French chef who taught the students how to flip *crèpes,* a French composer who spoke about music and was accompanied by a concert pianist, and the French consul. French students from UCLA have assisted in coaching soccer, and some parents volunteer to teach sewing and help students create costumes for their dramatic productions. Lycée students have visited local wineries to see the plant operations and discuss the wine industries of California and France, have gone on a guided tour in French of the Los Angeles International Airport as guests of TWA, and have visited the New Orleans section of Disneyland. A *foire française* and a *soirée* at a local French restaurant give students a chance to share their activities with parents and friends.

The general staff evaluation of the program seems to be summed up by this observation at the end of the Colegio's first session. "With the help of teachers and native speakers, [students] were able to reduce, even to eliminate, mistakes in pronunciation and phraseology. . . . FLES teachers unanimously attested to the fact that the students of Colegio '66 performed in a superior fashion after having been exposed to the Colegio experience. The Colegio staff is equally convinced that those who participated not only improved their Spanish to a considerable degree during the summer school but will continue to improve."[1] At the end of the first Lycée, only four out of 86 students said that the session did not help their study of French. All but two parents were enthusiastic at the end of the program and noted that their children showed an "at-homeness" in the language, a wider cultural understanding, and "great strides" in all skills.

318 - OPTIONS AND PERSPECTIVES

TARGET AUDIENCE

The criteria for selecting students in the Colegio are "good citizenship, command of the Spanish language, positive attitudes and willingness to participate in all activities, and interest in understanding people of other cultures." For acceptance in the Lycée, students must also "meet special requirements of attitude, ability, and achievement." Those Colegio students who participate in the field trip to Mexico are also specially selected.

FUNDING AND COSTS

Specific costs for teachers' salaries, facilities at the school, materials, the exchange teacher, transportation on field trips, and entrance fees were not available. There is no cost for students, except for some field trips, costumes for dances, and family dinner night. The district's average annual expenditure per pupil is $1756.

CONTACT PERSON

Albert W. JeKenta, Head, FLES Department, Beverly Hills Unified School District, 255 South Lasky Drive, Beverly Hills, California 90212 (213) 277-5900 Ext. 344

NOTE
[1] Quotations are from "A Report: Elementary Summer School" (Beverly Hills, Calif.: Beverly Hills Unified School District, 1967).

PROJECT
AWARE

Project Aware was begun in Braddock Junior High School in Cumberland, Maryland as an effort to integrate an investigation of the "world of work" and career opportunities into foreign language study. A French teacher from the school and a career counselor, the program coordinator, first met with specialists from the Maryland State Department on Career Development to discuss goals and procedures for the program. Working closely with the school principal, they then planned an approach that would incorporate into the eighth-grade French curriculum a study of vocational possibilities, needs, and problems—locally and in countries where French is spoken. The program was piloted in eighth-grade French classes in 1969; the coordinator has since transferred to another school, but the French teacher continues to use Project Aware in her five eighth-grade classes.

The French classes meet for three 45-minute sessions per week; the teacher uses an audiolingual approach and a standard text. Project Aware enters the curriculum not through additional materials, but through a new perspective applied to existing resources. Students are expected to develop an awareness of the occupational implications of French vocabulary words and pictures representative of French culture in texts and magazines. Conditions of the local world of work are studied in relation to those in countries where French is spoken, and students are led to explore a range of vocational opportunities, including vocations that employ speakers of a foreign language.

Career-related work may take the form of an entire lesson, a research project, or a single activity or "point of view" introduced during a regular class session. One career-oriented lesson focuses on a French language magazine, Ça Va (Scholastic Publications). The objectives of the lesson are: "To make students aware that problems in the world of work (in America) are the same as those in French culture. To make students aware that pictorial presentations have occupational connotations. To make students aware that the vocabulary of Ça Va has occupational denotations. To make a cross-cultural comparison of foreign language study and job performance."[1] In the issue of Ça Va used for the lesson, there is a front-page story on the need for more policemen in France and the necessity to recruit them. On the basis of the article and the teacher's explanations, the students discuss in French the routine of police, the duties of police in small towns as compared to those in large towns, a young policeman's reaction to his job, and an old policeman's concern about the future. The teacher introduces the subject of modernization and how it might affect people's jobs. There is also a list of occupations in the magazine; students compare those on the list with jobs in America, identify which jobs might require knowledge of a foreign language, and which jobs were once held only by men that women now hold as well. At the end of the lesson, they might construct a crossword puzzle using job-related words from the magazine.

Another activity involves looking through the vocabulary section of the textbook for such words as le boucher, le chimiste, l'écrivain, or l'actrice and defining the occupation associated with each word. Students also look through their texts for lessons that include a veterinarian, a bank teller, or people who work in restaurants, on the railroad, or in business and see to what extent employment figures into the contexts of their book. In the study of a dialogue about going to the theater, students might be asked to name, in addition to the parts of a theater and the types of plays shown, the different kinds of people who work in a theater. In a "Community Survey" the students investigate industries in the area that have international branches in order to see how much French is used by local firms. They have found, for example, that a local tire company that advertises with the saying, "The Sun Never Sets on Kelly Tires," employs speakers of French in Haiti, Lebanon, Madagascar, Switzerland, Syria, Trinidad, and Vietnam. In a related activity, the language club invited the vice-president for overseas sales from a nearby business to speak about how the knowledge of a foreign language helps his employees.

In a survey completed at the end of the project's first year, 94% of the participants in Project Aware and 91% of a control group felt that learning about jobs and the future world of work in the eighth grade was important. To the question "What do you think is more important in a job choice?" the most frequent response among the project students was "happiness"; among the control group, "chances of keeping a job." Both groups wanted more counselors as a way of improving the program, but the project group also specified that they wanted better counselors. The project coordinator says that in their overall response, the experimental groups "were much more realistic in career goals" than the control group. And one student said: "It started me thinking about what I want to be. It also got me to think of several jobs instead of one."

COSTS

There are no costs for the program. "No materials were added. The purpose [of the program] was to utilize existing materials to implement career awareness."

CONTACT PERSON

Mesach I. Browning, Career Counselor, Career Exploration Laboratory, Allegheny County Vo-Tech Center, Cresaptown, Maryland 21502 (301) 729-8100

NOTE
    [1] All quotations are from the survey questionnaire.

PURNELL
FOREIGN
LANGUAGE
IMMERSION
PROGRAM

All of the 93 students and most of the faculty members at the Purnell School in Pottersville, New Jersey learn French or Spanish —and go to France or Mexico to travel, study at foreign language institutes, and live with French and Mexican families. The program was developed with the help of the Experiment in International Living, a student- and teacher-exchange agency, and its School for International Training (SIT). It consists of three four-week phases in consecutive years; students receive one full-year language credit for each phase.

The first phase of the program takes place for one month— from late February to late March—during the students' sophomore year. The regular schedule of classes is suspended, and for the entire month the teachers and students study nothing but the foreign language and culture, six or seven hours a day, five and a half days a week. The classes are taught by three native-speaker instructors in Spanish and five in French, all recruited, trained, and supervised by the SIT. The students are grouped in classes of ten by ability only and may change groups at any time their progress warrants it. They usually sit in semi-circles in comfortable chairs and do drills and dialogues from texts developed by the SIT, sing foreign songs, put on skits, and watch filmstrips, films, and slides. Reading and writing are not taught. The students practice their listening and speaking skills in classroom and dinner-hour conversation sessions, and also use foreign language records and cassette tape recordings about 45 minutes a day. They have ten-minute breaks between the 50-minute class sessions and two or three hours of sports and free time each day. The school takes on a foreign atmosphere during the special four-week quarter: road signs are covered with their international equivalents; posters, maps, and photos of the foreign countries are on display everywhere; and foreign dishes are served at meals. After the special four-week quarter, the school returns to its regular academic program.

The second phase of the program takes place 11 months later. The faculty leaders from Purnell and the students, now juniors, study language and culture at foreign language institutes in Vichy, France or Cuernavaca, Mexico and live in pairs with French or Mexican families. The school arranges for all transportation, and the foreign language institutes in France and Mexico locate and select the host families. To supplement the language institute program, the students also take field trips to local wineries, museums, and other places. At the end of the four-week period, the students and faculty return to the regular academic program at the Purnell School.

The third phase takes place the following year. The students, now seniors, return to the same towns and live separately with host families. There is no formal schooling at this stage of the program; instead, the students are urged to spend as much time as possible exploring the foreign culture with their host families and by themselves. At the end of four weeks, the students return to the Purnell School.

In 1971–72, the first year of the immersion program, the students went abroad for the homestay experience immediately after the intensive language training program. They were given a pre- and post-test of both the LA and MA forms of the MLA Cooperative Foreign Language Tests in French or Spanish. The average scores of the French students in the four different categories of both test forms improved generally by at least 15 to 20 percentile points and in one speaking category improved by almost 70. No testing information was available for the Spanish students.

The intensive program has completely supplanted the full-year language program in the school; the cost of the intensive program approximately equals the cost of the other, so there is no extra charge to students for the first phase. The study abroad component costs each student an additional $525 each year for the second and third phases. The teachers' training, travel, and living expenses abroad are paid by the school. By 1974, all three phases of the program will be operating simultaneously.

TARGET AUDIENCE

All students in grades 10–12 at the Purnell School are required to take part in the program. The Purnell School is a private boarding and day school for girls.

ADAPTABILITY OF CONCEPT TO OTHER PLACES

The Experiment in International Living and similar agencies can be used in setting up programs of study abroad during the academic year. But one private boys' school has managed to create such a program on its own. Since 1966 Saint John's Preparatory School of the Benedictine Abbey in Collegeville, Minnesota has had a mutual exchange program with the *Gymnasium* school of a Benedictine monastery in Melk, Austria. Each year one teacher and a group of about 15 juniors and seniors who have completed at least one level of German spend an entire academic year at the *Gymnasium* in Melk, studying a broad variety of subjects in both German and English; the curriculum parallels that at Saint John's so that students may satisfy requirements and reintegrate themselves easily on their return. Some of the more advanced students attend the regular *Gymnasium* classes; the others study in a self-contained group taught by Austrian teachers and the American program director, who also teaches English to some of the Austrian students. In end-of-semester breaks, the students and the director tour Europe on group sightseeing and skiing trips; the rest of the year they room and board at the *Gymnasium* with their German-speaking Austrian peers, leaving for occasional weekend visits with friends whose homes are nearby. During this time, five to ten Austrian students spend a year at Saint John's. The cost of the program for the American students is $2400; this includes all group trips, but does not include personal expenses. The fees the students regularly pay for a year at Saint John's are $1750 for tuition, room, and board.

CONTACT PEOPLE

David T. O'Dell, Director of Studies, Purnell Foreign Language Immersion Program, Purnell School, Pottersville, New Jersey 07979 (201) 439-2154

Mark L. Thamert, Director of Foreign Study 1973, Saint John's Preparatory School, Collegeville, Minnesota 56321 (612) 363-3667

SATURATION
PROGRAM

The Saturation Program at Xaverian High School in Brooklyn, New York provides intensive contact with a foreign language from the very beginning of language study. It began in the spring of 1967 with 25 volunteer ninth-graders, most of above average ability, who had had no previous training in Spanish. For three months these students had daily language classes of 20 minutes that covered the basic sound system, sentence patterns, and grammatical structures of Spanish. The next fall two teachers of Cuban origin, assisted by eight Latin American student aides, conducted courses in Spanish for these students in history, ethics, and Spanish grammar. The participants also spoke the language during lunch and in 20-minute conversation sessions after lunch each day.

As a result of its initial popularity, the program now includes all ninth-grade students in the school (over 300) who begin saturation classes in Spanish, French, Italian, or Russian at the very

327

start of the school year. They take year-long courses, conducted in the target language, in Civilization and Literature, Conversation and Grammar, and Area Studies, all scheduled in a two and one-half hour block of time at the beginning of the day. The Conversation and Grammar course in each language introduces students to the four basic skills through audiolingual dialogues and drills, oral readings, and written compositions, and the use of records, tapes, and television presentations. Civilization and Literature courses begin with more work in grammar in the first few weeks to provide intensive reinforcement of the basic skills; later, these courses focus on writing paragraphs and on reading short stories, excerpts from major literary works, anecdotes, and cultural essays. The content of the Area Studies course is the same as that of the regular ninth-grade World Geography course, but the courses are conducted in the target language and special attention is paid to those regions where the language is spoken.

After the first year, the interdisciplinary aspect of Saturation is reduced for practical reasons: simply, if the monolingual teachers of history and the humanities who turned their ninth-grade classes over to the foreign language teachers were also asked to give up their classes in the other grades, there would be virtually no classes left for them. After the ninth grade, the Saturation Program, in all languages but Spanish, is limited to one or two saturation language and literature courses at each level that offer a more intensive study of the language than the regular language courses and aim at developing real fluency in all four skills. However, since there are Spanish-speaking social studies teachers, saturation classes in World History in grade 10 and U.S. History in grade 11 are conducted in Spanish and include the same course content as the regular history class taught in English. Finally, there is an elective twelfth-grade course in Caribbean Culture, which examines the history of the Caribbean world, emphasizing Puerto Rico and Cuba and their relations with the U.S. Classes are conducted in Spanish and include seminar discussions, readings, written reports, and guest speakers from the Spanish-speaking community. Projects that actively involve the students in the community are carried out in the second semester of the course.

There is much evidence of the success of the Saturation Program. In three years the original volunteers completed four levels of Spanish plus an advanced placement course. In May 1970, 13 of these students took the CEEB Spanish Achievement Test and scored an average of 200 points higher than students in the school who had had the same number of years of Spanish in the regular program. Two of the original participants received scholarships to study in Spain, many others who have been in the program since then have gone abroad to study and travel, and Saturation students have achieved high honors at language proficiency contests. Interest generated by the program has led to the development of an annual foreign language music and drama festival and an annual Spanish literary contest in the school. In 1973–74, the department plans to offer one-semester courses conducted in Spanish in such topics as "Spanish Love Literature," "The Spanish Civil War," "The Message of the Contemporary Spanish Novel," and a survey of Spanish art "From Altamira to Guernica."

TARGET AUDIENCE

Students of all abilities, grades 9–12; participation is required in grade 9 and optional in grades 10–12.

MATERIALS

Audio-visual center with language laboratory units, film and slide projectors, record player, and television; films, tapes, newspapers, workbooks, texts (Dale and Dale), and reference books and texts obtained abroad.

FUNDING AND COSTS

The program is funded through the regular school budget; estimates of initial costs for the Saturation Program are $1400 for print materials, tapes, audio-visual equipment, and establishment of the resource center, and $500 for teacher training.

CONTACT PERSON

Brother Edward Scott, C.F.X., Xaverian High School, 7100 Shore Road, Brooklyn, New York 11209 (212) TE6-7100

SELF-INSTRUCTION
IN
FLES SPANISH

The public schools in Tucson, Arizona have avoided the bugbear of high salary costs for FLES by setting up a program of self-instruction in Spanish for 365 volunteer sixth-graders in four schools. Each class meets three or five days a week (depending on the school) and is divided into two groups; while one group works with the regular classroom teacher in other subject areas, the second works with the printed and taped Spanish materials. After half an hour, the groups switch. Students may work alone in Spanish, but most choose to be in teams of three; at the beginning of the 30-minute period, the "captain" of each team checks a cassette playback unit out of the library, and, if the weather is good, the trio goes off to the patio or the playground to work under a tree. They use programmed materials developed by the Tucson Public Schools that are generously illustrated and require only minimal reading ability. Dialogues and drills are based on real-life situations, often set in the Tucson area; they are designed to promote strong student interaction. Print materials are kept in looseleaf binders so that special units on Christmas, Halloween, and other holidays can be added at the appropriate times. The tapes contain dialogues, verses, songs, drills, and cultural information. Students can check out the cassettes and playback units overnight, and in several homes whole families have started learning Spanish.

Two paraprofessionals, native speakers of Spanish, visit each school separately or as a team, depending on the student load. They circulate among the groups—indoors or outdoors—to provide any help students may request, check their progress, listen to oral tests, correct written tests, and see that the materials are adequate. Equally important, the paraprofessionals direct large group activities, such as staging a play for the Christmas pageant or making *piñatas* or *cascarones*. Although formal evaluation studies have not yet been completed, the district feels that the program is successful. The retention rate in the program is 92%, and the students' parents and the school administrators are enthusiastic and supportive; one mother even volunteers two hours a day to organize and dispense the Spanish materials in the school library. The program has been spotlighted in PTA meetings, and the local press and television have carried stories on it. In 1973–74, Tucson Public Schools will extend the program to over 1900 students—fifth-graders in the four pilot schools and sixth-graders in 12 additional schools. As the first year's students graduate, the program will be articulated more closely with the program of self-instruction in Spanish in the district's junior and senior high schools.

COSTS

The district's initial appropriation of $10,000 for the program was divided as follows: $5000 for the salaries of the two paraprofessionals ($2.37 per hour, 6 hours per day); $2500 for the cassette playback units ($18.00 each); $2500 for printing costs, cassette tapes, etc. The district has a cassette duplicator. Programming is done by the district coordinator on his own time.

The costs for the expanded program are estimated at $40,000. One third of the initial investment is a diminishing cost, since the cassettes and playback units can be re-used.

CONTACT PERSON

Felizardo L. Valencia, Coordinator of Modern and Classical Languages, Tucson Public Schools, Education Center, P.O. Box 4040, 1010 East Tenth Street, Tucson, Arizona 85717 (602) 791-6230

SHORT-TERM EXCHANGE: JAPANESE AND AMERICAN STUDENTS (STE–JAS)

East and West at least have a chance to meet each other in a growing exchange program between schools in Japan and schools in Montana, Oregon, and Washington state. STE—JAS began in 1967, when a Japanese high school teacher of English asked Tamako Niwa, a professor at the University of Washington, for help in placing 15 Japanese students in American homes for a brief stay. These homestay experiences proved to be so successful and happy that ten children from the American host families visited the Japanese students the following summer. During the next year, Niwa brought into the exchange program students in a Japanese language program in Spokane, Washington and made formal arrangements for recruiting Japanese exchange students and host families with the Association of Japanese Private Middle and High Schools. The exchange has grown each year; in 1973 50 Japanese students visited the United States and 20 American students went to Japan. Beyond that, the exchange has been instru-

334

mental in starting Japanese language programs in three American school districts.

The Japanese visitors are recruited from private schools all over Japan. They must be 15 to 18 years old, speak English well, and be of good character. The American students are recruited from about 25 school districts in the three states. To be selected for the exchange or as a host, a student must be 15 to 18, be of good character, and have a school and family situation that could profit from a Japanese exchange visitor. American students are not required to speak Japanese, but they must be interested in Japan and the purposes of STE—JAS. The students are paired on the basis of their probable compatibility. The Japanese students begin their visit in March, during their spring vacation, and stay for about six weeks. The American students visit Japan in July and stay for about the same length of time. A longer exchange was considered impractical from the Japanese viewpoint because the competition for places in good Japanese universities is so strong that parents are reluctant to let their children stay out of school very long.

The Japanese students meet in Tokyo and fly as a group to Seattle. There they meet their host families, and go with them to towns in Washington, Oregon, and Montana; the program organizers try to place two to four exchange students in each participating high school. The Japanese visitors attend the classes of their choice at their hosts' schools, and, if there is a Japanese language program, may talk with classes. (The exchange is having some unexpected side benefits; math teachers have developed a strong interest in Japanese instructional methods because of the Japanese students' high competence in mathematics.) Some group activities, visits to industrial plants and the harbor, for instance, are planned in Seattle, but students spend almost all their time with their hosts. At the end of the homestay, the Japanese students regroup in Seattle and fly to Disneyland for a day-long visit and then to Hawaii for two days of sightseeing and fun. And then back to school in Japan.

The American students return the visit during the summer, arriving after the Japanese students' final exams in the last week before summer vacation. In the first years of the program, only students who had studied Japanese went; they were given a two-week tour of southwestern Japan to acquaint them with some customs and foods. Later, when the program was opened to students who did not speak Japanese, this orientation was replaced by two weeks of classroom instruction in Tokyo in the language and customs. Lately, this too has been replaced—by four two-hour orientation sessions conducted by Niwa on the University of Washington campus before departure. About one-third of the students take Japanese in school, and need little orientation; the others have had some previous contact with Japan through their visitors. The students are met by their host families—in most cases, those of the same visitors they hosted earlier—and go with them to their homes.

PROGRAM ORGANIZATION

Administration of the STE—JAS is now carried out by the STE—JAS KAI (Committee), which is in fact three committees. The Working Committee recruits and places students and makes travel arrangements. The Advisory Committee is made up of businessmen, bankers, travel agents, lawyers, teachers, and university faculty who donate their time and special talents to the program; and the Honorary Committee is made up of prominent people who lend their prestige to the program. In Japan, the Association of Japanese Private Middle and High Schools, the *Nihon Shiritsu Chūkōren*, coordinates all activities.

FUNDING

In the beginning STE—JAS was partially supported by the Washington Foreign Language Program, a project funded until 1971 by the Ford Foundation to improve foreign language teaching in the state. Now STE—JAS is self-supporting: the host families provide room and board and take care of some minor expenses; the travel costs and other incidentals are paid by the students and their families; and all members of STE—JAS KAI volunteer their services without pay.

COSTS

The approximate cost of travel and other expenses in 1973 was about $800 per student. Contributions from several ethnic and travel organizations cover the cost of postage, telephone, and office expenses. Recently, with help from the STE—JAS KAI lawyer, STE—JAS was incorporated as a nonprofit organization, and is about to start a fund-raising drive so that it may expand. Eventually the program organizers hope to start a series of regionally-based American-Japanese exchange programs all over the United States.

CONTACT PERSON

Tamako Niwa, Department of Asian Languages, University of Washington, Seattle, Washington 98105 (206) 543-4925

SPANISH
CULTURE

At North Pitt High School in Bethel, North Carolina, a beginning-level Spanish Culture program has been developed specifically for students with low reading scores or low aptitude, with the purpose of exposing them to people whose language and lifestyles differ from their own. By "exploring a variety of methods which might allow the disadvantaged [student] to succeed," the program "attempts to make each learning activity a visual, hands-on experience" in which the student participates energetically. The approach to language instruction emphasizes oral rather than written work. The approach to culture relies heavily on the observations and experiences of Spanish-speaking people who are invited to the class, and on movies, slides, filmstrips, and other media "which to a great extent eliminate the student's having to learn 'facts' " by reading. In 1972–73, the first year of the program, 40 students are enrolled in two Spanish Culture classes that meet daily for 50 minutes.

The course consists of seven units: Introduction to the Spanish Language and to the Countries Where Spanish Is Spoken; the Geography of Latin America; the History of Latin America; Family Life of Spanish-Speaking People; Food and Clothing; Religion and Education; and Cultural Activities and Sports. Spanish-speakers who have lived in Spain or Latin America talk with the classes on such subjects as Spanish art, foods, home life in their countries, and bullfighting. University students show slides of their trips to foreign countries, and in the study of arts and crafts in Latin America, the students go to East Carolina University to observe pottery-making and weaving.

In the unit on Latin American geography, the teacher uses transparencies and blackboard demonstrations to explain the origin and nature of the major climate zones, and the students fill in a worksheet as the lesson progresses. Later, they construct a climate map of Latin America with an appropriate key using special pencils and outline maps. They also see slides and pictures illustrating different landforms in Latin America and compare an area on a physical map with a photograph of the same area. In conjunction with relief and population maps they discuss elevation and its effect on determining where people live. And they see movies on the peoples of the Andes, the Pampas, and the Highlands, compare the ways of life in the three regions, and discuss how the differences are determined by climate and landforms. Discussions and explanations are mostly in English.

Students learn the language through simple Spanish phrases and sentences. In one exercise, involving the description of a house, students first collect pictures of houses, floor plans, and rooms. Using the pictures as clues, the teacher presents the related vocabulary orally and then in writing. She teaches the construction of sentences through repetitive oral questions that require a structured answer. The students answer as a class, as small groups, and individually. After the vocabulary is fairly well mastered, the students use the same question-and-answer method with each other. Then they each give an oral description of a house, write out their descriptions, write another description from dictation, and translate the dictation back into English. As often as possible, language exercises are related to the cultural topic being discussed. In a unit on geography, students learn the vocabulary and phrases needed to talk about weather conditions, the seasons, and the months of the year; they collect pictures of different seasons and weather and describe them to the class in Spanish. In the same unit, the students learn the names of 20 classroom objects and play a game in which two teams compete to place labels on objects in the classroom in the shortest period of time.

Students are given a course description and meet with guidance counselors prior to enrolling in the program. High-ability students are discouraged from taking the course, and counselors make an effort to attract students who generally would not be interested in—or would be discouraged by—a standard language course. Classes are kept to a maximum of 25 students. The level of work and types of activities on which the students are evaluated are controlled so that all students, with a reasonable amount of effort, can pass the course—and feel successful. One unit of high school credit is given for completion of the course. Representatives of the North Carolina State Department of Public Instruction will review the program during the 1972–73 school year.

TARGET AUDIENCE

Students in grades 9–12 with low reading scores, low ability, or disinterest in standard language courses.

MATERIALS AND EQUIPMENT

Slides, maps, transparencies, records, and magazines are used extensively. Filmstrips, movies, and library resources are used somewhat less. The program's textbook is *Speaking Spanish* (Allyn & Bacon); it is supplemented by numerous worksheets prepared by the teacher.

FUNDING AND COSTS

The program is funded by the regular school budget; the average annual expenditure in the district is $633 per pupil. Costs for the program itself are minimal; about $120 has been spent on audio-visual aids.

CONTACT PERSON

Barbara R. Rogers, North Pitt High School, Bethel, North Carolina 28712 (919) 825-8741

SPANISH
FOR
DEAF STUDENTS

For the past year students at the Model Secondary School for the Deaf in Washington, D.C. have been learning not only to read and write Spanish but to lipread and speak it too with the help of a recently developed system called Cued Speech. The problems deaf students face in learning a second language are considerable, for they are "typically weak in analytical thinking and abstract reasoning powers, . . . do not use English, either in speech or in writing, with native language habits, . . . [and] experience a great deal of difficulty in reading . . . with comprehension."[1] The grammar-translation approach has been used successfully with college-level deaf students, but neither the techniques nor the objectives of this method are realistically attuned to the characteristics of the large majority of deaf students. And audiolingual materials and approaches are very difficult to use with any deaf students since the problems inherent in lipreading are compounded by the second language.

Cued Speech, however, allows deaf people to identify speech sounds in a visual form that complements and reinforces their understanding of lip movement. The system consists of eight different hand configurations that are placed in any of four different positions close to the mouth to indicate particular groups of three or four phonemes. When a deaf person sees both the speaker's normal lip movements and the hand cues, he can easily understand which specific phoneme is being spoken. Training in Cued Speech takes approximately 12 hours for a teacher and 30 to 40 hours for a deaf student.

The system of Cued Speech is used with the teaching approach and materials of *Vida y Diálogos de España* (Center for Curriculum Development). The teacher first presents a filmstrip of 21 frames and speaks and cues the entire accompanying dialogue in full view of the students to give them a global understanding of the dialogue situation. Then, for five to seven class meetings, the class goes over each of the dialogue frames separately. While the teacher is showing a frame, he speaks and cues the appropriate dialogue sentences and asks individual students questions; they answer with the words from the dialogue that they discover to be appropriate. After each student has answered, the class repeats after the teacher, in "echo fashion," the sentences for each frame. After every group of three or four frames, and at the end of all 21 frames, the students break up into groups or pairs to practice speaking the dialogue; they may work with the teacher or another student, cueing and speaking at the same time, or they may work with a videotape "replay" of the teacher's presentation, a flipchart (a book of pictures from the filmstrip with overlays of words spelled phonetically), or a filmstrip previewer and the flipchart. When a student decides that he is ready to be tested on the dialogue, the teacher shows him the filmstrip frames one-by-one and the student speaks and cues the appropriate dialogue sentences. When he has proved he can speak the dialogue accurately, he logs his achievement in a daily record book and may help the teacher in testing other students. These presentation and testing procedures are followed until all the students can speak the dialogue accurately.

The students then assign themselves the roles of characters in the dialogue and wear around their necks simple portraits of the characters' faces on laminated posterboard plaques. The teacher projects the filmstrip on the screen and the "actors" assume the proper poses and speak their characters' parts in the dialogue with appropriate kinetic behavior. The students then change roles and re-enact the situation, until each student can play any role with "ease, spontaneity, and naturalness." Reading and writing are introduced after the students have learned the dialogue well. The students may transcribe the dialogue, describe the pictures and make résumés of the story, write from cued oral dictation, or complete written work based on the dialogue in their workbooks.

The language class occasionally shares activities with such areas as home economics, drama, social studies, and art. Since the school is an "open" school, with unwalled subject areas rather than classrooms, these activities can be carried out fairly easily, and the teachers plan to expand them in the next couple of years. The class has gone on field trips to Spanish and Mexican restaurants, a Flamenco show, the Pan-American Union, and a film-lecture on Mexico at the National Geographic Society. The teachers make an effort to include daily activities related to Hispanic cultures in the U.S. and abroad. In addition, they are beginning to write instructional "packets" based on the CCD materials that will include interdisciplinary units on Hispanic cultures, as well as criterion-referenced tests, behavioral objectives, and self-paced learning activities.

TARGET AUDIENCE

Deaf students at the secondary school level who want to take Spanish. As the program has been in existence only one year, there is only one level. There are ten students and two teachers in the class.

CONTACT PERSON

Jay Diamant, Model Secondary School for the Deaf, Kendall Green, Washington, D.C. 20002 (202) 447-0411

NOTE
    [1] Quotations are from the survey questionnaire.

WEEKEND
FOREIGN
LANGUAGE
CAMPS

In Jefferson County, Colorado, in the Denver metropolitan area, weekend foreign language camps in the mountains are helping to make language study more exciting by bringing distant lands a little closer. The camps began in late 1970 when the county's Russian teachers got permission to turn a mountain ranch complex owned by the school district into a temporary foreign language camp. The teachers sent letters of invitation to all the county's high school Russian classes and to all the Russian-speaking residents and professors in the area. The response was good, and in the next several weeks the teachers spent some late evenings drawing up two days' worth of Russian menus and activities and making banners, flags, costumes, Russian language signs, "passports," and "radio-broadcast" tapes. Finally the ancient village of Sosnovka appeared at the ranch one busy Friday morning.

That afternoon, the students arrived by bus. A local police car blocked their road at a state fish and game inspection point three miles from the camp, allowing the Russian border guards, dressed in rented costumes, to inspect all luggage and documents and give welcoming speeches in Russian. The buses' license plates were changed, and the students went on to the Immigration Office to receive their visitors' documents (pleas to speak only Russian, schedules, and camp regulations) and their "hotel" assignments. It took students at least an hour to get through these bureaucratic hassles in what was sometimes agitated Russian, but finally they were officially welcomed to Sosnovka in a long and dramatic speech by the newly appointed commissar, a university professor.

The same entry procedures are now used in all the village camps—El Pinar, Tannenheim, Val-les-Pins, and Sosnovka—with suitable ethnic variations and costuming. Sometimes "contraband" is planted in students' luggage, causing great uproars and even some good-natured roughing-up of suspicious characters. Approximately 150 students go to each camp, along with 20 to 30 teachers and 10 to 20 native speakers. One native speaker is appointed mayor of each village, and teachers occasionally play the roles of parish priests or policemen. The German, French, and Spanish camps are each held on different weekends in the spring, while the Russian camp is held in winter.

In the camps, displays of photographs, realia, posters, artwork, and foreign language signs are everywhere; even Smokey the Bear becomes *Medved* in Sosnovka. Selected feature-length foreign language films are shown almost continuously, and colorful ethnic markets, cafés, and tea rooms sell pastries, *espresso*, food, perfumes, and souvenirs as well as craftwork made by the schools' language clubs. Some villagers while away the afternoons in the cafés, talking in the foreign language. Others help the teachers and food-service staff in the kitchens, preparing *piroski, alouette sans tête, paella, auschnit*, and other foreign dishes. At any one time, there are seven to fifteen different activities going on in the foreign language—macramé, lectures and discussions, card games, *Bébé Foot*, soccer, scrabble, painting ceramic tiles, *boules*, weaving, Ukrainian Easter-egg painting, chess tournaments, painting copies of Limoges patterns on paper plates, *Cordon Bleu* baking, candle-dipping, silkscreen painting, folk dancing, or rap sessions. At Val-les-Pins an artist-in-residence does caricatures, and some students have made *cidre à la normande* with an old apple press. There is a piano in the main building with at least one piano player usually on hand and foreign language songsheets scattered around for people who want to sing along.

The teachers are involved almost constantly with the students, sharing in the activities, telling them about their own experiences in the foreign cultures, or making up histories and legends about the villages. St. Denis de la Tour, for instance, struck the drought-stricken earth with his staff two centuries ago and brought forth a spring whose holy waters still cure the aches of sincere pilgrims to Val-les-Pins. San Marcelino found a cave full of red wine that lasted El Pinar 300 years! In gratitude the two saints are included frequently in the campers' paintings and drawings. The villagers of Val-les-Pins also hold somewhat sacred an old pottery kiln that is "in fact" the ruins of a once-glorious cathedral whose cemetery, recently resurrected by the villagers, shows the horrors of the 80-year war with Tannenheim.

The festivities on Saturday nights are the high points of village life. Students learn folk dances during the afternoon, and, after an elegant dinner, put on a show. Saturday nights wind up with a discotheque, and Sunday, after a lazy lunch, the villagers return to their homes.

TARGET AUDIENCE

Foreign language students at any level in all 30 secondary schools in Jefferson County. Participation is voluntary.

FUNDING AND COSTS

The cost for each teacher and student is $13.50, including $0.50 for round-trip transportation by school bus. Native speakers and guests are given room and board. Each camp usually rents three feature films with camp fees. The facilities are donated by the school district, but the camp fees cover the costs of food and kitchen and custodial staff. Some materials and equipment are purchased; some are brought from the participating schools.

AVAILABLE DESCRIPTIONS

Martha Quiat, a Jefferson County teacher, described the French language camps in the February 1972 issues of *PEALS*, the newsletter of the Colorado Congress of Foreign Language Teachers, and described Val-les-Pins in the April 1973 issue of *Accent on ACTFL*. A slide/tape presentation on the camps is available from the contact person for a rental fee of $10.

CONTACT PERSON

Larry McWilliams, Coordinator of Foreign Languages, Jefferson County Public Schools, 809 Quail Street, Lakewood, Colorado 80215 (303) 237-6971

WELD
COUNTY
BILINGUAL/BICULTURAL
PROJECT

In the "two-way" bilingual/bicultural project of the Letford Elementary School in Johnstown, Colorado, the 260 English-speaking children in the primary grades learn Spanish, the 80 Spanish-speaking children learn English, and their parents, grandparents, and others from the community are actively involved in planning the activities, developing materials, and helping in class in the extensive bicultural program. The project follows an open-classroom format and style of teaching; the students do a great deal of work on their own or in small groups under appointed group leaders, using worksheets and other printed and audio-visual materials developed by the school's teachers and by commercial firms. The eight bilingual teachers and nine bilingual teacher aides generally circulate among the students, helping them as needed, but the students meet in larger groups for the more usual type of teacher instruction whenever new concepts are introduced.

The 80 students whose "home" language is Spanish have

classes in arithmetic, social studies, and science—taught primarily in Spanish—as well as reading classes in both English and Spanish and several periods of English instruction each day. As the students advance from the pre-kindergarten level through the second grade, progressively more English is used in the classes, but even after the second grade they continue to learn all subject matter in both languages. The 260 children whose "home" language is English also have classes in reading, arithmetic, social studies, and science—taught in English and Spanish—as well as several periods of Spanish language instruction a day. At the pre-kindergarten level there are about 45 minutes a day of instruction in the second language, in kindergarten about 100 minutes, and in the second grade between 125 and 140 minutes; the periods are 20 to 25 minutes long. The students build from a completely oral-aural approach in pre-kindergarten classes to learning reading and writing in the second grade. The teacher aides work with both the ESL and SSL classes.

Second-language instruction is integrated as much as possible with the other curriculum areas at all levels. In second-grade arithmetic, for example, students learn, among other things, how to add, subtract, count, and measure, as well as how to tell time; much of this material and vocabulary—and even more conceptual work such as the relationship between numbers of objects and terms of quantity—is reinforced by the work in the second-language classes. The integration between language and other curriculum areas is strengthened by a special system of peer teaching; if an Anglo child, for instance, is having trouble with a lesson in arithmetic, he may be paired with a Mexican-American child who can help; if a Mexican American is having trouble with a concept in social studies, he may be paired with an Anglo. Such peer teaching also serves to bring the two groups together socially.

The students are brought into contact with the other language and culture in a variety of ways. The teachers try to bring a consciousness of both cultures into social studies classes and other activities; in fact several monolingual teachers have recently started learning Spanish so they can integrate both languages into their subject areas. The bilingual teachers and aides generally use a child's second language when speaking to him outside of class.

The teachers frequently put up room displays of both Anglo- and Mexican-American culture. And in Movement Education classes the students learn both Mexican- and Anglo-American folk dances. Every year, the school sponsors two Cultural Awareness Weeks. In one, centering on Mexican Independence Day (September 16), one hour a day is devoted exclusively to Mexican-American culture. Mexican-American professionals and other people talk with the students about their jobs, and university faculty and students speak about educational opportunities for Mexican Americans. There are assemblies with Mexican-American foods, songs, dances, and a parade with children from Letford and other schools in the area. The second Cultural Awareness Week is built around United Nations Day (October 24), with an hour a day devoted to the ethnic groups the Anglo children represent. The children wear appropriate ethnic costumes, their parents and grandparents speak with the classes, and foods, dances, and other activities make up the assemblies.

Community involvement in the project is substantial. A Parent Advisory Board of Anglo- and Mexican-American parents, educators, a student, and civic leaders meets once a year to confirm or develop the project's goals and activities. The project staff speaks with community groups frequently and maintains a liaison with the area's news media. The project hosts four one-evening "Mother Workshops" during each year, in which parents gather for a potluck supper and make games, puzzles, abacuses, ecology and educational toys, and instructional materials for both classroom and home use. The parents also draw up Language Experience Books that detail, in children's natural language, experiences children commonly have in school and at home. Parents also take part in the project's informal inservice meetings once a month and in the three-week preservice training program, primarily as cultural resource consultants. Additionally, the parents and grandparents work with the teachers in frequent Inservice Cultural Workshops; one cultural workshop wrote a cookbook for Mexican-American foods, another prepared materials on how Mexican superstitions and folklore evolved and how they have been changed in the United States. Similar materials for other ethnic groups are being developed this year. Approximately 80 percent of the parents—both Anglo- and Mexican-American—attend the Mother Workshops and other parent activities during the year, in part because of the staff's intensive efforts to induce them to come, in part because transportation and child care are provided free by volunteers, and in part because of the welcoming social atmosphere and real need for their help.

The children's grandparents are also frequently involved; Norwegian Americans, German Americans, and Mexican Americans have all talked with the classes about life in their countries of origin and told stories and folktales. In fact the staff is now compiling the stories told in class into reading books, called the Grandmother Series. Several of the teachers have extended open invitations to the parents and grandparents to come to the classes, and some of them do.

TARGET AUDIENCE

Students in pre-kindergarten through the second grade. Each year one more grade level will be included in the project until it extends from pre-kindergarten through the tenth grade. The project is now in its second year.

PROGRAM EVALUATION

Only a small amount of the project evaluation has been completed. An Educational Accomplishment Audit Team from Denver University gave the project's activities a very favorable evaluation. Further, in a recent administration of the Metropolitan Reading Examination 29 of 38 Spanish-speaking children were reading at or above grade level in English.

FUNDING

The entire program, including the costs of administration, staffing, materials, evaluation, and consultants, was funded through an ESEA Title VII grant of $180,584.

354 – OPTIONS AND PERSPECTIVES

AVAILABLE DESCRIPTIONS

The program has been described by Ernest Andrade in "Bilingual Education: An Answer," published in the October 1971 issue of the *Journal for Educational Research*. A manual for community relations, the "Parent Involvement Guide," is available from the contact person for $3.00.

CONTACT PERSON

Ernest Andrade, Project Director, Weld County Bilingual/ Bicultural Project, Letford Elementary School, Johnstown, Colorado 80534 (303) 587-4172

HOW
TO ORDER
ERIC
REPORTS

ORDERS MUST SPECIFY: ED numbers of documents, kinds of reproduction desired (hard copy or microfiche), number of copies, method of payment (cash with order, deposit account, charge).

ADDRESS ORDERS TO: ERIC Document Reproduction Service, P.O. Drawer O, Bethesda, Maryland 20014. (*The ERIC Document Reproduction Service will provide a convenient order form upon request.*)

The cost of *microfiche* is $.65 *per title*, regardless of the length of a document; the cost of *hard copy* is $3.29 per title, unless noted otherwise in the report citation. Payment must accompany orders totalling less than $10. The EDRS is registered to collect sales tax. Please add applicable sales tax or submit tax exemption certificate for the following states: Alabama, California, Colorado, Connecticut, District of Columbia, Florida, Georgia, Hawaii, Illinois, Indiana, Iowa, Kansas, Kentucky, Louisiana, Maine, Maryland, Massachusetts, Michigan, Missouri, New Jersey, New Mexico, New York, North Carolina, North Dakota, Ohio, Oklahoma, Pennsylvania, Rhode Island, South Carolina, South Dakota, Tennessee, Texas, Utah, Virginia, Washington, West Virginia, and Wisconsin.

INDEX

357

358 – INDEX